CANADA BUSINESS CORPORATIONS ACT
with
REGULATIONS

9th Edition, 1993

CCH CANADIAN LIMITED

6 Garamond Court, North York, Ontario M3C 1Z5
Telephone: 1-800-268-4522; Toronto only: (416) 441-0086
Fax No: (416) 444-9011

Published by CCH Canadian Limited

USA	Commerce Clearing House Inc., Riverwoods, Illinois.
UK and EUROPE	CCH Editions Limited, Bicester, Oxfordshire.
AUSTRALIA	CCH Australia Limited, North Ryde, NSW.
NEW ZEALAND	CCH New Zealand Limited, Auckland.
SINGAPORE, MALAYSIA and BRUNEI	CCH Asia Limited, Singapore.
JAPAN	CCH Japan Limited, Tokyo.

Important Disclaimer: This publication is sold with the understanding that (1) the author and editors are not responsible for the results of any actions taken on the basis of information in this work, nor for any errors or omissions; and (2) the publisher is not engaged in rendering legal, accounting or other professional services. The publisher, and the author and editors, expressly disclaim all and any liability to any person, whether a purchaser of this publication or not, in respect of anything and of the consequences of anything done or omitted to be done by any such person in reliance, whether whole or partial, upon the whole or any part of the contents of this publication. If legal advice or other expert assistance is required, the services of a competent professional person should be sought.

Ownership of Trade Marks

CCH ACCESS, COMPUTAX and **COMMERCE CLEARING HOUSE, INC.**

are the property of Commerce Clearing House Incorporated, Riverwoods, Illinois, U.S.A.

1st edition — April, 1975
2nd edition — June, 1975
3rd edition — March, 1976
4th edition — April, 1979
5th edition — April, 1983
6th edition — March, 1985
7th edition — January, 1989
8th edition — March, 1991
9th edition — April, 1993

ISBN 0-88796-916-X

© 1993, CCH Canadian Limited

 Typeset and printed in Canada by CCH Canadian Limited.

Foreword

The foundation for the *Canada Business Corporations Act* was laid in late 1967 when the federal government set up a Task Force with broad terms of reference to reconsider the philosophy, substance and administration of the *Canada Corporations Act*. The Task Force submitted its Report to the Department of Consumer and Corporate Affairs in early 1971 and the Report was published by Information Canada under the title "Proposals for a new Business Corporations Law for Canada".

Based on the Task Force Report, Bill C-213, an Act to provide for Canada Business Corporations, was introduced in 1973 by the Minister of Consumer and Corporate Affairs. The Bill died on the Order Paper but was re-introduced on October 21, 1974, as Bill C-29. Bill C-29 received Royal Assent on March 24, 1975, and became effective December 15, 1975 (S.C. 1974-75-76, c. 33). Under the *Canada Business Corporations Act*, companies which were incorporated under the *Canada Corporations Act* had to apply for a certificate of continuance within five years from the date the Act came into force, i.e., before December 15, 1980. If a company with share capital did not apply for continuance, it was automatically dissolved at the end of that period. The text of the *Canada Business Corporations Act* is revised to reflect the law as it is contained in the Revised Statutes of Canada, 1985, c. C-44, as amended, which was proclaimed in force on December 12, 1988, by P.C. 1988-2567 and P.C. 1988-2568, gazetted November 23, 1988. Amendments to the Act up to the date of publication have been consolidated with this edition.

Regulations under the *Canada Business Corporations Act* were first issued in 1975 (P.C. 1975-2820). These Regulations were subsequently amended and in 1979 they were consolidated and re-issued as P.C. 1979-1195 (SOR/79-316), gazetted April 25, 1979, and effective April 6, 1979. At the date this edition went to press no revised regulations under the Act have been published. Amendments to the Regulations up to the date of publication of this edition have been consolidated.

In the publication of this book, meticulous care has been exercised to attain an exact reproduction of the official text of the Act. Some changes in printing style have been adopted, however, for convenience. None of the changes affect the substance or wording of the Act.

For more extensive information on this subject, readers are directed to the loose-leaf CCH CANADA CORPORATIONS LAW REPORTER. This is a monthly reporting service which includes both law and commentary relating to federally incorporated companies, bankruptcy, winding-up, competition law, foreign investment controls, and the "doing business" provisions of the various provincial company Acts as they affect federally incorporated companies.

April, 1993   CCH Canadian Limited

Table of Contents

	Page
Foreword	iii

Canada Business Corporations Act

Interpretation and Application	1
Short Title	1
Interpretation	1
Application	4
Purposes of Act	4
Incorporation	5
Capacity and Powers	8
Registered Office and Records	9
Corporate Finance	12
Sale of Constrained Shares	23
Security Certificates, Registers and Transfers	25
Interpretation and General	25
Issue — Issuer	33
Purchase	34
Registration	40
Trust Indentures	43
Receivers and Receiver-Managers	47
Directors and Officers	48
Insider Trading	61
Shareholders	66
Proxies	73
Financial Disclosure	78
Fundamental Changes	86
Prospectus Qualification	103
Take-over Bids	103
Liquidation and Dissolution	111

	Page
Investigation	123
Remedies, Offences and Punishment	126
General	131

Canada Business Corporations Act Regulations

Short Title	139
Interpretation	139
General	139
Forms	139
Format of Documents	140
"Resident Canadian" Class of Persons Prescribed	141
Corporate Names	142
Interpretation	142
Confusion of Names	142
Consideration of Whole Name	143
Prohibited Names	143
Deceptively Misdescriptive Names	145
Certain Names Not Prohibited	145
Insider Trading	146
First Insider Report	146
Subsequent Insider Report	146
Deemed Insider Report	146
Notice Pursuant to Section 122.1 [128] of the Act	146
Proxies and Proxy Solicitation	147
Form of Proxy	147
Contents of Management Proxy Circular	148
Dissident's Proxy Circular	154
Contents of Dissident's Proxy Circular	155
Date of Proxy Circular and Information	156
Financial Statements in Proxy Circular	156
Financial Disclosure	157
General	157
Contents of Financial Statements	157
Reporting Classes of Business	157

Page

Exemption from Public Disclosure of Financial Statement..... 158

Interpretation.. 158

Prescribed Circumstances for Exemptions Under
Subsection 160(3) or 163(4) of the Act......................... 158

Constrained Share Corporations.. 160

Interpretation.. 160

Disclosure Required 161

Powers and Duties of Directors.. 161

Limitation on Voting Rights... 163

Sale of Constrained Shares... 163

Disclosure of Beneficial Ownership.................................. 168

References and Definitions for the Purposes of
Section 174 of the Act... 169

Take-Over Bids... 170

Exempt Offer Circumstances Prescribed 170

Take-Over Bid Circular Under Subsection 198(1)
of the Act... 171

Take-Over Bid Circular Under Section 200 of the Act 172

Where Offeror Has Effective Control................................. 173

Where Repurchase of Own Shares Involved...................... 173

Statement of Directors' Approval 175

Experts' Consent... 175

Certificate Required.. 175

Amendment to Take-Over Bid... 175

Contents of Directors' Circular... 175

Notice of Directors' Circular... 177

Report to Accompany Financial Statements...................... 178

Statement of Directors' Approval 178

Experts' Consent... 178

Certificate Required.. 178

Rules of Procedure for Applications for Exemptions.............. 178

Application... 178

Form for Application.. 179

Time of Filing Applications 179

Notice by Director of Decision 179

General.. 179

Prescribed Fees... 180

Page

Forms

List of Forms.. 181

Schedule I... 182

    Form 1: Articles of incorporation..................................... 182

    Form 2: Certificate of incorporation.................................. 184

    Form 3: Notice of registered office or notice of change
        of registered office.. 185

    Form 4: Articles of amendment... 187

    Form 5: Certificate of amendment..................................... 189

    Form 6: Notice of directors or notice of change of
        directors... 190

    Form 7: Restated articles of incorporation.......................... 192

    Form 8: Restated certificate of incorporation...................... 194

    Form 9: Articles of amalgamation...................................... 195

    Form 10: Certificate of amalgamation................................. 197

    Form 11: Articles of continuance....................................... 198

    Form 12: Certificate of continuance................................... 200

    Form 13: Certificate of discontinuance............................... 201

    Form 14: Articles of reorganization................................... 202

    Form 14.1: Articles of arrangement................................... 204

    Form 15: Articles of revival.. 206

    Form 16: Certificate of revival... 208

    Form 17: Articles of dissolution.. 209

    Form 18: Certificate of dissolution.................................... 211

    Form 19: Statement of intent to dissolve or statement of
        revocation of intent to dissolve.............................. 212

    Form 20: Certificate of intent to dissolve........................... 214

    Form 21: Certificate of revocation of intent to dissolve... 215

    Form 22: Annual return.. 216

    Form 24: Insider report.. 218

    Form 26: Statement of executive remuneration................ 220

    Form 27: Application for exemption................................... 222

Schedule II: Fees.. 224

Table of Concordance.. 227

Index.. 231

Canada Business Corporations Act

R.S.C. 1985, c. C-44, as amended by R.S.C. 1985 (1st Supp.), c. 27, Sch. V, item 3; R.S.C. 1985 (2nd Supp.), c. 27; S.C. 1988, c. 2; S.C. 1990, c. 17; S.C. 1991, c. 45, c. 46, c. 47; S.C. 1992, c. 1, c. 27, c. 51.

Part I

Interpretation and Application

Short Title

[¶23-001]

Sec. 1.   Short title. — This Act may be cited as the *Canada Business Corporations Act.*

Interpretation

[¶23-002]

Sec. 2.   Definitions. — (1) In this Act,

"affairs". — "affairs" means the relationships among a corporation, its affiliates and the shareholders, directors and officers of such bodies corporate but does not include the business carried on by such bodies corporate;

"affiliate". — "affiliate" means an affiliated body corporate within the meaning of subsection (2);

"articles". — "articles" means the original or restated articles of incorporation, articles of amendment, articles of amalgamation, articles of continuance, articles of reorganization, articles of arrangement, articles of dissolution, articles of revival and includes any amendments thereto;

"associate". — "associate" when used to indicate a relationship with any person means

   (a) a body corporate of which that person beneficially owns or controls, directly or indirectly, shares or securities currently convertible into shares carrying more than ten per cent of the voting rights under all circumstances or by reason of the occurrence of an event that has occurred and is continuing, or a currently exercisable option or right to purchase such shares or such convertible securities,

   (b) a partner of that person acting on behalf of the partnership of which they are partners,

   (c) a trust or estate in which that person has a substantial beneficial interest or in respect of which he serves as a trustee or in a similar capacity,

   (d) a spouse or child of that person, and

   (e) a relative of that person or of his spouse if that relative has the same residence as that person;

"auditor". — "auditor" includes a partnership of auditors;

"beneficial interest". — "beneficial interest" means an interest arising out of the beneficial ownership of securities;

"beneficial ownership". — "beneficial ownership" includes ownership through any trustee, legal representative, agent or other intermediary;

"body corporate". — "body corporate" includes a company or other body corporate wherever or however incorporated;

"call". — "call" means an option transferable by delivery to demand delivery of a specified number or amount of securities at a fixed price within a specified time but does not include an option or right to acquire securities of the corporation that granted the option or right to acquire;

"corporation". — "corporation" means a body corporate incorporated or continued under this Act and not discontinued under this Act;

"court". — "court" means

(a) in the Provinces of Newfoundland and Prince Edward Island, the trial division of the Supreme Court of the Province,

(a.1) in the Province of Ontario, the Ontario Court (General Division),

(b) in the Provinces of Nova Scotia and British Columbia, the Supreme Court of the Province,

(c) in the Provinces of Manitoba, Saskatchewan, Alberta and New Brunswick, the Court of Queen's Bench for the Province,

(d) in the Province of Quebec, the Superior Court of the Province, and

(e) in the Yukon Territory and the Northwest Territories, the Supreme Court thereof;

"court of appeal". — "court of appeal" means the court to which an appeal lies from an order of a court;

"debt obligation". — "debt obligation" means a bond, debenture, note or other evidence of indebtedness or guarantee of a corporation, whether secured or unsecured;

"Director". — "Director" means the Director appointed under section 260;

"director". — "director" means a person occupying the position of director by whatever name called and "directors" and "board of directors" includes a single director;

"incorporator". — "incorporator" means a person who signs articles of incorporation;

"individual". — "individual" means a natural person;

"liability". — "liability" includes a debt of a corporation arising under section 40, subsection 190(25) and paragraphs 241(3)(f) and (g);

"Minister". — "Minister" means such member of the Queen's Privy Council for Canada as is designated by the Governor in Council as the Minister for the purposes of this Act;

"ordinary resolution". — "ordinary resolution" means a resolution passed by a majority of the votes cast by the shareholders who voted in respect of that resolution;

"person". — "person" includes an individual, partnership, association, body corporate, trustee, executor, administrator or legal representative;

"prescribed". — "prescribed" means prescribed by the regulations;

"put". — "put" means an option transferable by delivery to deliver a specified number or amount of securities at a fixed price within a specified time;

"redeemable share". — "redeemable share" means a share issued by a corporation

(a) that the corporation may purchase or redeem on the demand of the corporation, or

(b) that the corporation is required by its articles to purchase or redeem at a specified time or on the demand of a shareholder;

"resident Canadian". — "resident Canadian" means an individual who is

(a) a Canadian citizen ordinarily resident in Canada,

(*b*) a Canadian citizen not ordinarily resident in Canada who is a member of a prescribed class of persons, or

(*c*) a permanent resident within the meaning of the *Immigration Act* and ordinarily resident in Canada, except a permanent resident who has been ordinarily resident in Canada for more than one year after the time at which he first became eligible to apply for Canadian citizenship;

"security". — "security" means a share of any class or series of shares or a debt obligation of a corporation and includes a certificate evidencing such a share or debt obligation;

"security interest". — "security interest" means an interest in or charge on property of a corporation to secure payment of a debt or performance of any other obligation of the corporation;

"send". — "send" includes deliver;

"series". — "series", in relation to shares, means a division of a class of shares;

"special resolution". — "special resolution" means a resolution passed by a majority of not less than two-thirds of the votes cast by the shareholders who voted in respect of that resolution or signed by all the shareholders entitled to vote on that resolution;

"unanimous shareholder agreement". — "unanimous shareholder agreement" means an agreement described in subsection 146(2) or a declaration of a shareholder described in subsection 146(3).

(S.C. 1986, c. 35, s. 14; 1992, c. 51, s. 30.)

[¶23-003]

(2) *Affiliated bodies corporate.* — For the purposes of this Act,

(*a*) one body corporate is affiliated with another body corporate if one of them is the subsidiary of the other or both are subsidiaries of the same body corporate or each of them is controlled by the same person; and

(*b*) if two bodies corporate are affiliated with the same body corporate at the same time, they are deemed to be affiliated with each other.

[¶23-004]

(3) *Control.* — For the purposes of this Act, a body corporate is controlled by a person if

(*a*) securities of the body corporate to which are attached more than fifty per cent of the votes that may be cast to elect directors of the body corporate are held, other than by way of security only, by or for the benefit of that person; and

(*b*) the votes attached to those securities are sufficient, if exercised, to elect a majority of the directors of the body corporate.

[¶23-005]

(4) *Holding body corporate.* — A body corporate is the holding body corporate of another if that other body corporate is its subsidiary.

[¶23-006]

(5) *Subsidiary body corporate.* — A body corporate is a subsidiary of another body corporate if it is controlled by that other body corporate.

[¶23-007]

(6) *Deemed distribution to the public.* — For the purposes of this Act, securities of a corporation

(*a*) issued on a conversion of other securities, or

(*b*) issued in exchange for other securities

are deemed to be securities that are part of a distribution to the public if those other securities were part of a distribution to the public.

[¶23-008]

(7) *Distribution to the public.* — Subject to subsection (8), for the purposes of this Act a security of a body corporate

(*a*) is part of a distribution to the public where, in respect of the security, there has been a filing of a prospectus, statement of material facts, registration statement, securities exchange take-over bid circular or similar document under the laws of Canada, a province or a jurisdiction outside Canada; or

(*b*) is deemed to be part of a distribution to the public, where the security has been issued and a filing referred to in paragraph (*a*) would be required if the security were being issued currently.

[¶23-009]

(8) *Exemption.* — On the application of a corporation, the Director may determine that a security of the corporation is not or was not part of a distribution to the public if he is satisfied that such determination would not prejudice any security holder of the corporation.

(S.C. 1986, c. 35, s. 14; 1992, c. 51, s. 30.)

Application

[¶23-015]

Sec. 3.   Application of Act. — (1) This Act applies to every corporation incorporated and every body corporate continued as a corporation under this Act that has not been discontinued under this Act.

[¶23-016]

(2) *Exceptions.* — [Repealed by S.C. 1991, c. 46, s. 593(1).]

[¶23-017]

(3) *Certain Acts do not apply.* — No provision of the *Canada Corporations Act*, chapter C-32 of the Revised Statutes of Canada, 1970, or the *Winding-up Act* applies to a corporation.

[¶23-018]

(4) *Limitations on business that may be carried on.* — No corporation shall carry on the business of

(*a*) a bank;

(*b*) a company to which the *Insurance Companies Act* applies; or

(*c*) a company to which the *Trust and Loan Companies Act* applies.

(1991, c. 45, s. 551(2); c. 46, s. 595(2)–(3); c. 47, s. 719(3).)

(1991, c. 45, s. 551(2); c. 46, s. 595(1)–(3); c. 47, s. 719(3).)

Purposes of Act

[¶23-019]

Sec. 4.   Purposes. — The purposes of this Act are to revise and reform the law applicable to business corporations incorporated to carry on business throughout Canada, to advance the cause of uniformity of business corporation law in Canada and to provide a means of allowing an orderly transference of certain federal companies incorporated under various Acts of Parliament to this Act.

Part II

Incorporation

[¶23-025]

Sec. 5.   Incorporators. — (1) One or more individuals not one of whom

(a) is less than eighteen years of age,

(b) is of unsound mind and has been so found by a court in Canada or elsewhere, or

(c) has the status of bankrupt,

may incorporate a corporation by signing articles of incorporation and complying with section 7.

[¶23-026]

(2) *Bodies corporate.* — One or more bodies corporate may incorporate a corporation by signing articles of incorporation and complying with section 7.

[¶23-027]

Sec. 6.   Articles of incorporation. — (1) Articles of incorporation shall follow the prescribed form and shall set out, in respect of the proposed corporation,

(a) the name of the corporation;

(b) the place within Canada where the registered office is to be situated;

(c) the classes and any maximum number of shares that the corporation is authorized to issue, and

(i) if there will be two or more classes of shares, the rights, privileges, restrictions and conditions attaching to each class of shares, and

(ii) if a class of shares may be issued in series, the authority given to the directors to fix the number of shares in, and to determine the designation of, and the rights, privileges, restrictions and conditions attaching to, the shares of each series;

(d) if the issue, transfer or ownership of shares of the corporation is to be restricted, a statement to that effect and a statement as to the nature of such restrictions;

(e) the number of directors or, subject to paragraph 107(a), the minimum and maximum number of directors of the corporation; and

(f) any restrictions on the businesses that the corporation may carry on.

[¶23-028]

(2) *Additional provisions in articles.* — The articles may set out any provisions permitted by this Act or by law to be set out in the by-laws of the corporation.

[¶23-029]

(3) *Special majorities.* — Subject to subsection (4), if the articles or a unanimous shareholder agreement require a greater number of votes of directors or shareholders than that required by this Act to effect any action, the provisions of the articles or of the unanimous shareholder agreement prevail.

Sec. 6(3)   ¶23-029

[¶23-029a]

(4) *Idem.* — The articles may not require a greater number of votes of shareholders to remove a director than the number required by section 109.

[¶23-030]

Sec. 7.   Delivery of articles of incorporation. — An incorporator shall send to the Director articles of incorporation and the documents required by sections 19 and 106.

[¶23-031]

Sec. 8.   Certificate of incorporation. — On receipt of articles of incorporation, the Director shall issue a certificate of incorporation in accordance with section 262.

[¶23-032]

Sec. 9.   Effect of certificate. — A corporation comes into existence on the date shown in the certificate of incorporation.

[¶23-033]

*Sec. 10.   Name of corporation. — (1) The word or expression "Limited", "Limitée", "Incorporated", "Incorporée", "Corporation", "Société par actions de régime fédéral" or "Société commerciale canadienne" or the abbreviation "Ltd.", "Ltée", "Inc.", "Corp.", "S.A.R.F." or "S.C.C." shall be part, other than only in a figurative or descriptive sense, of the name of every corporation, but a corporation may use and be legally designated by either the full or the abbreviated form. (1992, c. 1, s. 53(1).)

[¶23-034]

(2) *Exemption.* — The Director may exempt a body corporate continued as a corporation under this Act from the provisions of subsection (1).

[¶23-035]

(3) *Alternate name.* — Subject to subsection 12(1), a corporation may set out its name in its articles in an English form, a French form, an English form and a French form or in a combined English and French form and it may use and may be legally designated by any such form.

[¶23-036]

(4) *Alternative name outside Canada.* — Subject to subsection 12(1), a corporation may, for use outside Canada, set out its name in its articles in any language form and it may use and may be legally designated by any such form outside Canada.

[¶23-037]

(5) *Publication of name.* — A corporation shall set out its name in legible characters in all contracts, invoices, negotiable instruments and orders for goods or services issued or made by or on behalf of the corporation.

[¶23-038]

(6) *Other name.* — Subject to subsections (5) and 12(1), a corporation may carry on business under or identify itself by a name other than its corporate name.

(1992, c. 1, s. 53(1).)

---

* Sec. 10(1) as amended by S.C. 1992, c. 1, s. 53(1) is deemed to have come into force on December 12, 1988.

[¶23-039]

Sec. 11. Reserving name. — (1) The Director may, on request, reserve for ninety days a name for an intended corporation or for a corporation about to change its name.

[¶23-040]

(2) *Designating number.* — If requested to do so by the incorporators or a corporation, the Director shall assign to the corporation as its name a designating number determined by him.

[¶23-041]

Sec. 12. Prohibited name. — (1) A corporation shall not be incorporated with, have, carry on business under or identify itself by a name

(a) that is, as prescribed, prohibited or deceptively misdescriptive; or

(b) that is reserved for another corporation or intended corporation under section 11.

[¶23-042]

(2) *Directing change of name.* — If, through inadvertence or otherwise, a corporation

(a) comes into existence or is continued with a name, or

(b) on an application to change its name, is granted a name

that contravenes this section, the Director may direct the corporation to change its number in accordance with section 173.

[¶23-043]

(3) *Name of continued corporation.* — Notwithstanding subsections (1) and (2), a corporation that is continued under this Act is entitled to be continued with the name it had before such continuance unless that name is identical with or confusingly similar to the name of an existing body corporate.

[¶23-044]

(4) *Idem.* — If a corporation has a designating number as its name, the Director may direct the corporation to change its name to a name other than a designating number in accordance with section 173.

[¶23-045]

(5) *Revoking name.* — When a corporation has been directed under subsection (2) or (4) to change its name and has not within sixty days from the service of the directive to that effect changed its name to a name that complies with this Act, the Director may revoke the name of the corporation and assign to it a name and, until changed in accordance with section 173, the name of the corporation is thereafter the name so assigned.

[¶23-046]

Sec. 13. Certificate of amendment. — (1) When a corporation has had its name revoked and a name assigned to it under subsection 12(5), the Director shall issue a certificate of amendment showing the new name of the corporation and shall forthwith give notice of the change of name in the *Canada Gazette* or in the periodical referred to in section 129.

[¶23-047]

(2) *Effect of certificate.* — The articles of the corporation are amended accordingly on the date shown in the certificate of amendment.

[¶23-048]

Sec. 14.   Personal liability. — (1) Subject to this section, a person who enters into a written contract in the name of or on behalf of a corporation before it comes into existence is personally bound by the contract and is entitled to the benefits thereof.

[¶23-049]

(2) *Pre-incorporation and pre-amalgamation contracts.* — A corporation may, within a reasonable time after it comes into existence, by any action or conduct signifying its intention to be bound thereby, adopt a written contract made before it came into existence in its name or on its behalf, and on such adoption

(a) the corporation is bound by the contract and is entitled to the benefits thereof as if the corporation had been in existence at the date of the contract and had been a party thereto; and

(b) a person who purported to act in the name of or on behalf of the corporation ceases, except as provided in subsection (3), to be bound by or entitled to the benefits of the contract.

[¶23-050]

(3) *Application to court.* — Subject to subsection (4), whether or not a written contract made before the coming into existence of a corporation is adopted by the corporation, a party to the contract may apply to a court for an order fixing obligations under the contract as joint or joint and several or apportioning liability between or among the corporation and a person who purported to act in the name of or on behalf of the corporation and on such application the court may make any order it thinks fit.

[¶23-051]

(4) *Exemption from personal liability.* — If expressly so provided in the written contract, a person who purported to act in the name of or on behalf of the corporation before it came into existence is not in any event bound by the contract or entitled to the benefits thereof.

Part III

Capacity and Powers

[¶23-060]

Sec. 15.   Capacity of a corporation. — (1)   A corporation has the capacity and, subject to this Act, the rights, powers and privileges of a natural person.

[¶23-060a]

(2) *Idem.* — A corporation may carry on business throughout Canada.

[¶23-061]

(3) *Extra-territorial capacity.* — A corporation has the capacity to carry on its business, conduct its affairs and exercise its powers in any jurisdiction outside Canada to the extent that the laws of such jurisdiction permit.

[¶23-062]

Sec. 16.   Powers of a corporation. — (1) It is not necessary for a by-law to be passed in order to confer any particular power on the corporation or its directors.

[¶23-063]

(2) *Restricted business or powers.* — A corporation shall not carry on any business or exercise any power that it is restricted by its articles from carrying on or exercising, nor shall the corporation exercise any of its powers in a manner contrary to its articles.

[¶23-064]

(3) *Rights preserved.* — No act of a corporation, including any transfer of property to or by a corporation, is invalid by reason only that the act or transfer is contrary to its articles or this Act.

[¶23-065]

Sec. 17. No constructive notice. — No person is affected by or is deemed to have notice or knowledge of the contents of a document concerning a corporation by reason only that the document has been filed by the Director or is available for inspection at an office of the corporation.

[¶23-066]

Sec. 18. Authority of directors, officers and agents. — A corporation or a guarantor of an obligation of the corporation may not assert against a person dealing with the corporation or with any person who has acquired rights from the corporation that

(a) the articles, by-laws and any unanimous shareholder agreement have not been complied with,

(b) the persons named in the most recent notice sent to the Director under section 106 or 113 are not the directors of the corporation,

(c) the place named in the most recent notice sent to the Director under section 19 is not the registered office of the corporation,

(d) a person held out by a corporation as a director, an officer or an agent of the corporation has not been duly appointed or has no authority to exercise the powers and perform the duties that are customary in the business of the corporation or usual for such director, officer or agent,

(e) a document issued by any director, officer or agent of a corporation with actual or usual authority to issue the document is not valid or not genuine, or

(f) financial assistance referred to in section 44 or a sale, lease or exchange of property referred to in subsection 189(3) was not authorized,

except where the person has or ought to have by virtue of his position with or relationship to the corporation knowledge to the contrary.

Part IV

Registered Office and Records

[¶23-071]

Sec. 19. Registered office. — (1) A corporation shall at all times have a registered office in the place within Canada specified in its articles.

[¶23-072]

(2) *Notice of registered office.* — A notice of registered office in prescribed form shall be sent to the Director together with any articles that designate or change the place of the registered office of the corporation.

[¶23-073]

(3) *Change of address.* — The directors of a corporation may change the address of the registered office within the place specified in the articles.

[¶23-074]

(4) *Notice of change of address.* — A corporation shall send to the Director, within fifteen days of any change of address of its registered office, a notice in prescribed form and the Director shall file it.

[¶23-075]

Sec. 20.   Corporate records. — (1) A corporation shall prepare and maintain, at its registered office or at any other place in Canada designated by the directors, records containing

   (a) the articles and the by-laws, and all amendments thereto, and a copy of any unanimous shareholder agreement;

   (b) minutes of meetings and resolutions of shareholders;

   (c) copies of all notices required by section 106 or 113; and

   (d) a securities register that complies with section 50.

[¶23-076]

(2) *Directors records.* — In addition to the records described in subsection (1), a corporation shall prepare and maintain adequate accounting records and records containing minutes of meetings and resolutions of the directors and any committee thereof.

[¶23-077]

(3) *Records of continued corporations.* — For the purposes of paragraph (1)(b) and subsection (2), where a body corporate is continued under this Act, "records" includes similar records required by law to be maintained by the body corporate before it was so continued.

[¶23-078]

(4) *Place of directors records.* — The records described in subsection (2) shall be kept at the registered office of the corporation or at such other place as the directors think fit and shall at all reasonable times be open to inspection by the directors.

[¶23-079]

(5) *Records in Canada.* — Where accounting records of a corporation are kept at a place outside Canada, there shall be kept at the registered office or other office in Canada accounting records adequate to enable the directors to ascertain the financial position of the corporation with reasonable accuracy on a quarterly basis.

[¶23-080]

(6) *Offence.* — A corporation that, without reasonable cause, fails to comply with this section is guilty of an offence and liable on summary conviction to a fine not exceeding five thousand dollars.

[¶23-081]

Sec. 21.   Access to corporate records. — (1) Shareholders and creditors of a corporation, their agents and legal representatives and the Director may examine the records described in subsection 20(1) during the usual business hours of the corporation, and may take extracts therefrom, free of charge, and, where the corporation is a distributing corporation as defined in subsection 126(1), any other person may do so on payment of a reasonable fee.

[¶23-082]

(2) *Copies of corporate records.* — A shareholder of a corporation is entitled on request and without charge to one copy of the articles and by-laws and of any unanimous shareholder agreement.

[¶23-083]

(3) *Shareholder lists.* — Shareholders and creditors of a corporation, their agents and legal representatives, the Director and, where the corporation is a distributing corporation as defined in subsection 126(1), any other person, on payment of a reasonable fee and on sending to a corporation or its agent the affidavit referred to in subsection (7), may on application require the corporation or its agent to furnish within ten days from the receipt of the affidavit a list (in this section referred to as the "basic list") made up to a date not more than ten days before the date of receipt of the affidavit setting out the names of the shareholders of the corporation, the number of shares owned by each shareholder and the address of each shareholder as shown on the records of the corporation.

[¶23-084]

(4) *Supplemental lists.* — A person requiring a corporation to furnish a basic list may, if he states in the affidavit referred to in subsection (3) that he requires supplemental lists, require the corporation or its agent on payment of a reasonable fee to furnish supplemental lists setting out any changes from the basic list in the names or addresses of the shareholders and the number of shares owned by each shareholder for each business day following the date the basic list is made up to.

[¶23-085]

(5) *When supplemental lists to be furnished.* — The corporation or its agent shall furnish a supplemental list required under subsection (4)

    (a) on the date the basic list is furnished, where the information relates to changes that took place prior to that date; and

    (b) on the business day following the day to which the supplemental list relates, there the information relates to changes that take place on or after the date the basic list is furnished.

[¶23-086]

(6) *Holders of options.* — A person requiring a corporation to furnish a basic list or a supplemental list may also require the corporation to include in that list the name and address of any known holder of an option or right to acquire shares of the corporation.

[¶23-087]

(7) *Contents of affidavit.* — The affidavit required under subsection (3) shall state

    (a) the name and address of the applicant;

    (b) the name and address for service of the body corporate if the applicant is a body corporate; and

    (c) that the basic list and any supplemental lists obtained pursuant to subsection (4) will not be used except as permitted under subsection (9).

[¶23-088]

(8) *Idem.* — If the applicant is a body corporate, the affidavit shall be made by a director or officer of the body corporate.

[¶23-089]

(9) *Use of shareholder list.* — A list of shareholders obtained under this section shall not be used by any person except in connection with

(a) an effort to influence the voting of shareholders of the corporation;

(b) an offer to acquire shares of the corporation; or

(c) any other matter relating to the affairs of the corporation.

[¶23-090]

(10) *Offence.* — A person who, without reasonable cause, contravenes this section is guilty of an offence and liable on summary conviction to a fine not exceeding five thousand dollars or to imprisonment for a term not exceeding six months or to both.

[¶23-091]

Sec. 22.   Form of records. — (1) All registers and other records required by this Act to be prepared and maintained may be in a bound or loose-leaf form or in a photographic film form, or may be entered or recorded by any system of mechanical or electronic data processing or any other information storage device that is capable of reproducing any required information in intelligible written form within a reasonable time.

[¶23-092]

(2) *Precautions.* — A corporation and its agents shall take reasonable precautions to

(a) prevent loss or destruction of,

(b) prevent falsification of entries in, and

(c) facilitate detection and correction of inaccuracies in

the registers and other records required by this Act to be prepared and maintained.

[¶23-093]

(3) *Offence.* — A person who, without reasonable cause, contravenes this section is guilty of an offence and liable on summary conviction to a fine not exceeding five thousand dollars or to imprisonment for a term not exceeding six months or to both.

[¶23-094]

Sec. 23.   Corporate seal. — An instrument or agreement executed on behalf of a corporation by a director, an officer or an agent of the corporation is not invalid merely because a corporate seal is not affixed thereto.

Part V

Corporate Finance

[¶23-105]

Sec. 24.   Shares. — (1) Shares of a corporation shall be in registered form and shall be without nominal or par value.

[¶23-106]

(2) *Transitional.* — Where a body corporate is continued under this Act, a share with nominal or par value issued by the body corporate before it was so continued is, for the purpose of subsection (1), deemed to be a share without nominal or par value.

[¶23-107]

(3) *Rights attached to shares.* — Where a corporation has only one class of shares, the rights of the holders thereof are equal in all respects and include the rights

(a) to vote at any meeting of shareholders of the corporation;

(b) to receive any dividend declared by the corporation; and

(c) to receive the remaining property of the corporation on dissolution.

[¶23-108]

(4) *Rights to classes of shares.* — The articles may provide for more than one class of shares and, if they so provide,

(a) the rights, privileges, restrictions and conditions attaching to the shares of each class shall be set out therein; and

(b) the rights set out in subsection (3) shall be attached to at least one class of shares but all such rights are not required to be attached to one class.

[¶23-109]

Sec. 25. Issue of shares. — (1) Subject to the articles, the by-laws and any unanimous shareholder agreement and to section 28, shares may be issued at such times and to such persons and for such consideration as the directors may determine.

[¶23-110]

(2) *Shares non-assessable.* — Shares issued by a corporation are non-assessable and the holders are not liable to the corporation or to its creditors in respect thereof.

[¶23-111]

(3) *Consideration.* — A share shall not be issued until the consideration for the share is fully paid in money or in property or past services that are not less in value than the fair equivalent of the money that the corporation would have received if the share had been issued for money.

[¶23-112]

(4) *Consideration other than money.* — In determining whether property or past services are the fair equivalent of a money consideration, the directors may take into account reasonable charges and expenses of organization and re-organization and payments for property and past services reasonably expected to benefit the corporation.

[¶23-113]

(5) *Definition of "property".* — For the purposes of this section, "property" does not include a promissory note or a promise to pay.

[¶23-114]

Sec. 26. Stated capital account. — (1) A corporation shall maintain a separate stated capital account for each class and series of shares it issues.

[¶23-114a]

(2) *Entries in stated capital account.* — A corporation shall add to the appropriate stated capital account the full amount of any consideration it receives for any shares it issues.

Sec. 26(2)   ¶23-114a

[¶23-114b]

(3) *Exception for non-arm's length transactions.* — Notwithstanding subsection 25(3) and subsection (2), where a corporation issues shares

(*a*) in exchange for

(i) property of a person who immediately before the exchange did not deal with the corporation at arm's length within the meaning of that term in the *Income Tax Act,* or

(ii) shares of a body corporate that immediately before the exchange or that, because of the exchange, did not deal with the corporation at arm's length within the meaning of that term in the *Income Tax Act,* or

(*b*) pursuant to an agreement referred to in subsection 182(1) or an arrangement referred to in paragraph 192(1)(*b*) or (*c*) to shareholders of an amalgamating body corporate who receive the shares in addition to or instead of securities of the amalgamated body corporate,

the corporation may, subject to subsection (4), add to the stated capital accounts maintained for the shares of the classes or series issued the whole or any part of the amount of the consideration it received in the exchange.

[¶23-114c]

(4) *Limit on addition to a stated capital account.* — On the issue of a share a corporation shall not add to a stated capital account in respect of the share it issues an amount greater than the amount of the consideration it received for the share.

[¶23-114d]

(5) *Constraint on addition to a stated capital account.* — Where a corporation proposes to add any amount to a stated capital account it maintains in respect of a class or series of shares, if

(*a*) the amount to be added was not received by the corporation as consideration for the issue of shares, and

(*b*) the corporation has issued any outstanding shares of more than one class or series,

the addition to the stated capital account must be approved by special resolution unless all the issued and outstanding shares are shares of not more than two classes of convertible shares referred to in subsection 39(5).

[¶23-114e]

(6) *Other additions to stated capital.* — When a body corporate is continued under this Act, it may add to a stated capital account any consideration received by it for a share it issued and a corporation at any time may, subject to subsection (5), add to a stated capital account any amount it credited to a retained earnings or other surplus account.

[¶23-115]

(7) *Transitional.* — When a body corporate is continued under this Act, subsection (2) does not apply to the consideration received by it before it was so continued unless the share in respect of which the consideration is received is issued after the corporation is so continued.

[¶23-116]

(8) *Idem.* — When a body corporate is continued under this Act, any amount unpaid in respect of a share issued by the body corporate before it was so continued and paid after it was so continued shall be added to the stated capital account maintained for the shares of that class or series.

[¶23-117]

(9) *Idem.* — For the purposes of subsection 34(2), sections 38 and 42, subsection 44(1) and paragraph 185(2)(*a*), when a body corporate is continued under this Act its stated capital is deemed to include the amount that would have been included in stated capital if the body corporate had been incorporated under this Act.

[¶23-118]

(10) *Restriction.* — A corporation shall not reduce its stated capital or any stated capital account except in the manner provided in this Act.

[¶23-118a]

(11) *Exception for an open-end mutual fund.* — Subsections (1) to (10) and any other provisions of this Act relating to stated capital do not apply to an open-end mutual fund.

[¶23-118b]

(12) *Definition of "open-end mutual fund".* — For the purposes of this section, "open-end mutual fund" means a corporation that makes a distribution to the public of its shares and that carries on only the business of investing the consideration it receives for the shares it issues, and all or substantially all of those shares are redeemable on the demand of a shareholder.

[¶23-119]

Sec. 27. Shares in series. — (1) The articles may authorize the issue of any class of shares in one or more series and may authorize the directors to fix the number of shares in and to determine the designation, rights, privileges, restrictions and conditions attaching to, the shares of each series, subject to the limitations set out in the articles.

[¶23-120]

(2) *Series participation.* — If any cumulative dividends or amounts payable on return of capital in respect of a series of shares are not paid in full, the shares of all series of the same class participate rateably in respect of accumulated dividends and return of capital.

[¶23-121]

(3) *Restrictions on series.* — No rights, privileges, restrictions or conditions attached to a series of shares authorized under this section shall confer on a series a priority in respect of dividends or return of capital over any other series of shares of the same class that are then outstanding.

[¶23-122]

(4) *Amendment of articles.* — Before the issue of shares of a series authorized under this section, the directors shall send to the Director articles of amendment in prescribed form to designate a series of shares.

[¶23-123]

(5) *Certificate of amendment.* — On receipt of articles of amendment designating a series of shares, the Director shall issue a certificate of amendment in accordance with section 262.

[¶23-124]

(6) *Effect of certificate.* — The articles of the corporation are amended accordingly on the date shown in the certificate of amendment.

[¶23-125]

Sec. 28.   Pre-emptive right. — (1) If the articles so provide, no shares of a class shall be issued unless the shares have first been offered to the shareholders holding shares of that class, and those shareholders have a pre-emptive right to acquire the offered shares in proportion to their holdings of the shares of that class, at such price and on such terms as those shares are to be offered to others.

[¶23-126]

(2) *Exception.* — Notwithstanding that the articles provide the pre-emptive right referred to in subsection (1), shareholders have no pre-emptive right in respect of shares to be issued

(a) for a consideration other than money;

(b) as a share dividend; or

(c) pursuant to the exercise of conversion privileges, options or rights previously granted by the corporation.

[¶23-127]

Sec. 29.   Options and rights. — (1) A corporation may issue certificates, warrants or other evidences of conversion privileges, options or rights to acquire securities of the corporation, and shall set out the conditions thereof

(a) in the certificates, warrants or other evidences; or

(b) in certificates evidencing the securities to which the conversion privileges, options or rights are attached.

[¶23-128]

(2) *Transferable rights.* — Conversion privileges, options and rights to acquire securities of a corporation may be made transferable or non-transferable, and options and rights to acquire may be made separable or inseparable from any securities to which they are attached.

[¶23-129]

(3) *Reserved shares.* — Where a corporation has granted privileges to convert any securities issued by the corporation into shares, or into shares of another class or series, or has issued or granted options or rights to acquire shares, if the articles limit the number of authorized shares, the corporation shall reserve and continue to reserve sufficient authorized shares to meet the exercise of such conversion privileges, options and rights.

[¶23-130]

Sec. 30.   Corporation holding its own shares. — (1) Subject to subsection (2) and sections 31 to 36, a corporation

(a) shall not hold shares in itself or in its holding body corporate; and

(b) shall not permit any of its subsidiary bodies corporate to acquire shares of the corporation.

[¶23-130a]

(2) *Subsidiary holding shares of a corporation.* — A corporation shall cause a subsidiary body corporate of the corporation that holds shares of the corporation to sell or otherwise dispose of those shares within five years from the date

(a) the body corporate became a subsidiary of the corporation; or

(b) the corporation was continued under this Act.

[¶23-131]

Sec. 31. Exception. — (1) A corporation may in the capacity of a legal representative hold shares in itself or in its holding body corporate unless it or the holding body corporate or a subsidiary of either of them has a beneficial interest in the shares.

[¶23-132]

(2) *Idem.* — A corporation may hold shares in itself or in its holding body corporate by way of security for the purposes of a transaction entered into by it in the ordinary course of a business that includes the lending of money.

[¶23-133]

Sec. 32. Exception relating to Canadian ownership. — (1) Subject to subsection 39(8), a corporation may, for the purpose of assisting the corporation or any of its affiliates or associates to qualify under any prescribed law of Canada or a province to receive licences, permits, grants, payments or other benefits by reason of attaining or maintaining a specified level of Canadian ownership or control, hold shares in itself that

(a) are not constrained for the purpose of assisting the corporation or any of its affiliates or associates to so qualify; or

(b) are shares into which shares held under paragraph (a) were converted by the corporation that are constrained for the purpose of assisting the corporation to so qualify and that were not previously held by the corporation.

[¶23-133a]

(2) *Prohibited transfers.* — A corporation shall not transfer shares held under subsection (1) to any person unless the corporation is satisfied, on reasonable grounds, that the ownership of the shares as a result of the transfer would assist the corporation or any of its affiliates or associates to achieve the purpose set out in subsection (1).

[¶23-133b]

(3) *Offence.* — A corporation that, without reasonable cause, fails to comply with subsection (2) is guilty of an offence and liable on summary conviction to a fine not exceeding five thousand dollars.

[¶23-133c]

(4) *Directors of corporation.* — Where a corporation commits an offence under subsection (3), any director of the corporation who knowingly authorized, permitted or acquiesced in the commission of the offence is a party to and guilty of the offence and is liable on summary conviction to a fine not exceeding five thousand dollars or to imprisonment for a term not exceeding six months or to both, whether or not the corporation has been prosecuted or convicted.

[¶23-133d]

(5) *Where shares are transferred.* — Where shares held under subsection (1) are transferred by a corporation, subsections 25(1), (3), (4) and (5), paragraph 115(3)(c) and subsection 118(1) apply, with such modifications as the circumstances require, in respect of the transfer as if the transfer were an issue.

[¶23-133e]

(6) *Transfer not void.* — No transfer of shares by a corporation shall be void or voidable solely because the transfer is in contravention of subsection (2).

(1980-81-82, c. 115, s. 2.)

[¶23-133f]

Sec. 33.   Voting shares. — A corporation holding shares in itself or in its holding body corporate shall not vote or permit those shares to be voted unless the corporation

(a) holds the shares in the capacity of a legal representative; and

(b) has complied with section 153.

[¶ 23-134]

Sec. 34.   Acquisition of corporation's own shares. — (1) Subject to subsection (2) and to its articles, a corporation may purchase or otherwise acquire shares issued by it.

[¶23-135]

(2) *Limitation.* — A corporation shall not make any payment to purchase or otherwise acquire shares issued by it if there are reasonable grounds for believing that

(a) the corporation is, or would after the payment be, unable to pay its liabilities as they become due; or

(b) the realizable value of the corporation's assets would after the payment be less than the aggregate of its liabilities and stated capital of all classes.

[¶23-136]

Sec. 35.   Alternative acquisition of corporation's own shares. — (1) Notwithstanding subsection 34(2), but subject to subsection (3) and to its articles, a corporation may purchase or otherwise acquire shares issued by it to

(a) settle or compromise a debt or claim asserted by or against the corporation;

(b) eliminate fractional shares; or

(c) fulfil the terms of a non-assignable agreement under which the corporation has an option or is obliged to purchase shares owned by a director, an officer or an employee of the corporation.

[¶23-137]

(2) *Idem.* — Notwithstanding subsection 34(2), a corporation may purchase or otherwise acquire shares issued by it to

(a) satisfy the claim of a shareholder who dissents under section 190; or

(b) comply with an order under section 241.

[¶23-138]

(3) *Limitation.* — A corporation shall not make any payment to purchase or acquire under subsection (1) shares issued by it if there are reasonable grounds for believing that

(a) the corporation is, or would after the payment be, unable to pay its liabilities as they become due; or

(b) the realizable value of the corporation's assets would after the payment be less than the aggregate of

(i) its liabilities, and

(ii) the amount required for payment on a redemption or in a liquidation of all shares the holders of which have the right to be paid prior to the holders of the shares to be purchased or acquired.

[¶23-139]

Sec. 36.   Redemption of shares. — (1) Notwithstanding subsection 34(2) or 35(3), but subject to subsection (2) and to its articles, a corporation may purchase or redeem any redeemable shares issued by it at prices not exceeding the redemption price thereof stated in the articles or calculated according to a formula stated in the articles.

[¶23-140]

(2) *Limitation.* — A corporation shall not make any payment to purchase or redeem any redeemable shares issued by it if there are reasonable grounds for believing that

(a) the corporation is, or would after the payment be, unable to pay its liabilities as they become due; or

(b) the realizable value of the corporation's assets would after the payment be less than the aggregate of

(i) its liabilities, and

(ii) the amount that would be required to pay the holders of shares that have a right to be paid, on a redemption or in a liquidation, rateably with or prior to the holders of the shares to be purchased or redeemed.

[¶23-141]

Sec. 37. Donated shares. — A corporation may accept from any shareholder a share of the corporation surrendered to it as a gift, but may not extinguish or reduce a liability in respect of an amount unpaid on any such share except in accordance with section 38.

[¶23-142]

Sec. 38. Other reduction of stated capital. — (1) Subject to subsection (3), a corporation may by special resolution reduce its stated capital for any purpose including, without limiting the generality of the foregoing, for the purpose of

(a) extinguishing or reducing a liability in respect of an amount unpaid on any share;

(b) distributing to the holder of an issued share of any class or series of shares an amount not exceeding the stated capital of the class or series; and

(c) declaring its stated capital to be reduced by an amount that is not represented by realizable assets.

[¶23-143]

(2) *Contents of special resolution.* — A special resolution under this section shall specify the stated capital account or accounts from which the reduction of stated capital effected by the special resolution will be deducted.

[¶23-144]

(3) *Limitation.* — A corporation shall not reduce its stated capital for any purpose other than the purpose mentioned in paragraph (1)(c) if there are reasonable grounds for believing that

(a) the corporation is, or would after the reduction be, unable to pay its liabilities as they become due; or

(b) the realizable value of the corporation's assets would thereby be less than the aggregate of its liabilities.

[¶23-145]

(4) *Recovery.* — A creditor of a corporation is entitled to apply to a court for an order compelling a shareholder or other recipient

(a) to pay to the corporation an amount equal to any liability of the shareholder that was extinguished or reduced contrary to this section; or (*b*) to pay or deliver to the corporation any money or property that was paid or distributed to the shareholder or other recipient as a consequence of a reduction of capital made contrary to this section.

[¶23-146]

(5) *Limitation.* — An action to enforce a liability imposed by this section may not be commenced after two years from the date of the act complained of.

[¶23-147]

(6) *Remedy preserved.* — This section does not affect any liability that arises under section 118.

[¶23-148]

Sec. 39.   Adjustment of stated capital account. — (1) On a purchase, redemption or other acquisition by a corporation under sections 34, 35, 36, 45 or 190 or paragraph 241(3)(*f*), of shares or fractions thereof issued by it, the corporation shall deduct from the stated capital account maintained for the class or series of shares of which the shares purchased, redeemed or otherwise acquired form a part an amount equal to the result obtained by multiplying the stated capital of the shares of that class or series by the number of shares of that class or series or fractions thereof purchased, redeemed or otherwise acquired, divided by the number of issued shares of that class or series immediately before the purchase, redemption or other acquisition.

[¶23-149]

(2) *Idem.* — A corporation shall deduct the amount of a payment made by the corporation to a shareholder under paragraph 241(3)(*g*) from the stated capital account maintained for the class or series of shares in respect of which the payment was made.

[¶23-150]

(3) *Idem.* — A corporation shall adjust its stated capital account or accounts in accordance with any special resolution referred to in subsection 38(2).

[¶23-151]

(4) *Idem.* — On a conversion of issued shares of a corporation into shares of another class or series or a change under section 173, 191 or 241 of issued shares of a corporation into shares of another class or series, the corporation shall

(*a*) deduct from the stated capital account maintained for the class or series of shares converted or changed an amount equal to the result obtained by multiplying the stated capital of the shares of that class or series by the number of shares of that class or series converted or changed, divided by the number of issued shares of that class or series immediately before the conversion or change; and

(*b*) add the result obtained under paragraph (*a*) and any additional consideration received pursuant to the conversion or change to the stated capital account maintained or to be maintained for the class or series of shares into which the shares have been converted or changed.

[¶23-151a]

(5) *Stated capital of interconvertible shares.* — For the purposes of subsection (4) and subject to its articles, where a corporation issues two classes of shares and there is attached to each such class a right to convert a share of the one class into a share of the other class, if a share of one class is converted into a share of the other class, the amount of stated capital attributable to a share in either class is the aggregate of the stated capital of both classes divided by the number of issued shares of both classes immediately before the conversion.

[¶23-152]

(6) *Cancellation or restoration of shares.* — Shares or fractions thereof of any class or series of shares issued by a corporation and purchased, redeemed or otherwise acquired by it shall be cancelled or, if the articles limit the number of authorized shares, may be restored to the status of authorized but unissued shares of the class.

[¶23-153]

(7) *Exception.* — For the purposes of this section, a corporation holding shares in itself as permitted by subsections 31(1) and (2) is deemed not to have purchased, redeemed or otherwise acquired such shares.

[¶23-154]

(8) *Idem.* — For the purposes of this section, a corporation holding shares in itself as permitted by paragraph 32(1)(*a*) is deemed not to have purchased, redeemed or otherwise acquired the shares at the time they were acquired, but

(*a*) any of those shares that are held by the corporation at the expiration of two years, and

(*b*) any shares into which any of those shares were converted by the corporation and held under paragraph 32(1)(*b*) that are held by the corporation at the expiration of two years after the shares from which they were converted were acquired

are deemed to have been acquired at the expiration of the two years.

[¶23-155]

(9) *Conversion or change of shares.* — Shares issued by a corporation and converted into shares of another class or series or changed under section 173, 191 or 241 into shares of another class or series shall become issued shares of the class or series of shares into which the shares have been converted or changed.

[¶23-155a]

(10) *Effect of change of shares on number of unissued shares.* — Where the articles limit the number of authorized shares of a class of shares of a corporation and issued shares of that class or of a series of shares of that class have become, pursuant to subsection (9), issued shares of another class or series, the number of unissued shares of the first-mentioned class shall, unless the articles otherwise provide, be increased by the number of shares that, pursuant to subsection (9), became shares of another class or series.

[¶23-156]

(11) *Repayment.* — Debt obligations issued, pledged, hypothecated or deposited by a corporation are not redeemed by reason only that the indebtedness evidenced by the debt obligations or in respect of which the debt obligations are issued, pledged, hypothecated or deposited is repaid.

[¶23-157]

(12) *Acquisition and reissue of debt obligations.* — Debt obligations issued by a corporation and purchased, redeemed or otherwise acquired by it may be cancelled or, subject to any applicable trust indenture or other agreement, may be reissued, pledged or hypothecated to secure any obligation of the corporation then existing or thereafter incurred, and any such acquisition and reissue, pledge or hypothecation is not a cancellation of the debt obligations.

[¶23-158]

Sec. 40. Enforceability of contract. — (1) A contract with a corporation providing for the purchase of shares of the corporation is specifically enforceable against the corporation except to the extent that the corporation cannot perform the contract without thereby being in breach of section 34 or 35.

[¶23-159]

(2) *Burden of proof.* — In any action brought on a contract referred to in subsection (1), the corporation has the burden of proving that performance thereof is prevented by section 34 or 35.

[¶23-160]

(3) *Status of contracting party.* — Until the corporation has fully performed a contract referred to in subsection (1), the other party retains the status of a claimant entitled to be paid as soon as the corporation is lawfully able to do so or, in a liquidation, to be ranked subordinate to the rights of creditors but in priority to the shareholders.

[¶23-161]

Sec. 41. Commission for sale of shares. — The directors may authorize the corporation to pay a reasonable commission to any person in consideration of his purchasing or agreeing to purchase shares of the corporation from the corporation or from any other person, or procuring or agreeing to procure purchasers for any such shares.

[¶23-162]

Sec. 42. Dividends. — A corporation shall not declare or pay a dividend if there are reasonable grounds for believing that

(*a*) the corporation is, or would after the payment be, unable to pay its liabilities as they become due; or

(*b*) the realizable value of the corporation's assets would thereby be less than the aggregate of its liabilities and stated capital of all classes.

[¶23-163]

Sec. 43. Form of dividend. — (1) A corporation may pay a dividend by issuing fully paid shares of the corporation and, subject to section 42, a corporation may pay a dividend in money or property.

[¶23-164]

(2) *Adjustment of stated capital account.* — If shares of a corporation are issued in payment of a dividend, the declared amount of the dividend stated as an amount of money shall be added to the stated capital account maintained or to be maintained for the shares of the class or series issued in payment of the dividend.

[¶23-165]

Sec. 44. Prohibited loans and guarantees. — (1) Subject to subsection (2), a corporation or any corporation with which it is affiliated shall not, directly or indirectly, give financial assistance by means of a loan, guarantee or otherwise

(*a*) to any shareholder, director, officer or employee of the corporation or of an affiliated corporation or to an associate of any such person for any purpose, or

(*b*) to any person for the purpose of or in connection with a purchase of a share issued or to be issued by the corporation or affiliated corporation,

where there are reasonable grounds for believing that

(*c*) the corporation is or, after giving the financial assistance, would be unable to pay its liabilities as they become due, or

(*d*) the realizable value of the corporation's assets, excluding the amount of any financial assistance in the form of a loan and in the form of assets pledged or encumbered to secure a guarantee, after giving the financial assistance, would be less than the aggregate of the corporation's liabilities and stated capital of all classes.

[¶23-166]

(2) *Permitted loans and guarantees.* — A corporation may give financial assistance by means of a loan, guarantee or otherwise

(a) to any person in the ordinary course of business if the lending of money is part of the ordinary business of the corporation;

(b) to any person on account of expenditures incurred or to be incurred on behalf of the corporation;

(c) to a holding body corporate if the corporation is a wholly-owned subsidiary of the holding body corporate;

(d) to a subsidiary body corporate of the corporation; and

(e) to employees of the corporation or any of its affiliates

(i) to enable or assist them to purchase or erect living accommodation for their own occupation, or

(ii) in accordance with a plan for the purchase of shares of the corporation or any of its affiliates to be held by a trustee.

[¶23-167]

(3) *Enforceability.* — A contract made by a corporation in contravention of this section may be enforced by the corporation or by a lender for value in good faith without notice of the contravention.

[¶23-168]

Sec. 45. Shareholder immunity. — (1) The shareholders of a corporation are not, as shareholders, liable for any liability, act or default of the corporation except under subsection 38(4), 146(5) or 226(5).

[¶23-169]

(2) *Lien on shares.* — Subject to subsection 49(8), the articles may provide that the corporation has a lien on a share registered in the name of a shareholder or his legal representative for a debt of that shareholder to the corporation, including an amount unpaid in respect of a share issued by a body corporate on the date it was continued under this Act.

[¶23-170]

(3) *Enforcement of lien.* — A corporation may enforce a lien referred to in subsection (2) in accordance with its by-laws.

Part VI

Sale of Constrained Shares

[¶23-171]

Sec. 46. Sale of constrained shares by corporation. — (1) A corporation that has constraints on the issue, transfer or ownership of its shares of any class or series may,

(a) in order to assist the corporation or any of its affiliates or associates to qualify under any prescribed law of Canada or a province to receive licences, permits, grants, payments or other benefits by reason of attaining or maintaining a specified level of Canadian ownership or control, or

Sec. 46(1)   ¶23-171

(b) in order to assist the corporation to comply with

(i) section 379 of the *Trust and Loan Companies Act*, or

(ii) section 411 of the *Insurance Companies Act*,

sell, for that purpose or for the purpose of attaining or maintaining a level of Canadian ownership specified in its articles, under such conditions and after giving such notice as may be prescribed, as if it were the owner thereof, any of those constrained shares that are owned, or that the directors determine in such manner as may be prescribed may be owned, contrary to the constraints. (1991, c. 45, s. 552; c. 47, s. 720(1)–(2).)

[¶23-172]

(2) *Obligations of directors in sale.* — Where shares are to be sold by a corporation under subsection (1), the directors of the corporation shall select the shares for sale in good faith and in a manner that is not unfairly prejudicial to, and does not unfairly disregard the interests of, the holders of the shares in the constrained class or series taken as a whole.

[¶23-173]

(3) *Effect of sale.* — Where shares are sold by a corporation under subsection (1), the owner of the shares immediately prior to the sale shall by that sale be divested of his interest in the shares, and the person who, but for the sale, would be the registered owner of the shares or a person who satisfies the corporation that, but for the sale, he could properly be treated as the registered owner or registered holder of the shares under section 51 shall, from the time of the sale, be entitled to receive only the net proceeds of the sale, together with any income earned thereon from the beginning of the month next following the date of the receipt by the corporation of the proceeds of the sale, less any taxes thereon and any costs of administration of a trust fund constituted under subsection 47(1) in relation thereto.

[¶23-174]

(4) *Subsections 51(4) to (6) apply.* — Subsections 51(4) to (6) apply in respect of the person who is entitled under subsection (3) to receive the proceeds of a sale of shares under subsection (1) as if the proceeds were a security and the person were a registered holder or owner of the security.

(1991, c. 45, s. 552; c. 47, s. 720(1)–(2).)

[¶23-175]

Sec. 47. Proceeds of sale to be trust fund. — (1) The proceeds of a sale by a corporation under subsection 46(1) constitute a trust fund in the hands of the corporation for the benefit of the person entitled under subsection 46(3) to receive the proceeds of the sale, and any such trust fund may be commingled by the corporation with other such trust funds and shall be invested in such manner as may be prescribed.

[¶23-176]

(2) *Costs of administration.* — Reasonable costs of administration of a trust fund referred to in subsection (1) may be deducted from the trust fund and any income earned thereon.

[¶23-177]

(3) *Appointment of trust company.* — Subject to this section, a corporation may transfer any trust fund referred to in subsection (1), and the administration thereof, to a trust company in Canada registered as such under the laws of Canada or a province, and the corporation is thereupon discharged of all further liability in respect of the trust fund.

[¶23-178]

(4) *Discharge of corporation and trust company.* — A receipt signed by a person entitled under subsection 46(3) to receive the proceeds of a sale that constitute a trust fund under subsection (1) shall be a complete discharge of the corporation and of any trust company to which a trust fund is transferred under subsection (3), in respect of the trust fund and income earned thereon paid to such person.

[¶23-179]

(5) *Vesting in Crown.* — A trust fund described in subsection (1), together with any income earned thereon, less any taxes thereon and costs of administration, that has not been claimed by a person entitled under subsection 46(3) to receive the proceeds of a sale that constitute the trust fund for a period of ten years after the date of the sale vests in Her Majesty in right of Canada.

[¶23-180]

(6) *Escheats Act applies.* — Sections 3 to 5 of the *Escheats Act* apply in respect of a trust fund that vests in Her Majesty in right of Canada under subsection (5).

Part VII

Security Certificates, Registers and Transfers

Interpretation and General

[¶23-191]

Sec. 48. Application of Part. — (1) The transfer or transmission of a security shall be governed by this Part.

[¶23-192]

(2) *Definitions.* — In this Part,

"adverse claim". — "adverse claim" includes a claim that a transfer was or would be wrongful or that a particular adverse person is the owner of or has an interest in the security;

"bearer". — "bearer" means the person in possession of a security payable to bearer or endorsed in blank;

"bona fide purchaser". — "bona fide purchaser" means a purchaser for value in good faith and without notice of any adverse claim who takes delivery of a security in bearer form or order form or of a security in registered form issued to him or endorsed to him or endorsed in blank;

"broker". — "broker" means a person who is engaged for all or part of his time in the business of buying and selling securities and who, in the transaction concerned, acts for, or buys a security from, or sells a security to a customer;

"delivery". — "delivery" means voluntary transfer of possession;

"fiduciary". — "fiduciary" means a trustee, guardian, committee, curator, tutor, executor, administrator or representative of a deceased person, or any other person acting in a fiduciary capacity;

"fungible". — "fungible" in relation to securities, means securities of which any unit is, by nature or usage of trade, the equivalent of any other like unit;

"genuine". — "genuine" means free of forgery or counterfeiting;

"good faith". — "good faith" means honesty in fact in the conduct of the transaction concerned;

"holder". — "holder" means a person in possession of a security issued or endorsed to him or to bearer or in blank;

"issuer". — "issuer" includes a corporation

(a) that is required by this Act to maintain a securities register, or

(b) that directly or indirectly creates fractional interests in its rights or property and that issues securities as evidence of such fractional interests;

"overissue". — "overissue" means the issue of securities in excess of any maximum number of securities that the issuer is authorized by its articles or a trust indenture to issue;

"purchaser". — "purchaser" means a person who takes an interest in a security by sale, mortgage, hypothec, pledge, issue, reissue, gift or any other voluntary transaction;

"security" or "security certificate". — "security" or "security certificate" means an instrument issued by a corporation that is

(a) in bearer, order or registered form,

(b) of a type commonly dealt in on securities exchanges or markets or commonly recognized in any area in which it is issued or dealt in as a medium for investment,

(c) one of a class or series or by its terms divisible into a class or series of instruments, and

(d) evidence of a share, participation or other interest in or obligation of a corporation;

"transfer". — "transfer" includes transmission by operation of law;

"trust indenture". — "trust indenture" means a trust indenture as defined in section 82;

"unauthorized". — "unauthorized" in relation to a signature or an endorsement, means one made without actual, implied or apparent authority and includes a forgery;

"valid". — "valid" means issued in accordance with the applicable law and the articles of the issuer, or validated under section 52.

[¶23-193]

(3) *Negotiable instruments.* — Except where its transfer is restricted and noted on a security in accordance with subsection 49(8), a security is a negotiable instrument.

[¶23-194]

(4) *Registered form.* — A security is in registered form if

(a) it specifies a person entitled to the security or to the rights it evidences, and its transfer is capable of being recorded in a securities register; or

(b) it bears a statement that it is in registered form.

[¶23-194a]

(5) *Order form.* — A debt obligation is in order form where, by its terms, it is payable to the order or assigns of any person therein specified with reasonable certainty or to him or his order.

[¶23-195]

(6) *Bearer form.* — A security is in bearer form if it is payable to bearer according to its terms and not by reason of any endorsement.

[¶23-196]

(7) *Guarantor for issuer.* — A guarantor for an issuer is deemed to be an issuer to the extent of his guarantee whether or not his obligation is noted on the security.

¶23-193   Sec. 48(3)

Sec. 49. Rights of holder. — (1) Every security holder is entitled at his option to a security certificate that complies with this Act or a non-transferable written acknowledgment of his right to obtain such a security certificate from a corporation in respect of the securities of that corporation held by him.

(2) *Fee for certificate.* — A corporation may charge a fee of not more than three dollars for a security certificate issued in respect of a transfer.

(3) *Joint holders.* — A corporation is not required to issue more than one security certificate in respect of securities held jointly by several persons, and delivery of a certificate to one of several joint holders is sufficient delivery to all.

(4) *Signatures.* — A security certificate shall be signed manually by at least one director or officer of the corporation or by or on behalf of a registrar, transfer agent or branch transfer agent of the corporation, or by a trustee who certifies it in accordance with a trust indenture, and any additional signatures required on a security certificate may be printed or otherwise mechanically reproduced thereon.

(5) *No manual signature required.* — Notwithstanding subsection (4), a manual signature is not required on

(a) a security certificate representing

(i) a promissory note that is not issued under a trust indenture,

(ii) a fractional share, or

(iii) an option or a right to acquire a security; or

(b) a scrip certificate.

(6) *Continuation of signature.* — If a security certificate contains a printed or mechanically reproduced signature of a person, the corporation may issue the security certificate, notwithstanding that the person has ceased to be a director or an officer of the corporation, and the security certificate is as valid as if he were a director or an officer at the date of its issue.

(7) *Contents of share certificate.* — There shall be stated on the face of each share certificate issued by a corporation

(a) the name of the corporation;

(b) the words "Incorporated under the *Canada Business Corporations Act*";

(c) the name of the person to whom it was issued; and

(d) the number and class of shares and the designation of any series that the certificate represents.

(8) *Restrictions.* — If a security certificate issued by a corporation or by a body corporate before the body corporate was continued under this Act is or becomes subject to

(*a*) a restriction on its transfer other than a constraint under section 174,

(*b*) a lien in favour of the corporation,

(*c*) a unanimous shareholder agreement, or

(*d*) an endorsement under subsection 190(10),

such restriction, lien, agreement or endorsement is ineffective against a transferee of the security who has no actual knowledge of it, unless it or a reference to it is noted conspicuously on the security certificate.

[¶23-204a]

(9) *Limit on restriction.* — A corporation any of the issued shares of which are or were part of a distribution to the public and remain outstanding and are held by more than one person shall not have a restriction on the issue, transfer or ownership of its shares of any class or series except by way of a constraint permitted under section 174.

[¶23-204b]

(10) *Notation of constraint.* — Where the articles of a corporation constrain the issue, transfer or ownership of shares of any class or series in order to assist

(*a*) the corporation or any of its affiliates or associates to qualify under any prescribed law of Canada or a province to receive licences, permits, grants, payments or other benefits by reason of attaining or maintaining a specified level of Canadian ownership or control, or

(*b*) the corporation to comply with

(i) section 379 of the *Trust and Loan Companies Act*, or

(ii) section 411 of the *Insurance Companies Act*,

the constraint, or a reference to it, shall be conspicuously noted on every security certificate of the corporation evidencing a share that is subject to the constraint where the security certificate is issued after the day on which the share becomes subject to the constraint under this Act. (1991, c. 45, s. 553; c. 47, s. 721(1)–(2).)

[¶23-204c]

(11) *Failure to note.* — The failure to note a constraint or a reference to it pursuant to subsection (10) shall not invalidate any share or security certificate and shall not render a constraint ineffective against an owner, holder or transferee of the share or security certificate.

[¶23-205]

(12) *Transitional.* — If a body corporate continued under this Act has outstanding security certification, and if the words "private company" appear on the certificate, those words are deemed to be a notice of a restriction, lien, agreement or endorsement for the purpose of subsection (8).

[¶23-206]

(13) *Particulars of class.* — There shall be stated legibly on a share certificate issued by a corporation that is authorized to issue shares of more than one class or series

(*a*) the rights, privileges, restrictions and conditions attached to the shares of each class and series that exists when the share certificate is issued; or

(*b*) that the class or series of shares that it represents has rights, privileges, restrictions or conditions attached thereto and that the corporation will furnish a shareholder, on demand and without charge, with a full copy of the text of

(i) the rights, privileges, restrictions and conditions attached to each class author-ized to be issued and to each series in so far as the same have been fixed by the directors, and

(ii) the authority of the directors to fix the rights, privileges, restrictions and conditions of subsequent series.

[¶23-207]

(14) *Duty.* — Where a share certificate issued by a corporation contains the statement mentioned in paragraph (13)(*b*), the corporation shall furnish a shareholder on demand and without charge, a full copy of the text of

(*a*) the rights, privileges, restrictions and conditions attached to each class author-ized to be issued and to each series in so far as the same have been fixed by the directors; and

(*b*) the authority of the directors to fix the rights, privileges, restrictions and condi-tions of subsequent series.

[¶23-208]

(15) *Fractional share.* — A corporation may issue a certificate for a fractional share or may issue in place thereof scrip certificates in bearer form that entitle the holder to receive a certificate for a full share by exchanging scrip certificates aggregating a full share.

[¶23-209]

(16) *Scrip certificates.* — The directors may attach conditions to any scrip certificates issued by a corporation, including conditions that

(*a*) the scrip certificates become void if not exchanged for a share certificate repre-senting a full share before a specified date; and

(*b*) any shares for which such scrip certificates are exchangeable may, notwith-standing any pre-emptive right, be issued by the corporation to any person and the proceeds thereof distributed rateably to the holders of the scrip certificates

[¶23-210]

(17) *Holder of fractional share.* — A holder of a fractional share issued by a corporation is not entitled to exercise voting rights or to receive a dividend in respect of the fractional share, unless

(*a*) the fractional share results from a consolidation of shares; or

(*b*) the articles of the corporation otherwise provide.

[¶23-211]

(18) *Holder of scrip certificate.* — A holder of a scrip certificate is not entitled to exercise voting rights or to receive a dividend in respect of the scrip certificate.

(1991, c. 45, s. 553; c. 47, s. 721(1)–(2).)

[¶23-212]

Sec. 50. Securities records. — (1) a corporation shall maintain a securities register in which it records the securities issued by it in registered form, showing with respect to each class or series of securities

(*a*) the names, alphabetically arranged, and the latest known address of each person who is or has been a security holder;

(*b*) the number of securities held by each security holder; and

(*c*) the date and particulars of the issue and transfer of each security.

Sec. 50(1) ¶23-212

[¶23-213]

(2) *Central and branch registers.* — A corporation may appoint an agent to maintain a central securities register and branch securities registers.

[¶23-214]

(3) *Place of register.* — A central securities register shall be maintained by a corporation at its registered office or at any other place in Canada designated by the directors, and any branch securities registers may be kept at any place in or out of Canada designated by the directors.

[¶23-215]

(4) *Effect of registration.* — Registration of the issue or transfer of a security in the central securities register or in a branch securities register is complete and valid registration for all purposes.

[¶23-216]

(5) *Branch register.* — A branch securities register shall only contain particulars of securities issued or transferred at that branch.

[¶23-217]

(6) *Central register.* — Particulars of each issue or transfer of a security registered in a branch securities register shall also be kept in the corresponding central securities register.

[¶23-218]

(7) *Destruction of certificates.* — A corporation, its agent or a trustee defined in subsection 82(1) is not required to produce

(a) a cancelled security certificate in registered form, an instrument referred to in subsection 29(1) that is cancelled or a like cancelled instrument in registered form six years after the date of its cancellation;

(b) a cancelled security certificate in bearer form or an instrument referred to in subsection 29(1) that is cancelled or a like cancelled instrument in bearer form after the date of its cancellation; or

(c) an instrument referred to in subsection 29(1) or a like instrument, irrespective of its form, after the date of its expiry.

[¶23-219]

Sec. 51.   Dealings with registered holder. — (1) A corporation or a trustee defined in subsection 82(1) may, subject to sections 134, 135 and 138, treat the registered owner of a security as the person exclusively entitled to vote, to receive notices, to receive any interest, dividend or other payments in respect of the security, and otherwise to exercise all the rights and powers of an owner of the security.

[¶23-220]

(2) *Constructive registered holder.* — Notwithstanding subsection (1), a corporation whose articles restrict the right to transfer its securities shall, and any other corporation may, treat a person as a registered security holder entitled to exercise all the rights of the security holder he represents, if that person furnishes the Corporation with evidence as described in subsection 77(4) that he is

(a) the executor, administrator, heir or legal representative of the heirs, of the estate of a deceased security holder;

(*b*) a guardian, committee, trustee, curator or tutor representing a registered security holder who is an infant, an

(*c*) a liquidator of, or a trustee in bankruptcy for, a registered security holder, incompetent person or a missing person; or

[¶23-221]

(3) *Permissible registered holder.* — If a person on whom the ownership of a security devolves by operation of law, other than a person described in subsection (2), furnishes proof of his authority to exercise rights or privileges in respect of a security of the corporation that is not registered in his name, the corporation shall treat such person as entitled to exercise those rights or privileges.

[¶23-222]

(4) *Immunity of corporation.* — A corporation is not required to inquire into the existence of, or see to the performance or observance of, any duty owed to a third person by a registered holder of any of its securities or by anyone whom it treats, as permitted or required by this section, as the owner or registered holder thereof.

[¶23-223]

(5) *Infants.* — If an infant exercises any rights of ownership in the securities of a corporation, no subsequent repudiation or avoidance is effective against the corporation.

[¶23-224]

(6) *Joint holders.* — A corporation may treat as owner of a security the survivors of persons to whom the security was issued as joint holders, if it receives proof satisfactory to it of the death of any such joint holder.

[¶23-225]

(7) *Transmission of securities.* — Subject to any applicable law relating to the collection of taxes, a person referred to in paragraph (2)(*a*) is entitled to become a registered holder or to designate a registered holder, if he deposits with the corporation or its transfer agent

(*a*) the original grant of probate or of letters of administration, or a copy thereof certified to be a true copy by

(i) the court that granted the probate or letters of administration,

(ii) a trust company incorporated under the laws of Canada or a province, or

(iii) a lawyer or notary acting on behalf of the person referred to in paragraph (2)(*a*), or

(*b*) in the case of transmission by notarial will in the Province of Quebec, a copy thereof authenticated pursuant to the laws of that Province,

together with

(*c*) an affidavit or declaration of transmission made by a person referred to in paragraph (2)(*a*), stating the particulars of the transmission, and

(*d*) the security certificate that was owned by the deceased holder

(i) in case of a transfer to a person referred to in paragraph (2)(*a*), with or without the endorsement of that person, and

(ii) in case of a transfer to any other person, endorsed in accordance with section 65,

and accompanied by any assurance the corporation may require under section 77.

Sec. 51(7)   ¶23-225

[¶23-226]

(8) *Excepted transmissions.* — Notwithstanding subsection (7), if the laws of the jurisdiction governing the transmission of a security of a deceased holder do not require a grant of probate or of letters of administration in respect of the transmission, a legal representative of the deceased holder is entitled, subject to any applicable law relating to the collection of taxes, to become a registered holder or to designate a registered holder, if he deposits with the corporation or its transfer agent

(a) the security certificate that was owned by the deceased holder; and

(b) reasonable proof of the governing laws, of the deceased holder's interest in the security and of the right of the legal representative or the person he designates to become the registered holder.

[¶23-227]

(9) *Right of corporation.* — Deposit of the documents required by subsection (7) or (8) empowers a corporation or its transfer agent to record in a securities register the transmission of a security from the deceased holder to a person referred to in paragraph (2)(a) or to such person as the person referred to in that paragraph may designate and, thereafter, to treat the person who thus becomes a registered holder as the owner of those securities.

[¶23-228]

Sec. 52. Overissue. — (1) The provisions of this Part that validate a security or compel its issue or reissue do not apply to the extent that validation, issue or reissue would result in overissue, but

(a) if a valid security, similar in all respects to the security involved in the overissue, is reasonably available for purchase, the person entitled to the validation or issue may compel the issuer to purchase and deliver such a security to him against surrender of the security that he holds; or

(b) if a valid security, similar in all respects to the security involved in the overissue, is not reasonably available for purchase, the person entitled to the validation or issue may recover from the issuer an amount equal to the price the last purchaser for value paid for the invalid security.

[¶23-229]

(2) *Retroactive validation.* — When an issuer amends its articles or a trust indenture to which it is a party to increase its authorized securities to a number equal to or in excess of the number of securities previously authorized plus the amount of the securities overissued, the securities so overissued are valid from the date of their issue.

[¶23-230]

(3) *Payment not a purchase or redemption.* — A purchase or payment by an issuer under subsection (1) is not a purchase or payment to which section 34, 35, 36 or 39 applies.

[¶23-231]

Sec. 53. Burden of proof. — In an action on a security,

(a) unless specifically denied in the pleadings, each signature on the security or in a necessary endorsement is admitted;

(b) a signature on the security is presumed to be genuine and authorized but, if the effectiveness of the signature is put in issue, the burden of establishing that it is genuine and authorized is on the party claiming under the signature;

(c) if a signature is admitted or established, production of the instrument entitles a holder to recover on it unless the defendant establishes a defence or a defect going to the validity of the security; and

(d) if the defendant establishes that a defence or defect exists, the plaintiff has the burden of establishing that the defence or defect is ineffective against him or some person under whom he claims.

[¶23-232]

Sec. 54. Securities fungible. — Unless otherwise agreed, and subject to any applicable law, regulation or stock exchange rule, a person required to deliver securities may deliver any security of the specified issue in bearer form or registered in the name of the transferee or endorsed to him or in blank.

Issue — Issuer

[¶23-233]

Sec. 55. Notice of defect. — (1) Even against a purchaser for value and without notice of a defect going to the validity of a security, the terms of the security include those stated on the security and those incorporated therein by reference to another instrument, statute, rule, regulation or order to the extent that the terms so incorporated do not conflict with the stated terms, but such a reference is not of itself notice to a purchaser for value of a defect going to the validity of the security, notwithstanding that the security expressly states that a person accepting it admits such notice.

[¶23-234]

(2) *Purchaser for value.* — A security is valid in the hands of a purchaser for value without notice of any defect going to its validity.

[¶23-235]

(3) *Lack of genuineness.* — Subject to section 57, the fact that a security is not genuine is a complete defence even against a purchaser for value and without notice.

[¶23-236]

(4) *Ineffective defences.* — All other defences of an issuer, including non-delivery and conditional delivery of a security, are ineffective against a purchaser for value without notice of the particular defence.

[¶23-237]

Sec. 56. Staleness as notice of defect. — After an event that creates a right to immediate performance of the principal obligation evidenced by a security, or that sets a date on or after which a security is to be presented or surrendered for redemption or exchange, a purchaser is deemed to have notice of any defect in its issue or of any defence of the issuer,

(a) if the event requires the payment of money or the delivery of securities, or both, on presentation or surrender of the security, and such money or securities are available on the date set for payment or exchange, and he takes the security more than one year after that date; or

(b) if he takes the security more than two years after the date set for presentation or surrender or the date on which such performance became due.

[¶23-246]

Sec. 57. Unauthorized signature. — An unauthorized signature on a security before or in the course of issue is ineffective, except that the signature is effective in favour of a purchaser for value and without notice of the lack of authority, if the signing has been done by

(a) an authenticating trustee, registrar, transfer agent or other person entrusted by the issuer with the signing of the security, or of similar securities, or their immediate preparation for signing; or

(b) an employee of the issuer or of a person referred to in paragraph (a) who in the ordinary course of his duties handles the security.

[¶23-247]

Sec. 58. Completion or alteration. — (1) Where a security contains the signatures necessary for its issue or transfer but is incomplete in any other respect,

(a) any person may complete it by filling in the blanks in accordance with his authority; and

(b) notwithstanding that the blanks are incorrectly filled in, the security as completed is enforceable by a purchaser who took it for value and without notice of such incorrectness.

[¶23-248]

(2) *Enforceability*. — A completed security that has been improperly altered, even if fraudulently altered, remains enforceable but only according to its original terms.

[¶23-249]

Sec. 59. Warranties of agents. — (1) A person signing a security as authenticating trustee, registrar, transfer agent or other person entrusted by the issuer with the signing of the security, warrants to a purchaser for value without notice that

(a) the security is genuine;

(b) his acts in connection with the issue of the security are within his authority; and

(c) he has reasonable grounds for believing that the security is in the form and within the amount the issuer is authorized to issue.

[¶23-250]

(2) *Limitation of liability*. — Unless otherwise agreed, a person referred to in subsection (1) does not assume any further liability for the validity of a security.

Purchase

[¶23-251]

Sec. 60. Title of purchaser. — (1) On delivery of a security the purchaser acquires the rights in the security that his transferor had or had authority to convey, except that a purchaser who has been a party to any fraud or illegality affecting the security or who as a prior holder had notice of an adverse claim does not improve his position by taking from a later *bona fide* purchaser.

[¶23-252]

(2) *Title of bona fide purchaser*. — A *bona fide* purchaser, in addition to acquiring the rights of a purchaser, also acquires the security free from any adverse claim.

[¶23-253]

(3) *Limited interest*. — A purchaser of a limited interest acquires rights only to the extent of the interest purchased.

Sec. 61.   Deemed notice of adverse claim. — (1) A purchaser of a security, or any broker for a seller or purchaser, is deemed to have notice of an adverse claim if

(*a*) the security, whether in bearer or registered form, has been endorsed "for collection" or "for surrender" or for some other purpose not involving transfer; or

(*b*) the security is in bearer form and has on it a statement that it is the property of a person other than the transferor, except that the mere writing of a name on a security is not such a statement.

(2) *Notice of fiduciary duty.* — Notwithstanding that a purchaser, or any broker for a seller or purchaser, has notice that a security is held for a third person or is registered in the name of or endorsed by a fiduciary, he has no duty to inquire into the rightfulness of the transfer and has no notice of an adverse claim, except that where a purchaser knows that the consideration is to be used for, or that the transaction is for, the personal benefit of the fiduciary or is otherwise in breach of the fiduciary's duty, the purchaser is deemed to have notice of an adverse claim.

Sec. 62.   Staleness as notice of adverse claim. — An event that creates a right to immediate performance of the principal obligation evidenced by a security or that sets a date on or after which the security is to be presented or surrendered for redemption or exchange is not of itself notice of an adverse claim, except in the case of a purchase

(*a*) after one year from any date set for such presentation or surrender for redemption or exchange; or

(*b*) after six months from any date set for payment of money against presentation or surrender of the security if funds are available for payment on that date.

Sec. 63.   Warranties to issuer. — (1) A person who presents a security for registration of transfer or for payment or exchange warrants to the issuer that he is entitled to the registration, payment or exchange, except that a purchaser for value without notice of an adverse claim who receives a new, reissued or re-registered security on registration of transfer warrants only that he has no knowledge of any unauthorized signature in a necessary endorsement.

(2) *Warranties to purchaser.* — A person by transferring a security to a purchaser for value warrants only that

(*a*) the transfer is effective and rightful;

(*b*) the security is genuine and has not been materially altered; and

(*c*) he knows of nothing that might impair the validity of the security.

(3) *Warranties of intermediary.* — Where a security is delivered by an intermediary known by the purchaser to be entrusted with delivery of the security on behalf of another or with collection of a draft or other claim to be collected against such delivery, the intermediary by such delivery warrants only his own good faith and authority even if he has purchased or made advances against the draft or other claim to be collected against the delivery.

[¶23-260]

(4) *Warranties of pledgee.* — A pledgee or other holder for purposes of security who redelivers a security received, or after payment and on order of the debtor delivers that security to a third person, gives only the warranties of an intermediary under subsection (3).

[¶23-261]

(5) *Warranties of broker.* — A broker gives to his customer, to the issuer and to a purchaser, as the case may be, the warranties provided in this section and has the rights and privileges of a purchaser under this section, and those warranties of and in favour of the broker acting as an agent are in addition to warranties given by his customer and warranties given in favour of his customer.

[¶23-262]

Sec. 64. Right to compel endorsement. — When a security in registered form is delivered to a purchaser without a necessary endorsement, he may become a *bona fide* purchaser only as of the time the endorsement is supplied, but against the transferor the transfer is complete on delivery and the purchaser has a specifically enforceable right to have any necessary endorsement supplied.

[¶23-263]

Sec. 65. Definition of "appropriate person". — (1) In this section, "appropriate person" means

(a) the person specified by the security or by special endorsement to be entitled to the security;

(b) if a person described in paragraph (a) is described as a fiduciary but is no longer serving in the described capacity, either that person or his successor;

(c) if the security or endorsement mentioned in paragraph (a) specifies more than one person as fiduciaries and one or more are no longer serving in the described capacity, the remaining fiduciary or fiduciaries, whether or not a successor has been appointed or qualified;

(d) if a person described in paragraph (a) is an individual and is without capacity to act by reason of death, incompetence, infancy, minority or otherwise, his fiduciary;

(e) if the security or endorsement mentioned in paragraph (a) specifies more than one person with right of survivorship and by reason of death all cannot sign, the survivor or survivors;

(f) a person having power to sign under applicable law or a power of attorney; or

(g) to the extent that a person described in paragraphs (a) to (f) may act through an agent, his authorized agent.

[¶23-264]

(2) *Determining "appropriate person".* — Whether the person signing is an appropriate person is determined as of the time of signing and an endorsement by such a person does not become unauthorized for the purposes of this Part by reason of any subsequent change of circumstances.

[¶23-265]

(3) *Endorsement.* — An endorsement of a security in registered form is made when an appropriate person signs, either on the security or on a separate document, an assignment or transfer of the security or a power to assign or transfer it, or when the signature of an appropriate person is written without more on the back of the security.

[¶23-266]

(4) *Special or blank.* — An endorsement may be special or in blank.

[¶23-267]

(5) *Blank endorsement.* — An endorsement in blank includes an endorsement to bearer.

[¶23-268]

(6) *Special endorsement.* — A special endorsement specifies the person to whom the security is to be transferred, or who has power to transfer it.

[¶23-269]

(7) *Right of holder.* — A holder may convert an endorsement in blank into a special endorsement.

[¶23-270]

(8) *Immunity of endorser.* — Unless otherwise agreed, the endorser by his endorsement assumes no obligation that the security will be honoured by the issuer.

[¶23-271]

(9) *Partial endorsement.* — An endorsement purporting to be only of part of a security representing units intended by the issuer to be separately transferable is effective to the extent of the endorsement.

[¶23-272]

(10) *Failure of fiduciary to comply.* — Failure of a fiduciary to comply with a controlling instrument or with the law of the jurisdiction governing the fiduciary relationship, including any law requiring the fiduciary to obtain court approval of a transfer, does not render his endorsement unauthorized for the purposes of this Part.

[¶23-282]

Sec. 66. Effect of endorsement without delivery. — An endorsement of a security whether special or in blank does not constitute a transfer until delivery of the security on which it appears or, if the endorsement is on a separate document, until delivery of both the security and that document.

[¶23-283]

Sec. 67. Endorsement in bearer form. — An endorsement of a security in bearer form may give notice of an adverse claim under section 61 but does not otherwise affect any right to registration that the holder has.

[¶23-284]

Sec. 68. Effect of unauthorized endorsement. — (1) The owner of a security may assert the ineffectiveness of an endorsement against the issuer or any purchaser, other than a purchaser for value and without notice of an adverse claim who has in good faith received a new, reissued or re-registered security on registration of transfer, unless the owner

(a) has ratified an unauthorized endorsement of the security; or

(b) is otherwise precluded from impugning the effectiveness of an unauthorized endorsement.

Sec. 68(1)   ¶23-284

[¶23-285]

(2) *Liability of issuer.* — An issuer who registers the transfer of a security on an unauthorized endorsement is liable for improper registration.

[¶23-286]

Sec. 69. Warranties of guarantor of signature. — (1) A person who guarantees a signature of an endorser of a security warrants that at the time of signing

(a) the signature was genuine;

(b) the signer was an appropriate person as defined in section 65 to endorse; and

(c) the signer had legal capacity to sign.

[¶23-287]

(2) *Limitation of liability.* — A person who guarantees a signature of an endorser does not otherwise warrant the rightfulness of the particular transfer.

[¶23-288]

(3) *Warranties of guarantor of endorsement.* — A person who guarantees an endorsement of a security warrants both the signature and the rightfulness of the transfer in all respects, but an issuer may not require a guarantee of endorsement as a condition to registration of transfer.

[¶23-289]

(4) *Extent of liability.* — The warranties referred to in this section are made to any person taking or dealing with the security relying on the guarantee and the guarantor is liable to such person for any loss resulting from breach of warranty.

[¶23-290]

Sec. 70. Constructive delivery of a security. — (1) Delivery to a purchaser occurs when

(a) the purchaser or a person designated by him acquires possession of a security;

(b) the broker of the purchaser acquires possession of a security specially endorsed to or issued in the name of the purchaser;

(c) the broker of the purchaser sends him confirmation of the purchase and the broker in his records identifies a specific security as belonging to the purchaser; or

(d) with respect to an identified security to be delivered while still in the possession of a third person, that person acknowledges that he holds it for the purchaser.

[¶23-291]

(2) *Constructive ownership.* — A purchaser is the owner of a security held for him by his broker, but a purchaser is not a holder except in the cases referred to in paragraphs (1)(b) and (c).

[¶23-292]

(3) *Ownership of part of fungible bulk.* — If a security is part of a fungible bulk a purchaser of the security is the owner of a proportionate interest in the fungible bulk.

[¶23-293]

(4) *Notice to broker.* — Notice of an adverse claim received by a broker or by a purchaser after the broker takes delivery as a holder for value is not effective against the broker or the purchaser, except that, as between the broker and the purchaser, the

purchaser may demand delivery of an equivalent security as to which no notice of an adverse claim has been received.

[¶23-303]

Sec. 71.   Delivery of security. — (1) Unless otherwise agreed, if a sale of a security is made on an exchange or otherwise through brokers,

(a) the selling customer fulfils his duty to deliver when he delivers the security to the selling broker or to a person designated by the selling broker or causes an acknowledgment to be made to the selling broker that it is held for him; and

(b) the selling broker, including a correspondent broker, acting for a selling customer fulfils his duty to deliver by delivering the security or a like security to the buying broker or to a person designated by the buying broker or by effecting clearance of the sale in accordance with the rules of the exchange on which the transaction took place.

[¶23-304]

(2) *Duty to deliver.* — Subject to this section and unless otherwise agreed, a transferor's duty to deliver a security under a contract of purchase is not fulfilled until he delivers the security in negotiable form to the purchaser or to a person designated by the purchaser, or causes an acknowledgment to be made to the purchaser that the security is held for him.

[¶23-305]

(3) *Delivery to broker.* — A sale to a broker purchasing for his own account is subject to subsection (2) and not subsection (1), unless the sale is made on a stock exchange.

[¶23-306]

Sec. 72.   Right to reclaim possession. — (1) A person against whom the transfer of a security is wrongful for any reason, including his incapacity, may against anyone except a *bona fide* purchaser reclaim possession of the security or obtain possession of any new security evidencing all or part of the same rights or claim damages.

[¶23-307]

(2) *Recovery if unauthorized endorsement.* — If the transfer of a security is wrongful by reason of an unauthorized endorsement, the owner may reclaim possession of the security or a new security even from a *bona fide* purchaser if the ineffectiveness of the purported endorsement may be asserted against such purchaser under section 68.

[¶23-308]

(3) *Remedies.* — The right to reclaim possession of a security may be specifically enforced, its transfer may be restrained and the security may be impounded pending litigation.

[¶23-309]

Sec. 73.   Right to requisites for registration. — (1) Unless otherwise agreed, a transferor shall on demand supply a purchaser with proof of his authority to transfer or with any other requisite that is necessary to obtain registration of the transfer of a security, but if the transfer is not for value a transferor need not do so unless the purchaser pays the reasonable and necessary costs of the proof and transfer.

[¶23-310]

(2) *Rescission of transfer.* — If the transferor fails to comply with a demand under subsection (1) within a reasonable time, the purchaser may reject or rescind the transfer.

[¶23-311]

Sec. 74. Seizure of security. — No seizure of a security or other interest evidenced thereby is effective until the person making the seizure obtains possession of the security.

[¶23-311a]

Sec. 75. No conversion if good faith delivery by agent. — An agent or bailee who in good faith, including observance of reasonable commercial standards if he is in the business of buying, selling or otherwise dealing with securities of a corporation, has received securities and sold, pledged or delivered them according to the instructions of his principal is not liable for conversion or for participation in breach of fiduciary duty although the principal has no right to dispose of them.

Registration

[¶23-312]

Sec. 76. Duty to register transfer. — (1) Where a security in registered form is presented for transfer, the issuer shall register the transfer if

(a) the security is endorsed by an appropriate person as defined in section 65;

(b) reasonable assurance is given that endorsement is genuine and effective;

(c) the issuer has no duty to inquire into adverse claims or has discharged any such duty;

(d) any applicable law relating to the collection of taxes has been complied with;

(e) the transfer is rightful or is to a *bona fide* purchaser; and

(f) any fee referred to in subsection 49(2) has been paid.

[¶23-313]

(2) *Liability for delay.* — Where an issuer has a duty to register a transfer of a security, the issuer is liable to the person presenting it for registration for loss resulting from any unreasonable delay in registration or from failure or refusal to register the transfer.

[¶23-314]

Sec. 77. Assurance that endorsement effective. — (1) An issuer may require an assurance that each necessary endorsement on a security is genuine and effective by requiring a guarantee of the signature of the person endorsing, and by requiring

(a) if the endorsement is by an agent, reasonable assurance of authority to sign;

(b) if the endorsement is by a fiduciary, evidence of appointment or incumbency;

(c) if there is more than one fiduciary, reasonable assurance that all who are required to sign have done so; and

(d) in any other case, assurance that corresponds as closely as practicable to the foregoing.

[¶23-315]

(2) *Definition of "guarantee of the signature".* — For the purposes of subsection (1), a "guarantee of the signature" means a guarantee signed by or on behalf of a person reasonably believed by the issuer to be responsible.

[¶23-316]

(3) *Standards.* — An issuer may adopt reasonable standards to determine responsible persons for the purpose of subsection (2).

[¶23-317]

(4) *Definition of "evidence of appointment or incumbency"*. — In paragraph (1)(*b*), "evidence of appointment of incumbency" means

(*a*) in the case of a fiduciary appointed by a court, a copy of the order certified in accordance with subsection 51(7), and dated not earlier than sixty days before the date a security is presented for transfer; or

(*b*) in any other case, a copy of a document showing the appointment or other evidence believed by the issuer to be appropriate.

[¶23-318]

(5) *Standards.* — An issuer may adopt reasonable standards with respect to evidence for the purposes of paragraph (4)(*b*).

[¶23-319]

(6) *No notice to issuer.* — An issuer is deemed not to have notice of the contents of any document referred to in subsection (4) except to the extent that the contents relate directly to appointment or incumbency.

[¶23-320]

(7) *Notice from excess documentation.* — If an issuer demands assurance additional to that specified in this section for a purpose other than that specified in subsection (4) and obtains a copy of a will, trust or partnership agreement, by-law or similar document, the issuer is deemed to have notice of all matters contained therein affecting the transfer.

[¶23-329]

Sec. 78. Limited duty of inquiry. — (1) An issuer to whom a security is presented for registration has a duty to inquire into adverse claims if

(*a*) written notice of an adverse claim has been received at a time and in a manner that affords the issuer a reasonable opportunity to act on it before the issue of a new, reissued or re-registered security and the notice discloses the name and address of the claimant, the registered owner and the issue of which the security is a part; or

(*b*) the issuer is deemed to have notice of an adverse claim from a document that it obtained under subsection 77(7).

[¶23-330]

(2) *Discharge of duty.* — An issuer may discharge a duty of inquiry by any reasonable means, including notifying an adverse claimant by registered mail sent to the address furnished by him or, if no such address has been furnished, to his residence or regular place of business, that a security has been presented for registration of transfer by a named person, and that the transfer will be registered unless within thirty days from the date of mailing the notice either

(*a*) the issuer is served with a restraining order or other order of a court; or

(*b*) the issuer is provided with an indemnity bond sufficient in the issuer's judgment to protect the issuer and any registrar, transfer agent or other agent of the issuer from any loss that may be incurred by any of them as a result of complying with the adverse claim.

[¶23-331]

(3) *Inquiry into adverse claims.* — Unless an issuer is deemed to have notice of an adverse claim from a document that it obtained under subsection 77(7) or has received notice of an adverse claim under subsection (1), if a security presented for registration is

endorsed by the appropriate person as defined in section 65, the issuer has no duty to inquire into adverse claims, and in particular,

(*a*) an issuer registering a security in the name of a person who is a fiduciary or who is described as a fiduciary is not bound to inquire into the existence, extent or correct description of the fiduciary relationship and thereafter the issuer may assume without inquiry that the newly registered owner continues to be the fiduciary until the issuer receives written notice that the fiduciary is no longer acting as such with respect to the particular security;

(*b*) an issuer registering transfer on an endorsement by a fiduciary has no duty to inquire whether the transfer is made in compliance with the document or with the law of the jurisdiction governing the fiduciary relationship; and

(*c*) an issuer is deemed not to have notice of the contents of any court record or any registered document even if the record or document is in the issuer's possession and even if the transfer is made on the endorsement of a fiduciary to the fiduciary himself or to his nominee.

[¶23-332]

(4) *Duration of notice.* — A written notice of adverse claim received by an issuer is effective for twelve months from the date when it was received unless the notice is renewed in writing.

[¶23-333]

Sec. 79. Limitation of issuer's liability. — (1) Subject to any applicable law relating to the collection of taxes, the issuer is not liable to the owner or any other person who incurs a loss as a result of the registration of a transfer of a security if

(*a*) the necessary endorsements were on or with the security; and

(*b*) the issuer had no duty to inquire into adverse claims or had discharged any such duty.

[¶23-334]

(2) *Duty of issuer in default.* — If an issuer has registered a transfer of a security to a person not entitled to it, the issuer shall on demand deliver a like security to the owner unless

(*a*) subsection (1) applies;

(*b*) the owner is precluded by subsection 80(1) from asserting any claim; or

(*c*) the delivery would result in overissue, in which case the issuer's liability is governed by section 52.

[¶23-344]

Sec. 80. Notice of lost or stolen security. — (1) Where a security has been lost, apparently destroyed or wrongfully taken, and the owner fails to notify the issuer of that fact by giving the issuer written notice of his adverse claim within a reasonable time after he knows of the loss, destruction or taking and if the issuer has registered a transfer of the security before receiving such notice, the owner is precluded from asserting against the issuer any claim to a new security.

[¶23-345]

(2) *Duty of issuer to issue a new security.* — Where the owner of a security claims that the security has been lost, destroyed or wrongfully taken, the issuer shall issue a new security in place of the original security if the owner

(*a*) so requests before the issuer has notice that the security has been acquired by a *bona fide* purchaser;

(*b*) furnishes the issuer with a sufficient indemnity bond; and

(*c*) satisfies any other reasonable requirements imposed by the issuer.

[¶23-346]

(3) *Duty to register transfer.* — If, after the issue of a new security under subsection (2), a *bona fide* purchaser of the original security presents the original security for registration of transfer, the issuer shall register the transfer unless registration would result in over-issue, in which case the issuer's liability is governed by section 52.

[¶23-347]

(4) *Right of issuer to recover.* — In addition to any rights on an indemnity bond, the issuer may recover a new security issued under subsection (2) from the person to whom it was issued or any person taking under him other than a *bona fide* purchaser.

[¶23-348]

Sec. 81. Agent's duties, rights, etc. — (1) An authenticating trustee, registrar, transfer agent or other agent of an issuer has, in respect of the issue, registration of transfer and cancellation of a security of the issuer,

(*a*) a duty to the issuer to exercise good faith and reasonable diligence; and

(*b*) the same obligations to the holder or owner of a security and the same rights, privileges and immunities as the issuer.

[¶23-349]

(2) *Notice to agent.* — Notice to an authenticating trustee, registrar, transfer agent or other agent of an issuer is notice to the issuer with respect to the functions performed by the agent.

Part VIII
Trust Indentures

[¶23-365]

Sec. 82. Definitions. — (1) In this Part,

"event of default". — "event of default" means an event specified in a trust indenture on the occurrence of which

(*a*) a security interest constituted by the trust indenture becomes enforceable, or

(*b*) the principal, interest and other moneys payable thereunder become or may be declared to be payable before maturity,

but the event is not an event of default until all conditions prescribed by the trust indenture in connection with such event for the giving of notice or the lapse of time or otherwise have been satisfied;

"trustee". — "trustee" means any person appointed as trustee under the terms of a trust indenture to which a corporation is a party and includes any successor trustee;

"trust indenture". — "trust indenture" means any deed, indenture or other instrument, including any supplement or amendment thereto, made by a corporation after its incorporation or continuance under this Act, under which the corporation issues debt obligations and in which a person is appointed as trustee for the holders of the debt obligations issued thereunder.

[¶23-366]

(2) *Application.* — This Part applies to a trust indenture if the debt obligations issued or to be issued under the trust indenture are part of a distribution to the public.

[¶23-367]

(3) *Exemption.* — The Director may exempt a trust indenture from this Part if the trust indenture, the debt obligations issued thereunder and the security interest effected thereby are subject to a law of a province or a country other than Canada that is substantially equivalent to this Part.

[¶23-368]

Sec. 83.   Conflict of interest. — (1) No person shall be appointed as trustee if there is a material conflict of interest between his role as trustee and his role in any other capacity.

[¶23-369]

(2) *Eliminating conflict of interest.* — A trustee shall, within ninety days after he becomes aware that a material conflict of interest exists

(a) eliminate such conflict of interest; or

(b) resign from office.

[¶23-370]

(3) *Validity.* — A trust indenture, any debt obligations issued thereunder and a security interest effected thereby are valid notwithstanding a material conflict of interest of the trustee.

[¶23-371]

(4) *Removal of trustee.* — If a trustee contravenes subsection (1) or (2), any interested person may apply to a court for an order that the trustee be replaced, and the court may make an order on such terms as it thinks fit.

[¶23-372]

Sec. 84.   Qualification of trustee. — A trustee, or at least one of the trustees if more than one is appointed, shall be a body corporate incorporated under the laws of Canada or a province and authorized to carry on the business of a trust company.

[¶23-383]

Sec. 85.   List of security holders. — (1) A holder of debt obligations issued under a trust indenture may, on payment to the trustee of a reasonable fee, require the trustee to furnish, within fifteen days after delivering to the trustee the statutory declaration referred to in subsection (4), a list setting out

(a) the names and addresses of the registered holders of the outstanding debt obligations,

(b) the principal amount of outstanding debt obligations owned by each such holder, and

(c) the aggregate principal amount of debt obligations outstanding

as shown on the records maintained by the trustee on the day that the statutory declaration is delivered to that trustee.

[¶23-384]

(2) *Duty of issuer.* — On the demand of a trustee, the issuer of debt obligations shall furnish the trustee with the information required to enable the trustee to comply with subsection (1).

[¶23-385]

(3) *Corporate applicant.* — If the person requiring the trustee to furnish a list under subsection (1) is a body corporate, the statutory declaration required under that subsection shall be made by a director or officer of the body corporate.

[¶23-386]

(4) *Contents of statutory declaration.* — The statutory declaration required under subsection (1) shall state

(a) the name and address of the person requiring the trustee to furnish the list and, if the person is a body corporate, the address for service thereof; and

(b) that the list will not be used except as permitted under subsection (5).

[¶23-387]

(5) *Use of list.* — A list obtained under this section shall not be used by any person except in connection with

(a) an effort to influence the voting of the holders of debt obligations;

(b) an offer to acquire debt obligations; or

(c) any other matter relating to the debt obligations or the affairs of the issuer or guarantor thereof.

[¶23-388]

(6) *Offence.* — A person who, without reasonable cause, contravenes subsection (5) is guilty of an offence and liable on summary conviction to a fine not exceeding five thousand dollars or to imprisonment for a term not exceeding six months or to both.

[¶23-389]

Sec. 86.   Evidence of compliance. — (1) An issuer or a guarantor of debt obligations issued or to be issued under a trust indenture shall, before doing any act under paragraph (a), (b) or (c), furnish the trustee with evidence of compliance with the conditions in the trust indenture relating to

(a) the issue, certification and delivery of debt obligations under the trust indenture;

(b) the release or release and substitution of property subject to a security interest constituted by the trust indenture; or

(c) the satisfaction and discharge of the trust indenture.

[¶23-390]

(2) *Duty of issuer or guarantor.* — On the demand of a trustee, the issuer or guarantor of debt obligations issued or to be issued under a trust indenture shall furnish the trustee with evidence of compliance with the trust indenture by the issuer or guarantor in respect of any act to be done by the trustee at the request of the issuer or guarantor.

[¶23-391]

Sec. 87.   Contents of declaration, etc. — Evidence of compliance as required by section 86 shall consist of

(a) a statutory declaration or certificate made by a director or an officer of the issuer or guarantor stating that the conditions referred to in that section have been complied with; and

(b) where the trust indenture requires compliance with conditions that are subject to review

(i) by legal counsel, an opinion of legal counsel that such conditions have been complied with, and

(ii) by an auditor or accountant, an opinion or report of the auditor of the issuer or guarantor, or such other accountant as the trustee may select, that such conditions have been complied with.

[¶23-392]

Sec. 88.   Further evidence of compliance. — The evidence of compliance referred to in section 87 shall include a statement by the person giving the evidence

(a) declaring that he has read and understands the conditions of the trust indenture described in section 86;

(b) describing the nature and scope of the examination or investigation on which he based the certificate, statement or opinion; and

(c) declaring that he has made such examination or investigation as he believes necessary to enable him to make the statements or give the opinions contained or expressed therein.

[¶23-393]

Sec. 89.   Trustee may require evidence of compliance. — (1) On the demand of a trustee, the issuer or guarantor of debt obligations issued under a trust indenture shall furnish the trustee with evidence in such form as the trustee may require as to compliance with any condition thereto relating to any action required or permitted to be taken by the issuer or guarantor under the trust indenture.

[¶23-394]

(2) *Certificate of compliance.* — At least once in each twelve-month period beginning on the date of the trust indenture and at any other time on the demand of a trustee, the issuer or guarantor of debt obligations issued under a trust indenture shall furnish the trustee with a certificate that the issuer or guarantor has complied with all requirements contained in the trust indenture that, if not complied with, would, with the giving of notice, lapse of time or otherwise, constitute an event of default, or, if there has been failure to so comply, giving particulars thereof.

[¶23-395]

Sec. 90.   Notice of default. — The trustee shall give to the holders of debt obligations issued under a trust indenture, within thirty days after the trustee becomes aware of the occurrence thereof, notice of every event of default arising under the trust indenture and continuing at the time the notice is given, unless the trustee reasonably believes that it is in the best interests of the holders of the debt obligations to withhold such notice and so informs the issuer and guarantor in writing.

[¶23-396]

Sec. 91.   Duty of care. — A trustee in exercising his powers and discharging his duties shall

(a) act honestly and in good faith with a view to the best interests of the holders of the debt obligations issued under the trust indenture; and

(b) exercise the care, diligence and skill of a reasonably prudent trustee.

[¶23-397]

Sec. 92. Reliance on statements. — Notwithstanding section 91, a trustee is not liable if he relies in good faith on statements contained in a statutory declaration, certificate, opinion or report that complies with this Act or the trust indenture.

[¶23-398]

Sec. 93. No exculpation. — No term of a trust indenture or of any agreement between a trustee and the holders of debt obligations issued thereunder or between the trustee and the issuer or guarantor shall operate so as to relieve a trustee from the duties imposed on him by section 91.

Part IX
Receivers and Receiver-Managers

[¶23-405]

Sec. 94. Functions of receiver. — A receiver of any property of a corporation may, subject to the rights of secured creditors, receive the income from the property and pay the liabilities connected with the property and realize the security interest of those on behalf of whom he is appointed, but, except to the extent permitted by a court, he may not carry on the business of the corporation.

[¶23-406]

Sec. 95. Functions of receiver-manager. — A receiver of a corporation may, if he is also appointed receiver-manager of the corporation, carry on any business of the corporation to protect the security interest of those on behalf of whom he is appointed

[¶23-407]

Sec. 96. Directors' powers cease. — If a receiver-manager is appointed by a court or under an instrument, the powers of the directors of the corporation that the receiver-manager is authorized to exercise may not be exercised by the directors until the receiver-manager is discharged.

[¶23-408]

Sec. 97. Duty to act. — A receiver or receiver-manager appointed by a court shall act in accordance with the directions of the court.

[¶23-409]

Sec. 98. Duty under instrument. — A receiver or receiver-manager appointed under an instrument shall act in accordance with that instrument and any direction of a court made under section 100.

[¶23-410]

Sec. 99. Duty of care. — A receiver or receiver-manager of a corporation appointed under an instrument shall

(a) act honestly and in good faith; and

(b) deal with any property of the corporation in his possession or control in a commercially reasonable manner.

[¶23-415]

Sec. 100. Directions given by court. — On an application by a receiver or receiver-manager, whether appointed by a court or under an instrument, or on an application by any interested person, a court may make any order it thinks fit including, without limiting the generality of the foregoing,

(a) an order appointing, replacing or discharging a receiver or receiver-manager and approving his accounts;

(b) an order determining the notice to be given to any person or dispensing with notice to any person;

(c) an order fixing the remuneration of the receiver or receiver-manager;

(d) an order requiring the receiver or receiver-manager, or a person by or on behalf of whom he is appointed, to make good any default in connection with the receiver's or receiver-manager's custody or management of the property and business of the corporation, or to relieve any such person from any default on such terms as the court thinks fit, and to confirm any act of the receiver or receiver-manager;

(e) an order giving directions on any matter relating to the duties of the receiver or receiver-manager.

[¶23-416]

Sec. 101.   Duties of receiver and receiver-manager. — A receiver or receiver-manager shall

(a) immediately notify the Director of his appointment and discharge;

(b) take into his custody and control the property of the corporation in accordance with the court order or instrument under which he is appointed;

(c) open and maintain a bank account in his name as receiver or receiver-manager of the corporation for the moneys of the corporation coming under his control;

(d) keep detailed accounts of all transactions carried out by him as receiver or receiver-manager;

(e) keep accounts of his administration that shall be available during usual business hours for inspection by the directors of the corporation;

(f) prepare at least once in every six-month period after the date of his appointment financial statements of his administration as far as is practicable in the form required by section 155; and

(g) on completion of his duties, render a final account of his administration in the form adopted for interim accounts under paragraph (f).

Part X
Directors and Officers

[¶23-426]

Sec. 102.   Power to manage. — (1) Subject to any unanimous shareholder agreement, the directors shall manage the business and affairs of a corporation.

[¶23-427]

(2) *Number of directors.* — A corporation shall have one or more directors but a corporation, any of the issued securities of which are or were part of a distribution to the public and remain outstanding and are held by more than one person, shall have not fewer than three directors, at least two of whom are not officers or employees of the corporation or its affiliates.

[¶23-428]

Sec. 103. By-laws. — (1) Unless the articles, by-laws or a unanimous shareholder agreement otherwise provide, the directors may, by resolution, make, amend, or repeal any by-laws that regulate the business or affairs of the corporation.

[¶23-429]

(2) *Shareholder approval.* — The directors shall submit a by-law, or an amendment or a repeal of a by-law, made under subsection (1) to the shareholders at the next meeting of shareholders, and the shareholders may, by ordinary resolution, confirm, reject or amend the by-law, amendment or repeal.

[¶23-430]

(3) *Effective date.* — A by-law, or an amendment or a repeal of a by-law, is effective from the date of the resolution of the directors under subsection (1) until it is confirmed, confirmed as amended or rejected by the shareholders under subsection (2) or until it ceases to be effective under subsection (4) and, where the by-law is confirmed or confirmed as amended, it continues in effect in the form in which it was so confirmed.

[¶23-431]

(4) *Idem.* — If a by-law, an amendment or a repeal is rejected by the shareholders, or if the directors do not submit a by-law, an amendment or a repeal to the shareholders as required under subsection (2), the by-law, amendment or repeal ceases to be effective and no subsequent resolution of the directors to make, amend or repeal a by-law having substantially the same purpose or effect is effective until it is confirmed or confirmed as amended by the shareholders.

[¶23-432]

(5) *Shareholder proposal.* — A shareholder entitled to vote at an annual meeting of shareholders may, in accordance with section 137, make a proposal to make, amend or repeal a by-law.

[¶23-433]

Sec. 104. Organization meeting. — (1) After issue of the certificate of incorporation, a meeting of the directors of the corporation shall be held at which the directors may

(a) make by-laws;

(b) adopt forms of security certificates and corporate records;

(c) authorize the issue of securities;

(d) appoint officers;

(e) appoint an auditor to hold office until the first annual meeting of shareholders;

(f) make banking arrangements; and

(g) transact any other business.

[¶23-433a]

(2) *Exception.* — Subsection (1) does not apply to a body corporate to which a certificate of amalgamation has been issued under subsection 185(4) or to which a certificate of continuance has been issued under subsection 187(4).

[¶23-434]

(3) *Calling meeting.* — An incorporator or a director may call the meeting of directors referred to in subsection (1) by giving not less than five days notice thereof by mail to each director, stating the time and place of the meeting.

[¶23-435]

Sec. 105.   Qualifications of directors. — (1) The following persons are disqualified from being a director of a corporation:

(a) anyone who is less than eighteen years of age;

(b) anyone who is of unsound mind and has been so found by a court in Canada or elsewhere;

(c) a person who is not an individual; or

(d) a person who has the status of bankrupt.

[¶23-436]

(2) *Further qualifications.* — Unless the articles otherwise provide, a director of a corporation is not required to hold shares issued by the corporation.

[¶23-437]

(3) *Residency.* — A majority of the directors of a corporation must be resident Canadians.

[¶23-438]

(4) *Exception for holding corporation.* — Notwithstanding subsection (3), not more than one-third of the directors of a holding corporation need be resident Canadians if the holding corporation earns in Canada directly or through its subsidiaries less than five per cent of the gross revenues of the holding corporation and all of its subsidiary bodies corporate together as shown in

(a) the most recent consolidated financial statements of the holding corporation referred to in section 157; or

(b) the most recent financial statements of the holding corporation and its subsidiary bodies corporate as at the end of the last completed financial year of the holding corporation.

[¶23-443]

Sec. 106.   Notice of directors. — (1) At the time of sending articles of incorporation, the incorporators shall send to the Director a notice of directors in prescribed form and the Director shall file the notice.

[¶23-444]

(2) *Term of office.* — Each director named in the notice referred to in subsection (1) holds office from the issue of the certificate of incorporation until the first meeting of shareholders.

[¶23-445]

(3) *Election of directors.* — Subject to paragraph 107(b), shareholders of a corporation shall, by ordinary resolution at the first meeting of shareholders and at each succeeding annual meeting at which an election of directors is required, elect directors to hold office for a term expiring not later than the close of the third annual meeting of shareholders following the election.

[¶23-446]

(4) *Staggered terms.* — It is not necessary that all directors elected at a meeting of shareholders hold office for the same term.

[¶23-447]

(5) *No stated terms.* — A director not elected for an expressly stated term ceases to hold office at the close of the first annual meeting of shareholders following his election.

[¶23-448]

(6) *Incumbent directors.* — Notwithstanding subsections (2), (3) and (5), if directors are not elected at a meeting of shareholders the incumbent directors continue in office until their successors are elected.

[¶23-449]

(7) *Vacancy among candidates.* — If a meeting of shareholders fails to elect the number or the minimum number of directors required by the articles by reason of the disqualification, incapacity or death of any candidates, the directors elected at that meeting may exercise all the powers of the directors if the number of directors so elected constitutes a quorum.

[¶23-450]

Sec. 107. Cumulative voting. — Where the articles provide for cumulative voting,

(a) the articles shall require a fixed number and not a minimum and maximum number of directors;

(b) each shareholder entitled to vote at an election of directors has the right to cast a number of votes equal to the number of votes attached to the shares held by him multiplied by the number of directors to be elected, and he may cast all such votes in favour of one candidate or distribute them among the candidates in any manner;

(c) a separate vote of shareholders shall be taken with respect to each candidate nominated for director unless a resolution is passed unanimously permitting two or more persons to be elected by a single resolution;

(d) if a shareholder has voted for more than one candidate without specifying the distribution of his votes among the candidates, he is deemed to have distributed his votes equally among the candidates for whom he voted;

(e) if the number of candidates nominated for director exceeds the number of positions to be filled, the candidates who receive the least number of votes shall be eliminated until the number of candidates remaining equals the number of positions to be filled;

(f) each director ceases to hold office at the close of the first annual meeting of shareholders following his election;

(g) a director may not be removed from office if the votes cast against his removal would be sufficient to elect him and such votes could be voted cumulatively at an election at which the same total number of votes were cast and the number of directors required by the articles were then being elected; and

(h) the number of directors required by the articles may not be decreased if the votes cast against the motion to decrease would be sufficient to elect a director and such votes could be voted cumulatively at an election at which the same total number of votes were cast and the number of directors required by the articles were then being elected.

[¶23-451]

Sec. 108. Ceasing to hold office. — (1) A director of a corporation ceases to hold office when

(a) he dies or resigns;

(b) he is removed in accordance with section 109; or

(c) he becomes disqualified under subsection 105(1)

[¶23-456]

(2) *Effective date of resignation.* — A resignation of a director becomes effective at the time a written resignation is sent to the corporation, or at the time specified in the resignation, whichever is later.

[¶23-457]

Sec. 109.   Removal of directors. — (1) Subject to paragraph 107(*g*), the shareholders of a corporation may by ordinary resolution at a special meeting remove any director or directors from office.

[¶23-458]

(2) *Exception.* — Where the holders of any class or series of shares of a corporation have an exclusive right to elect one or more directors, a director so elected may only be removed by an ordinary resolution at a meeting of the shareholders of that class or series.

[¶23-459]

(3) *Vacancy.* — Subject to paragraphs 107(*b*) to (*e*), a vacancy created by the removal of a director may be filled at the meeting of the shareholders at which the director is removed or, if not so filled, may be filled under section 111.

[¶23-460]

Sec. 110.   Attendance at meeting. — (1) A director of a corporation is entitled to receive notice of and to attend and be heard at every meeting of shareholders.

[¶23-461]

(2) *Statement of director.* — A director who

(*a*) resigns,

(*b*) receives a notice or otherwise learns of a meeting of shareholders called for the purpose of removing him from office, or

(*c*) receives a notice or otherwise learns of a meeting of directors or shareholders at which another person is to be appointed or elected to fill the office of director, whether because of his resignation or removal or because his term of office has expired or is about to expire,

is entitled to submit to the corporation a written statement giving the reasons for his resignation or the reasons why he opposes any proposed action or resolution.

[¶23-462]

(3) *Circulating statement.* — A corporation shall forthwith send a copy of the statement referred to in subsection (2) to every shareholder entitled to receive notice of any meeting referred to in subsection (1) and to the Director unless the statement is included in or attached to a management proxy circular required by section 150.

[¶23-463]

(4) *Immunity.* — No corporation or person acting on its behalf incurs any liability by reason only of circulating a director's statement in compliance with subsection (3).

[¶23-464]

Sec. 111.   Filling vacancy. — (1) Notwithstanding subsection 114(3), but subject to subsections (3) and (4), a quorum of directors may fill a vacancy among the directors, except a vacancy resulting from an increase in the number or minimum number of directors or from a failure to elect the number or minimum number of directors required by the articles.

[¶23-465]

(2) *Calling meeting.* — If there is not a quorum of directors, or if there has been a failure to elect the number or minimum number of directors required by the articles, the directors then in office shall forthwith call a special meeting of shareholders to fill the vacancy and, if they fail to call a meeting or if there are no directors then in office, the meeting may be called by any shareholder.

[¶23-466]

(3) *Class director.* — Where the holders of any class or series of shares of a corporation have an exclusive right to elect one or more directors and a vacancy occurs among those directors,

(a) subject to subsection (4), the remaining directors elected by that class or series may fill the vacancy except a vacancy resulting from an increase in the number or minimum number of directors for that class or series or from a failure to elect the number or minimum number of directors for that class or series; or

(b) if there are no such remaining directors any holder of shares of that class or series may call a meeting of the holders thereof for the purpose of filling the vacancy.

[¶23-467]

(4) *Shareholders filling vacancy.* — The articles may provide that a vacancy among the directors shall only be filled by a vote of the shareholders, or by a vote of the holders of any class or series of shares having an exclusive right to elect one or more directors if the vacancy occurs among the directors elected by that class or series.

[¶23-468]

(5) *Unexpired term.* — A director appointed or elected to fill a vacancy holds office for the unexpired term of his predecessor.

[¶23-469]

Sec. 112.   Number of directors. — (1) The shareholders of a corporation may amend the articles to increase or, subject to paragraph 107(h), to decrease the number of directors, or the minimum or maximum number of directors, but no decrease shall shorten the term of an incumbent director.

[¶23-469a]

(2) *Electing additional number of directors where articles amended.* — Where the shareholders adopt an amendment to the articles of a corporation to increase the number or minimum number of directors, the shareholders may, at the meeting at which they adopt the amendment, elect the additional number of directors authorized by the amendment, and for that purpose, notwithstanding subsections 179(1) and 262(3), on the issue of a certificate of amendment the articles are deemed to be amended as of the date the shareholders adopt the amendment to the articles.

[¶23-470]

Sec. 113.   Notice of change of directors. — (1) Within fifteen days after a change is made among its directors, a corporation shall send to the Director a notice in prescribed form setting out the change and the Director shall file the notice.

[¶23-471]

(2) *Application to court.* — Any interested person, or the Director, may apply to a court for an order to require a corporation to comply with subsection (1), and the court may so order and make any further order it thinks fit.

[¶23-472]

Sec. 114.   Meeting of directors. — (1) Unless the articles or by-laws otherwise provide, the directors may meet at any place and upon such notice as the by-laws require.

[¶23-473]

(2) *Quorum.* — Subject to the articles or by-laws, a majority of the number of directors or minimum number of directors required by the articles constitutes a quorum at any meeting of directors, and, notwithstanding any vacancy among the directors, a quorum of directors may exercise all the powers of the directors.

[¶23-474]

(3) *Canadian majority.* — Directors, other than directors of a corporation referred to in subsection 105(4), shall not transact business at a meeting of directors unless a majority of directors present are resident Canadians.

[¶23-475]

(4) *Exception.* — Notwithstanding subsection (3), directors may transact business at a meeting of directors where a majority of resident Canadian directors is not present if

(a) a resident Canadian director who is unable to be present approves in writing or by telephone or other communications facilities the business transacted at the meeting; and

(b) a majority of resident Canadian directors would have been present had that director been present at the meeting.

[¶23-476]

(5) *Notice of meeting.* — A notice of a meeting of directors shall specify any matter referred to in subsection 115(3) that is to be dealt with at the meeting but, unless the by-laws otherwise provide, need not specify the purpose of or the business to be transacted at the meeting.

[¶23-477]

(6) *Waiver of notice.* — A director may in any manner waive a notice of a meeting of directors; and attendance of a director at a meeting of directors is a waiver of notice of the meeting, except where a director attends a meeting for the express purpose of objecting to the transaction of any business on the grounds that the meeting is not lawfully called.

[¶23-478]

(7) *Adjournment.* — Notice of an adjourned meeting of directors is not required to be given if the time and place of the adjourned meeting is announced at the original meeting.

[¶23-479]

(8) *One director meeting.* — Where a corporation has only one director, that director may constitute a meeting.

[¶23-480]

(9) *Participation by telephone.* — Subject to the by-laws, a director may, if all the directors of the corporation consent, participate in a meeting of directors or of a committee of directors by means of such telephone or other communications facilities as permit all persons participating in the meeting to hear each other, and a director participating in such a meeting by such means is deemed for the purposes of this Act to be present at that meeting.

[¶23-488]

Sec. 115. Delegation. — (1) Directors of a corporation may appoint from their number a managing director who is a resident Canadian or a committee of directors and delegate to such managing director or committee any of the powers of the directors.

[¶23-489]

(2) *Canadian majority.* — If the directors of a corporation, other than a corporation referred to in subsection 105(4), appoint a committee of directors, a majority of the members of the committee must be resident Canadians.

[¶23-490]

(3) *Limits on authority.* — Notwithstanding subsection (1), no managing director and no committee of directors has authority to

(a) submit to the shareholders any question or matter requiring the approval of the shareholders;

(b) fill a vacancy among the directors or in the office of auditor;

(c) issue securities except in the manner and on the terms authorized by the directors;

(d) declare dividends;

(e) purchase, redeem or otherwise acquire shares issued by the corporation;

(f) pay a commission referred to in section 41;

(g) approve a management proxy circular referred to in Part XIII;

(h) approve a take-over bid circular or directors' circular referred to in Part XVII;

(i) approve any financial statements referred to in section 155; or

(j) adopt, amend or repeal by-laws.

[¶23-492]

Sec. 116. Validity of acts of directors and officers. — An act of a director or officer is valid notwithstanding an irregularity in his election or appointment or a defect in his qualification.

[¶23-493]

Sec. 117. Resolution in lieu of meeting. — (1) A resolution in writing, signed by all the directors entitled to vote on that resolution at a meeting of directors or committee of directors, is as valid as if it had been passed at a meeting of directors or committee of directors.

[¶23-494]

(2) *Filing resolution.* — A copy of every resolution referred to in subsection (1) shall be kept with the minutes of the proceedings of the directors or committee of directors.

[¶23-495]

Sec. 118. Directors' liability. — (1) Directors of a corporation who vote for or consent to a resolution authorizing the issue of a share under section 25 for a consideration other than money are jointly and severally liable to the corporation to make good any amount by which the consideration received is less than the fair equivalent of the money that the corporation would have received if the share had been issued for money on the date of the resolution.

[¶23-496]

(2) *Further directors' liabilities.* — Directors of a corporation who vote for or consent to a resolution authorizing

(a) a purchase, redemption or other acquisition of shares contrary to section 34, 35 or 36,

(b) a commission contrary to section 41,

(c) a payment of a dividend contrary to section 2,

(d) financial assistance contrary to section 44,

(e) a payment of an indemnity contrary to section 124, or

(f) a payment to a shareholder contrary to section 190 or 241,

are jointly and severally liable to restore to the corporation any amounts so distributed or paid and not otherwise recovered by the corporation.

[¶23-497]

(3) *Contribution.* — A director who has satisfied a judgment rendered under this section is entitled to contribution from the other directors who voted for or consented to the unlawful act on which the judgment was founded.

[¶23-498]

(4) *Recovery.* — A director liable under subsection (2) is entitled to apply to a court for an order compelling a shareholder or other recipient to pay or deliver to the director any money or property that was paid or distributed to the shareholder or other recipient contrary to section 34, 35, 36, 41, 42, 44, 124, 190 or 241.

[¶23-499]

(5) *Order of court.* — In connection with an application under subsection (4) a court may, if it is satisfied that it is equitable to do so,

(a) order a shareholder or other recipient to pay or deliver to a director any money or property that was paid or distributed to the shareholder or other recipient contrary to section 34, 35, 36, 41, 42, 44, 124, 190 or 241;

(b) order a corporation to return or issue shares to a person from whom the corporation has purchased, redeemed or otherwise acquired shares; or

(c) make any further order it thinks fit.

[¶23-500]

(6) *No liability.* — A director is not liable under subsection (1) if he proves that he did not know and could not reasonably have known that the share was issued for a consideration less than the fair equivalent of the money that the corporation would have received if the share had been issued for money.

[¶23-501]

(7) *Limitation.* — An action to enforce a liability imposed by this section may not be commenced after two years from the date of the resolution authorizing the action complained of.

[¶23-502]

Sec. 119. Liability of directors for wages. — (1) Directors of a corporation are jointly and severally liable to employees of the corporation for all debts not exceeding six months wages payable to each such employee for services performed for the corporation while they are such directors respectively.

[¶23-503]

(2) *Conditions precedent to liability.* — A director is not liable under subsection (1) unless

(a) the corporation has been sued for the debt within six months after it has become due and execution has been returned unsatisfied in whole or in part;

(b) the corporation has commenced liquidation and dissolution proceedings or has been dissolved and a claim for the debt has been proved within six months after the earlier of the date of commencement of the liquidation and dissolution proceedings and the date of dissolution; or

(c) the corporation has made an assignment or a receiving order has been made against it under the *Bankruptcy and Insolvency Act* and a claim for the debt has been proved within six months after the date of the assignment or receiving order.

(1992, c. 27, s. 90(1)(h).)

[¶23-504]

(3) *Limitation.* — A director is not liable under this section unless he is sued for a debt referred to in subsection (1) while he is a director or within two years after he has ceased to. be a director.

[¶23-505]

(4) *Amount due after execution.* — Where execution referred to in paragraph (2)(a) has issued, the amount recoverable from a director is the amount remaining unsatisfied after execution.

[¶23-506]

(5) *Subrogation of director.* — Where a director pays a debt referred to in subsection (1) that is proved in liquidation and dissolution or bankruptcy proceedings, he is entitled to any preference that the employee would have been entitled to, and where a judgment has been obtained he is entitled to an assignment of the judgment.

[¶23-507]

(6) *Contribution.* — A director who has satisfied a claim under this section is entitled to contribution from the other directors who were liable for the claim.

(1992, c. 27, s. 90(1)(h).)

[¶23-508]

Sec. 120.   Disclosure of interested director contract. — (1) A director or officer of a corporation who

(a) is a party to a material contract or proposed material contract with the corporation, or

(b) is a director or an officer of or has a material interest in any person who is a party to a material contract or proposed material contract with the corporation,

shall disclose in writing to the corporation or request to have entered in the minutes of meetings of directors the nature and extent of his interest.

[¶23-509]

(2) *Time of disclosure for director.* — The disclosure required by subsection (1) shall be made, in the case of a director,

(a) at the meeting at which a proposed contract is first considered;

(b) if the director was not then interested in a proposed contract, at the first meeting after he becomes so interested;

(c) if the director becomes interested after a contract is made, at the first meeting after he becomes so interested; or

(d) if a person who is interested in a contract later becomes a director, at the first meeting after he becomes a director.

[¶23-510]

(3) *Time of disclosure for officer.* — The disclosure required by subsection (1) shall be made, in the case of an officer who is not a director,

(a) forthwith after he becomes aware that the contract or proposed contract is to be considered or has been considered at a meeting of directors;

(b) if the officer becomes interested after a contract is made, forthwith after he becomes so interested; or

(c) if a person who is interested in a contract later becomes an officer, forthwith after he becomes an officer.

[¶23-511]

(4) *Time of disclosure for director or officer.* — If a material contract or proposed material contract is one that, in the ordinary course of the corporation's business, would not require approval by the directors or shareholders, a director or officer shall disclose in writing to the corporation or request to have entered in the minutes of meetings of directors the nature and extent of his interest forthwith after the director or officer becomes aware of the contract or proposed contract.

[¶23-512]

(5) *Voting.* — A director referred to in subsection (1) shall not vote on any resolution to approve the contract unless the contract is

(a) an arrangement by way of security for money lent to or obligations undertaken by him for the benefit of the corporation or an affiliate;

(b) one relating primarily to his remuneration as a director, officer, employee or agent of the corporation or an affiliate;

(c) one for indemnity or insurance under section 124; or

(d) one with an affiliate.

[¶23-513]

(6) *Continuing disclosure.* — For the purposes of this section, a general notice to the directors by a director or officer, declaring that he is a director or officer of or has a material interest in a person and is to be regarded as interested in any contract made with that person, is a sufficient declaration of interest in relation to any contract so made.

[¶23-514]

(7) *Avoidance standards.* — A material contract between a corporation and one or more of its directors or officers, or between a corporation and another person of which a director or officer of the corporation is a director or officer or in which he has a material interest, is neither void nor voidable by reason only of that relationship or by reason only that a director with an interest in the contract is present at or is counted to determine the presence of a quorum at a meeting of directors or committee of directors that authorized the contract, if the director or officer disclosed his interest in accordance with subsection (2), (3), (4) or (6), as the case may be, and the contract was approved by the directors or the shareholders and it was reasonable and fair to the corporation at the time it was approved.

[¶23-515]

(8) *Application to court.* — Where a director or officer of a corporation fails to disclose his interest in a material contract in accordance with this section, a court may, on the application of the corporation or a shareholder of the corporation, set aside the contract on such terms as it thinks fit.

[¶23-520]

Sec. 121. Officers. — Subject to the articles, the by-laws or any unanimous shareholder agreement,

(a) the directors may designate the offices of the corporation, appoint as officers persons of full capacity, specify their duties and delegate to them powers to manage the business and affairs of the corporation, except powers to do anything referred to in subsection 115(3);

(b) a director may be appointed to any office of the corporation; and

(c) two or more offices of the corporation may be held by the same person.

[¶23-521]

Sec. 122. Duty of care of directors and officers. — (1) Every director and officer of a corporation in exercising his powers and discharging his duties shall

(a) act honestly and in good faith with a view to the best interest of the corporation; and

(b) exercise the care, diligence and skill that a reasonably prudent person would exercise in comparable circumstances.

[¶23-522]

(2) *Duty to comply.* — Every director and officer of a corporation shall comply with this Act, the regulations, articles, by-laws and any unanimous shareholder agreement.

[¶23-523]

(3) *No exculpation.* — Subject to subsection 146(5), no provision in a contract, the articles, the by-laws or a resolution relieves a director or officer from the duty to act in accordance with this Act or the regulations or relieves him from liability for a breach thereof.

[¶23-524]

Sec. 123. Dissent. — (1) A director who is present at a meeting of directors or committee of directors is deemed to have consented to any resolution passed or action taken thereat unless

(a) he requests that his dissent be or his dissent is entered in the minutes of the meeting;

(b) he sends his written dissent to the secretary of the meeting before the meeting is adjourned; or

(c) he sends his dissent by registered mail or delivers it to the registered office of the corporation immediately after the meeting is adjourned.

[¶23-525]

(2) *Loss of right to dissent.* — A director who votes for or consents to a resolution is not entitled to dissent under subsection (1).

[¶23-526]

(3) *Dissent of absent director.* — A director who was not present at a meeting at which a resolution was passed or action taken is deemed to have consented thereto unless within seven days after he becomes aware of the resolution he

(a) causes his dissent to be placed with the minutes of the meeting; or

(b) sends his dissent by registered mail or delivers it to the registered office of the corporation.

[¶23-527]

(4) *Reliance on statements.* — A director is not liable under section 118, 119 or 122, if he relies in good faith on

(a) financial statements of the corporation represented to him by an officer of the corporation or in a written report of the auditor of the corporation fairly to reflect the financial condition of the corporation; or

(b) a report of a lawyer, accountant, engineer, appraiser or other person whose profession lends credibility to a statement made by him.

[¶23-528]

Sec. 124.   Indemnification. — (1) Except in respect of an action by or on behalf of the corporation or body corporate to procure a judgment in its favour, a corporation may indemnify a director or officer of the corporation, a former director or officer of the corporation or a person who acts or acted at the corporation's request as a director or officer of a body corporate of which the corporation is or was a shareholder or creditor, and his heirs and legal representatives, against all costs, charges and expenses, including an amount paid to settle an action or satisfy a judgment, reasonably incurred by him in respect of any civil, criminal or administrative action or proceeding to which he is made a party by reason of being or having been a director or officer of such corporation or body corporate, if

(a) he acted honestly and in good faith with a view to the best interests of the corporation; and

(b) in the case of a criminal or administrative action or proceeding that is enforced by a monetary penalty, he had reasonable grounds for believing that his conduct was lawful.

[¶23-529]

(2) *Indemnification in derivative actions.* — A corporation may with the approval of a court indemnify a person referred to in subsection (1) in respect of an action by or on behalf of the corporation or body corporate to procure a judgment in its favour, to which he is made a party by reason of being or having been a director or an officer of the corporation or body corporate, against all costs, charges and expenses reasonably incurred by him in connection with such action if he fulfils the conditions set out in paragraphs (1)(a) and (b).

[¶23-530]

(3) *Indemnity as of right.* — Notwithstanding anything in this section, a person referred to in subsection (1) is entitled to indemnity from the corporation in respect of all costs, charges and expenses reasonably incurred by him in connection with the defence of any civil, criminal or administrative action or proceeding to which he is made a party by reason of being or having been a director or officer of the corporation or body corporate, if the person seeking indemnity

(a) was substantially successful on the merits in his defence of the action or proceeding; and

(b) fulfils the conditions set out in paragraphs (1)(a) and (b).

[¶23-531]

(4) *Directors' and officers' insurance.* — A corporation may purchase and maintain insurance for the benefit of any person referred to in subsection (1) against any liability incurred by him

    (a) in his capacity as a director or officer of the corporation, except where the liability relates to his failure to act honestly and in good faith with a view to the best interests of the corporation; or

    (b) in his capacity as a director or officer of another body corporate where he acts or acted in that capacity at the corporation's request, except where the liability relates to his failure to act honestly and in good faith with a view to the best interests of the body corporate.

[¶23-532]

(5) *Application to court.* — A corporation or a person referred to in subsection (1) may apply to a court for an order approving an indemnity under this section and the court may so order and make any further order it thinks fit.

[¶23-533]

(6) *Notice to Director.* — An applicant under subsection (5) shall give the Director notice of the application and the Director is entitled to appear and be heard in person or by counsel.

[¶23-534]

(7) *Other notice.* — On an application under subsection (5), the court may order notice to be given to any interested person and such person is entitled to appear and be heard in person or by counsel.

[¶23-535]

Sec. 125. Remuneration. — Subject to the articles, the by-laws or any unanimous shareholder agreement, the directors of a corporation may fix the remuneration of the directors, officers and employees of the corporation.

Part XI
Insider Trading

[¶23-545]

Sec. 126. Definitions. — (1) In this Part,

"distributing corporation". — "distributing corporation" means a corporation, any of the issued securities of which are or were part of a distribution to the public and remain outstanding and are held by more than one person;

"insider". — "insider" means, except in section 131,

    (a) a director or officer of a distributing corporation,

    (b) a distributing corporation that purchases or otherwise acquires, except by means of a redemption under section 36, shares issued by it,

    (c) a distributing corporation that purchases or otherwise acquires or sells shares issued by any of its affiliates or

    (d) a person who beneficially owns more than ten per cent of the shares of a distributing corporation or who exercises control or direction over more than ten per cent of the votes attached to shares of a distributing corporation, excluding shares owned by an underwriter under an underwriting agreement while those shares are in the course of a distribution to the public;

"officer". — *"officer"* means

    (a) the chairman, president, vice-president, secretary, treasurer, comptroller, general counsel, general manager, managing director or any other individual who performs functions for a corporation similar to those normally performed by an individual occupying any such office, and

    (b) each of the five highest paid employees of a corporation including any individual mentioned in paragraph (a);

"share". — *"share"* means a share carrying voting rights under all circumstances or by reason of the occurrence of an event that has occurred and that is continuing, and includes

    (a) a security currently convertible into such a share, and

    (b) currently exercisable options and rights to acquire such a share or such a convertible security.

[¶23-546]

(2) *Further interpretation.* — For the purposes of this Part,

    (a) a director or an officer of a body corporate that is an insider of a distributing corporation is deemed to be an insider of the distributing corporation;

    (b) a director or an officer of a body corporate that is a subsidiary is deemed to be an insider of its holding distributing corporation;

    (c) a person is deemed to own beneficially shares beneficially owned by a body corporate controlled by him directly or indirectly;

    (d) a body corporate is deemed to own beneficially shares beneficially owned by its affiliates; and

    (e) the acquisition or disposition by an insider of an option or right to acquire a share is deemed to be a change in the beneficial ownership of the share to which the option or right to acquire relates.

[¶23-547]

(3) *Deemed insiders.* — For the purposes of this Part,

    (a) if a body corporate becomes an insider of a distributing corporation, or enters into a business combination with a distributing corporation, a director or an officer of the body corporate or a shareholder of the body corporate who is a person referred to in paragraph (d) of the definition "insider" is deemed to have been an insider of the distributing corporation for the previous six months or for such shorter period as he was a director, an officer or such a shareholder of the body corporate; and

    (b) if a distributing corporation becomes an insider of a body corporate or enters into a business combination with a body corporate, a director or an officer of the body corporate or a shareholder of the body corporate who is a person referred to in paragraph (d) of the definition "insider" is deemed to have been an insider of the distributing corporation for the previous six months or for such shorter period as he was a director, an officer or such a shareholder of the body corporate.

[¶23-548]

(4) *Definition of "business combination".* — In subsection (3), "business combination" means an acquisition of all or substantially all the property of one body corporate by another or an amalgamation of two or more bodies corporate.

¶23-546   Sec. 126(2)

[¶23-549]

Sec. 127. First insider report. — (1) Unless he has filed or has been exempted from filing an insider report under the, *Canada Corporations Act*, chapter C-32, of the Revised Statutes of Canada, 1970, or has been exempted from filing an insider report by the regulations, a person who is an insider of a body corporate on the day on which it is continued as a corporation under this Act shall, if the corporation is a distributing corporation, send to the Director an insider report in prescribed form within ten days after the end of the month in which such day occurs.

[¶23-550]

(2) *Idem.* — A person who becomes an insider shall, within ten days after the end of the month in which he becomes an insider, send to the Director an insider report in the prescribed form.

[¶23-551]

(3) *Constructive insider report.* — A person who is deemed to have been an insider under subsection 126(3) shall, within ten days after the end of the month in which he is deemed to have become an insider, send to the Director the insider reports for the period in respect of which he is deemed to have been an insider that he would have been required to send under this section had he been otherwise an insider for such period.

[¶23-552]

(4) *Subsequent insider reports.* — An insider whose interest in securities of a distributing corporation changes from that shown or required to be shown in the last insider report sent or required to be sent by him shall, within ten days after the end of the month in which such change takes place, send to the Director an insider report in the prescribed form.

[¶23-553]

(5) *One insider report.* — An insider report of a person that includes securities deemed to be beneficially owned by that person is deemed to be an insider report of a body corporate referred to in paragraph 126(2)(c) and the body corporate is not required to send a separate insider report.

[¶23-554]

(6) *Idem.* — An insider report of a body corporate that includes securities deemed to be beneficially owned by the body corporate is deemed to be an insider report of an affiliate referred to in paragraph 126(2)(d) and the affiliate is not required to send a separate insider report.

[¶23-555]

(7) *Contents.* — An insider report of a person that includes securities deemed beneficially owned by that person shall disclose separately

(a) the number or amount of the securities owned by a body corporate; and

(b) the name of the body corporate.

[¶23-556]

(8) *Exemption order.* — Upon an application by or on behalf of an insider, the Director may make an order on such terms as he thinks fit exempting the insider from any of the requirements of this section, which order may have retrospective effect.

Sec. 127(8) ¶23-556

[¶23-557]

(9) *Offence.* — A person who, without reasonable cause, fails to comply with this section is guilty of an offence and liable on summary conviction to a fine not exceeding five thousand dollars or to imprisonment for a term not exceeding six months or to both.

[¶23-558]

(10) *Officers, etc., of bodies corporate.* — Where a body corporate commits an offence under subsection (9), any director or officer of the body corporate who knowingly authorized, permitted or acquiesced in the commission of the offence is a party to and guilty of the offence and is liable on summary conviction to a fine not exceeding five thousand dollars or to imprisonment for a term not exceeding six months or to both, whether or not the body corporate has been prosecuted or convicted.

[¶23-560]

Sec. 128. Notice of purchase of own shares. — A corporation that proposes to purchase or otherwise acquire its own shares otherwise than by means of a purchase or redemption under section 36 shall, in the prescribed circumstances, give notice to the Director of the proposed purchase or other acquisition in the manner prescribed.

[¶23-563]

Sec. 129. Publication. — The Director shall summarize in a periodical available to the public the information contained in insider reports sent to him under sections 127 and 128 and the particulars of exemptions granted under subsection 127(8) together with the reasons therefor.

[¶23-564]

Sec. 130. Prohibition of short sale. — (1) An insider shall not knowingly sell, directly or indirectly, a share of the distributing corporation or any of its affiliates if the insider selling the share does not own or has not fully paid for the share to be sold.

[¶23-565]

(2) *Calls and puts.* — An insider shall not, directly or indirectly, buy or sell a call or put in respect of a share of the corporation or any of its affiliates.

[¶23-566]

(3) *Exception.* — Notwithstanding subsection (1), an insider may sell a share he does not own if he owns another share convertible into the share sold or an option or right to acquire the share sold and, within ten days after the sale, he

(a) exercises the conversion privilege, option or right and delivers the share so acquired to the purchaser; or

(b) transfers the convertible share, option or right to the purchaser.

[¶23-567]

(4) *Offence.* — An insider who contravenes subsection (1) or (2) is guilty of an offence and liable on summary conviction to a fine not exceeding five thousand dollars or to imprisonment for a term not exceeding six months or to both.

[¶23-568]

Sec. 131. Definition of "insider". — (1) In this section, "insider" means, with respect to a corporation,

(a) the corporation;

(b) an affiliate of the corporation;

(*c*) a director or an officer of the corporation;

(*d*) a person who beneficially owns more than ten per cent of the shares of the corporation or who exercises control or direction over more than ten per cent of the votes attached to the shares of the corporation;

(*e*) a person employed or retained by the corporation; and

(*f*) a person who receives specific confidential information from a person described in this subsection or in subsection (2), including a person described in this paragraph, and who has knowledge that the person giving the information is a person described in this subsection or in subsection (2), including a person described in this paragraph.

[¶23-570]

(2) *Deemed insiders.* — For the purposes of this section,

(*a*) if a body corporate becomes an insider of a corporation, or enters into a business combination with a corporation, a director or officer of the body corporate is deemed to have been an insider of the corporation for the previous six months or for such shorter period as he was a director or an officer of the body corporate; and

(*b*) if a corporation becomes an insider of a body corporate, or enters into a business combination with a body corporate, a director or an officer of the body corporate is deemed to have been an insider of the corporation for the previous six months or for such shorter period as he was a director or officer of the body corporate.

[¶23-571]

(3) *Definition of "business combination".* — In subsection (2), "business combination" means an acquisition of all or substantially all the property of one body corporate by another or an amalgamation of two or more bodies corporate.

[¶23-572]

(4) *Civil liability.* — An insider who, in connection with a transaction in a security of the corporation or any of its affiliates, makes use of any specific confidential information for his own benefit or advantage that, if generally known, might reasonably be expected to affect materially the value of the security

(*a*) is liable to compensate any person for any direct loss suffered by that person as a result of the transaction, unless the information was known or in the exercise of reasonable diligence should have been known to that person; and

(*b*) is accountable to the corporation for any direct benefit or advantage received or receivable by the insider as a result of the transaction.

[¶23-573]

(5) *Limitation.* — An action to enforce a right created by subsection (4) may be commenced

(*a*) only within two years after discovery of the facts that gave rise to the cause of action; or

(*b*) if the transaction was required to be reported under section 127, only within two years from the time of reporting under that section.

Part XII
Shareholders

[¶23-584]

Sec. 132. Place of meetings. — (1) Meetings of shareholders of a corporation shall be held at the place within Canada provided in the by-laws or, in the absence of such provision, at the place within Canada that the directors determine.

[¶23-585]

(2) *Meeting outside Canada.* — Notwithstanding subsection (1), a meeting of shareholders of a corporation may be held outside Canada if all the shareholders entitled to vote at that meeting so agree, and a shareholder who attends a meeting of shareholders held outside Canada is deemed to have so agreed except when he attends the meeting for the express purpose of objecting to the transaction of any business on the grounds that the meeting is not lawfully held.

[¶23-586]

Sec. 133. Calling meetings. — The directors of a corporation

(a) shall call an annual meeting of shareholders not later than eighteen months after the corporation comes into existence and subsequently not later than fifteen months after holding the last preceding annual meeting; and

(b) may at any time call a special meeting of shareholders.

[¶23-587]

Sec. 134. Fixing record date. — (1) For the purpose of determining shareholders

(a) entitled to receive payment of a dividend,

(b) entitled to participate in a liquidation distribution, or

(c) for any other purpose except the right to receive notice of or to vote at a meeting,

the directors may fix in advance a date as the record date for such determination of shareholders, but such record date shall not precede by more than fifty days the particular action to be taken.

[¶23-588]

(2) *Notice of meeting.* — For the purpose of determining shareholders entitled to receive notice of a meeting of shareholders, the directors may fix in advance a date as the record date for such determination of shareholders, but such record date shall not precede by more than fifty days or by less than twenty-one days the date on which the meeting is to be held.

[¶23-589]

(3) *No record date fixed.* — If no record date is fixed,

(a) the record date for the determination of shareholders entitled to receive notice of a meeting of shareholders shall be

(i) at the close of business on the day immediately preceding the day on which the notice is given, or

(ii) if no notice is given, the day on which the meeting is held; and

(b) the record date for the determination of shareholders for any purpose other than to establish a shareholder's right to receive notice of a meeting or to vote shall be at the close of business on the day on which the directors pass the resolution relating thereto.

[¶23-590]

(4) *When record date fixed.* — If a record date is fixed, unless notice of the record date is waived in writing by every holder of a share of the class or series affected whose name is set out in the securities register at the close of business on the day the directors fix the record date, notice thereof shall, not less than seven days before the date so fixed, be given

(a) by advertisement in a newspaper published or distributed in the place where the corporation has its registered office and in each place in Canada where it has a transfer agent or where a transfer of its shares may be recorded; and

(b) by written notice to each stock exchange in Canada on which the shares of the corporation are listed for trading.

[¶23-591]

Sec. 135. Notice of meeting. — (1) Notice of the time and place of a meeting of shareholders shall be sent not less than twenty-one days nor more than fifty days before the meeting,

(a) to each shareholder entitled to vote at the meeting;

(b) to each director; and

(c) to the auditor of the corporation.

[¶23-592]

(2) *Exception.* — A notice of a meeting is not required to be sent to shareholders who were not registered on the records of the corporation or its transfer agent on the record date determined under subsection 134(2) or (3), but failure to receive a notice does not deprive a shareholder of the right to vote at the meeting.

[¶23-593]

(3) *Adjournment.* — If a meeting of shareholders is adjourned for less than thirty days it is not necessary, unless the by-laws otherwise provide, to give notice of the adjourned meeting, other than by announcement at the earliest meeting that is adjourned.

[¶23-594]

(4) *Notice of adjourned meeting.* — If a meeting of shareholders is adjourned by one or more adjournments for an aggregate of thirty days or more, notice of the adjourned meeting shall be given as for an original meeting but, unless the meeting is adjourned by one or more adjournments for an aggregate of more than ninety days, subsection 149(1) does not apply.

[¶23-595]

(5) *Business.* — All business transacted at a special meeting of shareholders and all business transacted at an annual meeting of shareholders. except consideration of the financial statements, auditor's report, election of directors and reappointment of the incumbent auditor, is deemed to be special business.

[¶23-596]

(6) *Notice of business.* — Notice of a meeting of shareholders at which special business is to be transacted shall state

(a) the nature of that business in sufficient detail to permit the shareholder to form a reasoned judgment thereon; and,

(b) the text of any special resolution to be submitted to the meeting.

[¶23-597]

Sec. 136. Waiver of notice. — A shareholder and any other person entitled to attend a meeting of shareholders may in any manner waive notice of a meeting of shareholders, and attendance of any such person at a meeting of shareholders is a waiver of notice of the meeting, except where he attends a meeting for the express purpose of objecting to the transaction of any business on the grounds that the meeting is not lawfully called.

[¶23-598]

Sec. 137. Shareholder proposal. — (1) A shareholder entitled to vote at an annual meeting of shareholders may

(a) submit to the corporation notice of any matter that he proposes to raise at the meeting, hereinafter referred to as a "proposal"; and

(b) discuss at the meeting any matter in respect of which he would have been entitled to submit a proposal.

[¶23-599]

(2) *Information circular.* — A corporation that solicits proxies shall set out the proposal in the management proxy circular required by section 150 or attach the proposal thereto.

[¶23-600]

(3) *Supporting statement.* — If so requested by the shareholder, the corporation shall include in the management proxy circular or attach thereto a statement by the shareholder of not more than two hundred words in support of the proposal, and the name and address of the shareholder.

[¶23-601]

(4) *Nomination for director.* — A proposal may include nominations for the election of directors if the proposal is signed by one or more holders of shares representing in the aggregate not less than five per cent of the shares or five per cent of the shares of a class of shares of the corporation entitled to vote at the meeting to which the proposal is to be presented, but this subsection does not preclude nominations made at a meeting of shareholders.

[¶23-602]

(5) *Exemptions.* — A corporation is not required to comply with subsections (2) and (3) if

(a) the proposal is not submitted to the corporation at least ninety days before the anniversary date of the previous annual meeting of shareholders;

(b) it clearly appears that the proposal is submitted by the shareholder primarily for the purpose of enforcing a personal claim or redressing a personal grievance against the corporation or its directors, officers or security holders, or primarily for the purpose of promoting general economic, political, racial, religious, social or similar causes;

(c) the corporation, at the shareholder's request, included a proposal in a management proxy circular relating to a meeting of shareholders held within two years preceding the receipt of such request, and the shareholder failed to present the proposal, in person or by proxy, at the meeting;

(d) substantially the same proposal was submitted to shareholders in a management proxy circular or a dissident's proxy circular relating to a meeting of shareholders held within two years preceding the receipt of the shareholder's request and the proposal was defeated; or

(e) the rights conferred by this section are being abused to secure publicity.

[¶23-603]

(6) *Immunity.* — No corporation or person acting on its behalf incurs any liability by reason only of circulating a proposal or statement in compliance with this section.

[¶23-604]

(7) *Notice of refusal.* — If a corporation refuses to include a proposal in a management proxy circular, the corporation shall, within ten days after receiving the proposal, notify the shareholder submitting the proposal of its intention to omit the proposal from the management proxy circular and send to him a statement of the reasons for the refusal.

[¶23-605]

(8) *Shareholder application to court.* — On the application of a shareholder claiming to be aggrieved by a corporation's refusal under subsection (7), a court may restrain the holding of the meeting to which the proposal is sought to be presented and make any further order it thinks fit.

[¶23-606]

(9) *Corporation's application to court.* — The corporation or any person claiming to be aggrieved by a proposal may apply to a court for an order permitting the corporation to omit the proposal from the management proxy circular, and the court, if it is satisfied that subsection (5) applies, may make such order as it thinks fit.

[¶23-607]

(10) *Director entitled to notice.* — An applicant under subsection (8) or (9) shall give the Director notice of the application and the Director is entitled to appear and be heard in person or by counsel.

[¶23-612]

Sec. 138. Shareholder list. — (1) A corporation shall prepare a list of shareholders entitled to receive notice of a meeting. arranged in alphabetical order and showing the number of shares held by each shareholder,

(a) if a record date is fixed under subsection 134(2), not later than ten days after that date; or

(b) if no record date is fixed

(i) at the close of business on the day immediately preceding the day on which the notice is given, or

(ii) where no notice is given, on the day on which the meeting is held.

[¶23-613]

(2) *Effect of list.* — Where a corporation fixes a record date under subsection 134(2) a person named in the list prepared under paragraph (1)(a) is entitled to vote the shares shown opposite his name at the meeting to which the list relates, except to the extent that

(a) the person has transferred the ownership of any of his shares after the record date, and

(b) the transferee of those shares

(i) produces properly endorsed share certificates, or

(ii) otherwise establishes that he owns the shares

and demands, not later than ten days before the meeting or such shorter period before the meeting as the by-laws of the corporation may provide, that his name be included in the list before the meeting

in which case the transferee is entitled to vote his shares at the meeting,

[¶23-614]

(3) *Effect of list.* — Where a corporation does not fix a record date under subsection 134(2), a person named in a list prepared under paragraph (1)(*b*) is entitled to vote the shares shown opposite his name at the meeting to which the list relates except to the extent that

(*a*) the person has transferred the ownership of any of his shares after the date on which a list referred to in subparagraph (1)(*b*)(i) is prepared, and

(*b*) the transferee of those shares

(i) produces properly endorsed share certificates, or otherwise establishes that he owns the shares,

(ii) and demands, not later than ten days before the meeting or such shorter period before the meeting as the by-laws of the corporation may provide, that his name be included in the list before the meeting

in which case the transferee is entitled to vote his shares at the meeting.

[¶23-615]

(4) *Examination of list.* — A shareholder may examine the list of shareholders

(*a*) during usual business hours at the registered office of the corporation or at the place where its central securities register is maintained; and

(*b*) at the meeting of shareholders for which the list was prepared.

[¶23-616]

Sec. 139.   Quorum. — (1) Unless the by-laws otherwise provide, a quorum of shareholders is present at a meeting of shareholders, irrespective of the number of persons actually present at the meeting, if the holders of a majority of the shares entitled to vote at the meeting are present in person or represented by proxy.

[¶23-617]

(2) *Opening quorum sufficient.* — If a quorum is present at the opening of a meeting of shareholders, the shareholders present may, unless the by-laws otherwise provide, proceed with the business of the meeting, notwithstanding that a quorum is not present throughout the meeting.

[¶23-618]

(3) *Adjournment.* — If a quorum is not present at the opening of a meeting of shareholders, the shareholders present may adjourn the meeting to a fixed time and place but may not transact any other business.

[¶23-619]

(4) *One shareholder meeting.* — If a corporation has only one shareholder, or only one holder of any class or series of shares, the shareholder present in person or by proxy constitutes a meeting.

[¶23-620]

Sec. 140.   Right to vote. — (1) Unless the articles otherwise provide, each share of a corporation entitles the holder thereof to one vote at a meeting of shareholders.

[¶23-621]

(2) *Representative.* — If a body corporate or association is a shareholder of a corporation, the corporation shall recognize any individual authorized by a resolution of the

directors or governing body of the body corporate or association to represent it at meetings of shareholders of the corporation.

[¶23-622]

(3) *Powers of representative.* — An individual authorized under subsection (2) may exercise on behalf of the body corporate or association he represents all the powers it could exercise if it were an individual shareholder.

[¶23-623]

(4) *Joint shareholders.* — Unless the by-laws otherwise provide, if two or more persons hold shares jointly, one of those holders present at a meeting of shareholders may in the absence of the others vote the shares, but if two or more of those persons who are present, in person or by proxy, vote, they shall vote as one on the shares jointly held by them.

[¶23-628]

Sec. 141. Voting. — (1) Unless the by-laws otherwise provide, voting at a meeting of shareholders shall be by show of hands except where a ballot is demanded by a shareholder or proxyholder entitled to vote at the meeting.

[¶23-629]

(2) *Ballot.* — A shareholder or proxyholder may demand a ballot either before or after any vote by show of hands.

[¶23-630]

Sec. 142. Resolution in lieu of meeting. — (1) Except where a written statement is submitted by a director under subsection 110(2) or by an auditor under subsection 168(5),

(a) a resolution in writing signed by all the shareholders entitled to vote on that resolution at a meeting of shareholders is as valid as if it had been passed at a meeting of the shareholders; and

(b) a resolution in writing dealing with all matters required by this Act to be dealt with at a meeting of shareholders, and signed by all the shareholders entitled to vote at that meeting, satisfies all the requirements of this Act relating to meetings of shareholders.

[¶23-631]

(2) *Filing resolution.* — A copy of every resolution referred to in subsection (1) shall be kept with the minutes of the meetings of shareholders.

[¶23-632]

Sec. 143. Requisition of meeting. — (1) The holders of not less than five per cent of the issued shares of a corporation that carry the right to vote at a meeting sought to be held may requisition the directors to call a meeting of shareholders for the purposes stated in the requisition.

[¶23-633]

(2) *Form.* — The requisition referred to in subsection (1), which may consist of several documents of like form each signed by one or more shareholders, shall state the business to be transacted at the meeting and shall be sent to each director and to the registered office of the corporation.

[¶23-634]

(3) *Directors calling meeting.* — On receiving the requisition referred to in subsection (1), the directors shall call a meeting of shareholders to transact the business stated in the requisition, unless

(a) a record date has been fixed under subsection 134(2) and notice thereof has been given under subsection 134(4);

(b) the directors have called a meeting of shareholders and have given notice thereof under section 135; or

(c) the business of the meeting as stated in the requisition includes matters described in paragraphs 137(5)(b) to (e).

[¶23-635]

(4) *Shareholder calling meeting.* — If the directors do not within twenty-one days after receiving the requisition referred to in subsection (1) call a meeting, any shareholder who signed the requisition may call the meeting.

[¶23-636]

(5) *Procedure.* — A meeting called under this section shall be called as nearly as possible in the manner in which meetings are to be called pursuant to the by-laws, this Part and Part XIII.

[¶23-637]

(6) *Reimbursement.* — Unless the shareholders otherwise resolve at a meeting called under subsection (4), the corporation shall reimburse the shareholders the expenses reasonably incurred by them in requisitioning, calling and holding the meeting.

[¶23-638]

Sec. 144. Meeting called by court. — (1) If for any reason it is impracticable to call a meeting of shareholders of a corporation in the manner in which meetings of those shareholders may be called, or to conduct the meeting in the manner prescribed by the by-laws and this Act, or if for any other reason a court thinks fit, the court, on the application of a director, a shareholder entitled to vote at the meeting or the Director, may order a meeting to be called, held and conducted in such manner as the court directs.

[¶23-639]

(2) *Varying quorum.* — Without restricting the generality of subsection (1), the court may order that the quorum required by the by-laws or this Act be varied or dispensed with at a meeting called, held and conducted pursuant to this section.

[¶23-640]

(3) *Valid meeting.* — A meeting called, held and conducted pursuant to this section is for all purposes a meeting of shareholders of the corporation duly called, held and conducted.

[¶23-641]

Sec. 145. Court review of election. — (1) A corporation or a shareholder or director may apply to a court to determine any controversy with respect to an election or appointment of a director or auditor of the corporation.

[¶23-642]

(2) *Powers of court.* — On an application under this section, the court may make any order it thinks fit including, without limiting the generality of the foregoing,

(*a*) an order restraining a director or auditor whose election or appointment is challenged from acting pending determination of the dispute;

(*b*) an order declaring the result of the disputed election or appointment;

(*c*) an order requiring a new election or appointment, and including in the order directions for the management of the business and affairs of the corporation until a new election is held or appointment made;

(*d*) an order determining the voting rights of shareholders and of persons claiming to own shares.

[¶23-643]

Sec. 146. Pooling agreement. — (1) A written agreement between two or more shareholders may provide that in exercising voting rights the shares held by them shall be voted as therein provided.

[¶23-644]

(2) *Unanimous shareholder agreement.* — An otherwise lawful written agreement among all the shareholders of a corporation, or among all the shareholders and a person who is not a shareholder, that restricts, in whole or in part, the powers of the directors to manage the business and affairs of the corporation is valid.

[¶23-644a]

(3) *Declaration by single shareholder.* — Where a person who is the beneficial owner of all the issued shares of a corporation makes a written declaration that restricts in whole or in part the powers of the directors to manage the business and affairs of a corporation, the declaration is deemed to be a unanimous shareholder agreement.

[¶23-645]

(4) *Constructive party.* — Subject to subsection 49(8), a transferee of shares subject to a unanimous shareholder agreement is deemed to be a party to the agreement.

[¶23-646]

(5) *Rights of shareholders.* — A shareholder who is a party to a unanimous shareholder agreement has all the rights, powers and duties of a director of the corporation to which the agreement relates to the extent that the agreement restricts the powers of the directors to manage the business and affairs of the corporation, and the directors are thereby relieved of their duties and liabilities, including any liabilities under section 119, to the same extent.

Part XIII
Proxies

[¶23-664]

Sec. 147. Definitions. — In this Part,

"form of proxy". — "form of proxy" means a written or printed form that, on completion and execution by or on behalf of a shareholder, becomes a proxy;

"proxy". — "proxy" means a completed and executed form of proxy by means of which a shareholder appoints a proxyholder to attend and act on his behalf at a meeting of shareholders;

"registrant". — "registrant" means a securities broker or dealer required to be registered to trade or deal in securities under the laws of any jurisdiction;

"solicit". — "solicit" or "solicitation" includes

(*a*) a request for a proxy whether or not accompanied by or included in a form of proxy,

(*b*) a request to execute or not to execute a form of proxy or to revoke a proxy,

(*c*) the sending of a form of proxy or other communication to a shareholder under circumstances reasonably calculated to result in the procurement, withholding or revocation of a proxy, and

(*d*) the sending of a form of proxy to a shareholder under section 149,

but does not include

(*e*) the sending of a form of proxy in response to an unsolicited request made by or on behalf of a shareholder,

(*f*) the performance of administrative acts or professional services on behalf of a person soliciting a proxy,

(*g*) the sending by a registrant of the documents referred to in section 153, or

(*h*) a solicitation by a person in respect of shares of which he is the beneficial owner;

"solicitation by or on behalf of the management of a corporation". — "solicitation by or on behalf of the management of a corporation" means a solicitation by any person pursuant to a resolution or instructions of, or with the acquiescence of, the directors or a committee of the directors.

[¶23-665]

Sec. 148.   Appointing proxyholder. — (1) A shareholder entitled to vote at a meeting of shareholders may by means of a proxy appoint a proxyholder or one or more alternate proxyholders who are not required to be shareholders, to attend and act at the meeting in the manner and to the extent authorized by the proxy and with the authority conferred by the proxy.

[¶23-666]

(2) *Execution of proxy.* — A proxy shall be executed by the shareholder or by his attorney authorized in writing.

[¶23-667]

(3) *Validity of proxy.* — A proxy is valid only at the meeting in respect of which it is given or any adjournment thereof.

[¶23-668]

(4) *Revocation of proxy.* — A shareholder may revoke a proxy

(*a*) by depositing an instrument in writing executed by him or by his attorney authorized in writing

(i) at the registered office of the corporation at any time up to and including the last business day preceding the day of the meeting, or an adjournment thereof, at which the proxy is to be used, or

(ii) with the chairman of the meeting on the day of the meeting or an adjournment thereof; or

(*b*) in any other manner permitted by law.

[¶23-669]

(5) *Deposit of proxies.* — The directors may specify in a notice calling a meeting of shareholders a time not exceeding forty-eight hours, excluding Saturdays and holidays, preceding the meeting or an adjournment thereof before which time proxies to be used at the meeting must be deposited with the corporation or its agent.

[¶23-670]

Sec. 149. Mandatory solicitation. — (1) Subject to subsection (2), the management of a corporation shall, concurrently with giving notice of a meeting of shareholders, send a form of proxy in prescribed form to each shareholder who is entitled to receive notice of the meeting.

[¶23-671]

(2) *Exception.* — Where a corporation has fewer than fifteen shareholders, two or more joint holders being counted as one shareholder, the management of the corporation is not required to send a form of proxy under subsection (1).

[¶23-672]

(3) *Offence.* — If the management of a corporation fails to comply, without reasonable cause, with subsection (1), the corporation is guilty of an offence and liable on summary conviction to a fine not exceeding five thousand dollars.

[¶23-673]

(4) *Officers, etc., of corporations.* — Where a corporation commits an offence under subsection (3), any director or officer of the corporation who knowingly authorized, permitted or acquiesced in the commission of the offence is a party to and guilty of the offence and is liable on summary conviction to a fine not exceeding five thousand dollars or to imprisonment for a term not exceeding six months or to both, whether or not the corporation has been prosecuted or convicted.

[¶23-679]

Sec. 150. Soliciting proxies. — (1) A person shall not solicit proxies unless

(a) in the case of solicitation by or on behalf of the management of a corporation, a management proxy circular in prescribed form, either as an appendix to or as a separate document accompanying the notice of the meeting, or

(b) in the case of any other solicitation, a dissident's proxy circular in prescribed form stating the purposes of the solicitation

is sent to the auditor of the corporation, to each shareholder whose proxy is solicited, to each director and, if paragraph (b) applies, to the corporation. (1992, c. 1, s. 54.)

[¶23-680]

(2) *Copy to Director.* — A person required to send a management proxy circular or dissident's proxy circular shall send concurrently a copy thereof to the Director together with a statement in prescribed form, a copy of the notice of meeting, the form of proxy and any other documents for use in connection with the meeting. (1992, c. 1, s. 54.)

[¶23-681]

(3) *Offence.* — A person who fails to comply with subsections (1) and (2) is guilty of an offence and liable on summary conviction to a fine not exceeding five thousand dollars or to imprisonment for a term not exceeding six months or to both, whether or not the body corporate has been prosecuted or convicted.

[¶23-682]

(4) *Officers, etc., of bodies corporate.* — Where a body corporate commits an offence under subsection (3), any director or officer of the body corporate who knowingly authorized, permitted or acquiesced in the commission of the offence is a party to and guilty of the offence and is liable on summary conviction to a fine not exceeding five thousand

Sec. 150(4)   ¶23-682

dollars or to imprisonment for a term not exceeding six months or to both, whether or not the body corporate has been prosecuted or convicted.

(1992, c. 1, s. 54.)

[¶23-683]

Sec. 151.   Exemption order. — (1) On the application of an interested person, the Director may make an order on such terms as he thinks fit exempting such person from any of the requirements of section 149 or subsection 150(1), which order may have retrospective effect.

[¶23-684]

(2) *Publication.* — The Director shall set out in the periodical referred to in section 129 the particulars of exemptions granted under this section together with the reasons therefor.

[¶23-685]

Sec. 152.   Attendance at meeting. — (1) A person who solicits a proxy and is appointed proxyholder shall attend in person or cause an alternate proxyholder to attend the meeting in respect of which the proxy is given and comply with the directions of the shareholder who appointed him.

[¶23-685a]

(2) *Right of a proxyholder.* — A proxyholder or an alternate proxyholder has the same rights as the shareholder who appointed him to speak at a meeting of shareholders in respect of any matter, to vote by way of ballot at the meeting and, except where a proxyholder or an alternate proxyholder has conflicting instructions from more than one shareholder, to vote at such a meeting in respect of any matter by way of any show of hands.

[¶23-685b]

(3) *Idem.* — Notwithstanding subsections (1) and (2), where the chairman of a meeting of shareholders declares to the meeting that, if a ballot is conducted, the total number of votes attached to shares represented at the meeting by proxy required to be voted against what to his knowledge will be the decision of the meeting in relation to any matter or group of matters is less than five per cent of all the votes that might be cast at the meeting on such ballot, unless a shareholder or proxyholder demands a ballot,

(a) the chairman may conduct the vote in respect of that matter or group of matters by a show of hands; and

(b) a proxyholder or alternate proxyholder may vote in respect of that matter or group of matters by a show of hands.

[¶23-686]

(4) *Offence.* — A proxyholder or alternate proxyholder who without reasonable cause fails to comply with the directions of a shareholder under this section is guilty of an offence and liable on summary conviction to a fine not exceeding five thousand dollars or to imprisonment for a term not exceeding six months or to both.

[¶23-687]

Sec. 153.   Duty of registrant. — (1) Shares of a corporation that are registered in the name of a registrant or his nominee and not beneficially owned by the registrant shall not be voted unless the registrant, forthwith after receipt of the notice of the meeting, financial statements, management proxy circular, dissident's proxy circular and any other documents other than the form of proxy sent to shareholders by or on behalf of any person for use in connection with the meeting, sends a copy thereof to the beneficial owner and, except where the registrant has received written voting instructions from the beneficial owner, a written request for such instructions.

[¶23-688]

(2) *Beneficial owner unknown.* — A registrant shall not vote or appoint a proxyholder to vote shares registered in his name or in the name of his nominee that he does not beneficially own unless he receives voting instructions from the beneficial owner.

[¶23-689]

(3) *Copies.* — A person by or on behalf of whom a solicitation is made shall, at the request of a registrant, forthwith furnish to the registrant at that person's expense the necessary number of copies of the documents referred to in subsection (1) other than copies of the document requesting voting instructions.

[¶23-690]

(4) *Instructions to registrant.* — A registrant shall vote or appoint a proxyholder to vote any shares referred to in subsection (1) in accordance with any written voting instructions received from the beneficial owner.

[¶23-691]

(5) *Beneficial owner as proxyholder.* — If requested by a beneficial owner, a registrant shall appoint the beneficial owner or a nominee of the beneficial owner as proxyholder.

[¶23-692]

(6) *Validity.* — The failure of a registrant to comply with this section does not render void any meeting of shareholders or any action taken thereat.

[¶23-693]

(7) *Limitation.* — Nothing in this section gives a registrant the right to vote shares that he is otherwise prohibited from voting.

[¶23-694]

(8) *Offence.* — A registrant who knowingly fails to comply with this section is guilty of an offence and liable on summary conviction to a fine not exceeding five thousand dollars or to imprisonment for a term not exceeding six months or to both.

[¶23-695]

(9) *Officers, etc., of bodies corporate.* — Where a registrant who is a body corporate commits an offence under subsection (8), any director or officer of the body corporate who knowingly authorized, permitted or acquiesced in the commission of the offence is a party to and guilty of the offence and is liable on summary conviction to a fine not exceeding five thousand dollars or to imprisonment for a term not exceeding six months or to both, whether or not the body corporate has been prosecuted or convicted.

[¶23-696]

Sec. 154. Restraining order. — (1) If a form of proxy, management proxy circular or dissident's proxy circular contains an untrue statement of a material fact or omits to state a material fact required therein or necessary to make a statement contained therein not misleading in the light of the circumstances in which it was made, an interested person or the Director may apply to a court and the court may make any order it thinks fit including, without limiting the generality of the foregoing, (*a*) an order restraining the solicitation, the holding of the meeting, or any person from implementing or acting on any resolution passed at the meeting to which the form of proxy, management proxy circular or dissident's proxy circular relates;

(*b*) an order requiring correction of any form of proxy or proxy circular and a further solicitation;

(*c*) an order adjourning the meeting.

[¶23-697]

(2) *Notice to Director.* — An applicant under this section shall give to the Director notice of the application and the Director is entitled to appear and to be heard in person or by counsel.

Part XIV
Financial Disclosure

[¶23-710]

Sec. 155.   Annual financial statements. — (1) Subject to section 156, the directors of a corporation shall place before the shareholders at every annual meeting

(*a*) comparative financial statements as prescribed relating separately to

(i) the period that began on the date the corporation came into existence and ended not more than six months before the annual meeting or, if the corporation has completed a financial year, the period that began immediately after the end of the last completed financial year and ended not more than six months before the annual meeting, and

(ii) the immediately preceding financial year;

(*b*) the report of the auditor, if any; and

(*c*) any further information respecting the financial position of the corporation and the results of its operations required by the articles, the by-laws or any unanimous shareholder agreement.

[¶23-711]

(2) *Exception.* — Notwithstanding paragraph (1)(*a*), the financial statements referred to in subparagraph (1)(*a*)(ii) may be omitted if the reason for the omission is set out in the financial statements, or in a note thereto, to be placed before the shareholders at an annual meeting.

[¶23-712]

Sec. 156.   Exemption. — A corporation may apply to the Director for an order authorizing the corporation to omit from its financial statements any item prescribed, or to dispense with the publication of any particular financial statement prescribed, and the Director may, if he reasonably believes that disclosure of the information therein contained would be detrimental to the corporation, permit such omission on such reasonable conditions as he thinks fit.

[¶23-713]

Sec. 157.   Consolidated statements. — (1) A corporation shall keep at its registered office a copy of the financial statements of each of its subsidiary bodies corporate and of each body corporate the accounts of which are consolidated in the financial statements of the corporation.

[¶23-714]

(2) *Examination.* — Shareholders of a corporation and their agents and legal representatives may on request therefor examine the statements referred to in subsection (1) during the usual business hours of the corporation and may make extracts therefrom free of charge.

[¶23-715]

(3) *Barring examination.* — A corporation may, within fifteen days of a request to examine under subsection (2), apply to a court for an order barring the right of any person to so examine, and the court may, if it is satisfied that such examination would be detrimental to the corporation or a subsidiary body corporate, bar such right and make any further order it thinks fit.

[¶23-716]

(4) *Notice to Director.* — A corporation shall give the Director and the person asking to examine under subsection (2) notice of an application under subsection (3), and the Director and such person may appear and be heard in person or by counsel.

[¶23-717]

Sec. 158. Approval of financial statements. — (1) The directors of a corporation shall approve the financial statements referred to in section 155 and the approval shall be evidenced by the signature of one or more directors.

[¶23-718]

(2) *Condition precedent.* — A corporation shall not issue, publish or circulate copies of the financial statements referred to in section 155 unless the financial statements are

(a) approved and signed in accordance with subsection (1); and

(b) accompanied by the report of the auditor of the corporation, if any.

[¶23-719]

Sec. 159. Copies to shareholders. — (1) A corporation shall, not less than twenty-one days before each annual meeting of shareholders or before the signing of a resolution under paragraph 142(1)(b) in lieu of the annual meeting, send a copy of the documents referred to in section 155 to each shareholder, except to a shareholder who has informed the corporation in writing that he does not want a copy of those documents.

[¶23-720]

(2) *Offence.* — A corporation that, without reasonable cause, fails to comply with subsection (1) is guilty of an offence and liable on summary conviction to a fine not exceeding five thousand dollars.

[¶23-725]

Sec. 160. Copies to Director. — (1) A corporation

(a) any of the securities of which are or were part of a distribution to the public, remain outstanding and are held by more than one person, or

(b) the gross revenues of which, as shown in the most recent financial statements referred to in section 155, exceed ten million dollars or the assets of which as shown in those financial statements exceed five million dollars

shall, not less than twenty-one days before each annual meeting of shareholders or forthwith after the signing of a resolution under paragraph 142(1)(b) in lieu of the annual meeting, and in any event not later than fifteen months after the last date when the last preceding annual meeting should have been held or a resolution in lieu of the meeting

Sec. 160(1) ¶23-725

should have been signed, send a copy of the documents referred to in section 155 to the Director.

[¶23-726]

(2) *Affiliates.* — For the purposes of paragraph (1)(*b*), the gross revenues and assets of the corporation include the gross revenues and assets of its affiliates.

[¶23-727]

(3) *Exemption.* — On the application of a corporation, the Director may make an order on such reasonable conditions as the Director thinks fit exempting the corporation from the application of subsection (2) in such circumstances as may be prescribed. (1992, c. 1, s. 55.)

[¶23-728]

(4) *Further disclosure.* — If a corporation referred to in subsection (1)

(*a*) sends to its shareholders, or

(*b*) is required to file with or send to a public authority or a stock exchange

interim financial statements or related documents, the corporation shall forthwith send copies thereof to the Director.

[¶23-729]

(5) *Subsidiary corporation exemption.* — A subsidiary corporation is not required to comply with this section if

(*a*) the financial statements of its holding corporation are in consolidated or combined form and include the accounts of the subsidiary; and

(*b*) the consolidated or combined financial statements of the holding corporation are included in the documents sent to the Director by the holding corporation in compliance with this section.

[¶23-730]

(6) *Offence.* — A corporation that fails to comply with this section is guilty of an offence and liable on summary conviction to a fine not exceeding five thousand dollars.

(1992, c. 1, s. 55.)

[¶23-731]

Sec. 161. Qualification of auditor. — (1) Subject to subsection (5), a person is disqualified from being an auditor of a corporation if he is not independent of the corporation, any of its affiliates, or the directors or officers of any such corporation or its affiliates.

[¶23-732]

(2) *Independence.* — For the purposes of this section,

(*a*) independence is a question of fact; and

(*b*) a person is deemed not to be independent if he or his business partner

(i) is a business partner, a director, an officer or an employee of the corporation or any of its affiliates, or a business partner of any director, officer or employee of any such corporation or any of its affiliates,

(ii) beneficially owns or controls, directly or indirectly, a material interest in the securities of the corporation or any of its affiliates, or

(iii) has been a receiver, receiver-manager, liquidator or trustee in bankruptcy of the corporation or any of its affiliates within two years of his proposed appointment as auditor of the corporation.

[¶23-733]

(3) *Duty to resign.* — An auditor who becomes disqualified under this section shall, subject to subsection (5), resign forthwith after becoming aware of his disqualification.

[¶23-734]

(4) *Disqualification order.* — An interested person may apply to a court for an order declaring an auditor to be disqualified under this section and the office of auditor to be vacant.

[¶23-735]

(5) *Exemption order.* — An interested person may apply to a court for an order exempting an auditor from disqualification under this section and the court may, if it is satisfied that an exemption would not unfairly prejudice the shareholders, make an exemption order on such terms as it thinks fit, which order may have retrospective effect.

[¶23-736]

Sec. 162. Appointment of auditor. — (1) Subject to section 163, shareholders of a corporation shall, by ordinary resolution, at the first annual meeting of shareholders and at each succeeding annual meeting, appoint an auditor to hold office until the close of the next annual meeting.

[¶23-737]

(2) *Eligibility.* — An auditor appointed under section 104 is eligible for appointment under subsection (1).

[¶23-738]

(3) *Incumbent auditor.* — Notwithstanding subsection (1), if an auditor is not appointed at a meeting of shareholders, the incumbent auditor continues in office until his successor is appointed.

[¶23-739]

(4) *Remuneration.* — The remuneration of an auditor may be fixed by ordinary resolution of the shareholders or, if not so fixed, may be fixed by the directors.

[¶23-745]

Sec. 163. Dispensing with auditor. — (1) The shareholders of a corporation that is not required to comply with section 160 may resolve not to appoint an auditor.

[¶23-746]

(2) *Limitation.* — A resolution under subsection (1) is valid only until the next succeeding annual meeting of shareholders.

[¶23-747]

(3) *Unanimous consent.* — A resolution under subsection (1) is not valid unless it is consented to by all the shareholders, including shareholders not otherwise entitled to vote.

Sec. 163(3)   ¶23-747

(4) *Exemption from appointing auditor.* — On the application of a corporation that is a wholly-owned subsidary of a holding body corporate, the Director may make an order on such reasonable conditions as the Director thinks fit exempting the corporation from appointing an auditor in such circumstances as may be prescribed. (1992, c. 1, s. 56.)

(1992, c. 1, s. 56.)

Sec. 164.   Ceasing to hold office. — (1) An auditor of a corporation ceases to hold office when

(*a*) he dies or resigns; or

(*b*) he is removed pursuant to section 165.

(2) *Effective date of resignation.* — A resignation of an auditor becomes effective at the time a written resignation is sent to the corporation, or at the time specified in the resignation, whichever is later.

Sec. 165.   Removal of auditor. — (1) The shareholders of a corporation may by ordinary resolution at a special meeting remove from office the auditor other than an auditor appointed by a court under section 167.

(2) *Vacancy.* — A vacancy created by the removal of an auditor may be filled at the meeting at which the auditor is removed or, if not so filled, may be filled under section 166.

Sec. 166.   Filling vacancy. — (1) Subject to subsection (3), the directors shall forthwith fill a vacancy in the office of auditor.

(2) *Calling meeting.* — If there is not a quorum of directors, the directors then in office shall, within twenty-one days after a vacancy in the office of auditor occurs, call a special meeting of shareholders to fill the vacancy and, if they fail to call a meeting or if there are no directors, the meeting may be called by any shareholder.

(3) *Shareholders filling vacancy.* — The articles of a corporation may provide that a vacancy in the office of auditor shall only be filled by vote of the shareholders.

(4) *Unexpired term.* — An auditor appointed to fill a vacancy holds office for the unexpired term of his predecessor.

Sec. 167.   Court appointed auditor. — (1) If a corporation does not have an auditor, the court may, on the application of a shareholder or the Director, appoint and fix the remuneration of an auditor who holds office until an auditor is appointed by the shareholders.

[¶23-757]

(2) *Exception.* — Subsection (1) does not apply if the shareholders have resolved under section 163 not to appoint an auditor.

[¶23-758]

Sec. 168.   Right to attend meeting. — (1) The auditor of a corporation is entitled to receive notice of every meeting of shareholders and, at the expense of the corporation, to attend and be heard thereat on matters relating to his duties as auditor.

[¶23-759]

(2) *Duty to attend.* — If a director or shareholder of a corporation, whether or not the shareholder is entitled to vote at the meeting, gives written notice not less than ten days before a meeting of shareholders to the auditor or a former auditor of the corporation, the auditor or former auditor shall attend the meeting at the expense of the corporation and answer questions relating to his duties as auditor.

[¶23-760]

(3) *Notice to corporation.* — A director or shareholder who sends a notice referred to in subsection (2) shall send concurrently a copy of the notice to the corporation.

[¶23-761]

(4) *Offence.* — An auditor or former auditor of a corporation who fails without reasonable cause to comply with subsection (2) is guilty of an offence and liable on summary conviction to a fine not exceeding five thousand dollars or to imprisonment for a term not exceeding six months or to both.

[¶23-762]

(5) *Statement of auditor.* — An auditor who

(*a*) resigns,

(*b*) receives a notice or otherwise learns of a meeting of shareholders called for the purpose of removing him from office,

(*c*) receives a notice or otherwise learns of a meeting of directors or shareholders at which another person is to be appointed to fill the office of auditor, whether because of the resignation or removal of the incumbent auditor or because his term of office has expired or is about to expire, or

(*d*) receives a notice or otherwise learns of a meeting of shareholders at which a resolution referred to in section 163 is to be proposed,

is entitled to submit to the corporation a written statement giving the reasons for his resignation or the reasons why he opposes any proposed action or resolution.

[¶23-763]

(6) *Circulating statement.* — The corporation shall forthwith send a copy of the statement referred to in subsection (5) to every shareholder entitled to receive notice of any meeting referred to in subsection (1) and to the Director unless the statement is included in or attached to a management proxy circular required by section 150.

[¶23-764]

(7) *Replacing auditor.* — No person shall accept appointment or consent to be appointed as auditor of a corporation if he is replacing an auditor who has resigned, been removed or whose term of office has expired or is about to expire until he has requested and received from that auditor a written statement of the circumstances and the reasons why, in that auditor's opinion, he is to be replaced.

[¶23-765]

(8) *Exception.* — Notwithstanding subsection (7), a person otherwise qualified may accept appointment or consent to be appointed as auditor of a corporation if, within fifteen days after making the request referred to in that subsection, he does not receive a reply.

[¶23-766]

(9) *Effect of non-compliance.* — Unless subsection (8) applies, an appointment as auditor of a corporation of a person who has not complied with subsection (7) is void.

[¶23-775]

Sec. 169.   Examination. — (1) An auditor of a corporation shall make the examination that is in his opinion necessary to enable him to report in the prescribed manner on the financial statements required by this Act to be placed before the shareholders, except such financial statements or part thereof that relate to the period referred to in subparagraph 155(1)(*a*)(ii).

[¶23-776]

(2) *Reliance on other auditor.* — Notwithstanding section 170, an auditor of a corporation may reasonably rely upon the report of an auditor of a body corporate or an unincorporated business the accounts of which are included in whole or in part in the financial statements of the corporation.

[¶23-777]

(3) *Reasonableness.* — For the purpose of subsection (2), reasonableness is a question of fact.

[¶23-778]

(4) *Application.* — Subsection (2) applies whether or not the financial statements of the holding corporation reported on by the auditor are in consolidated form.

[¶23-779]

Sec. 170.   Right to information. — (1) On the demand of an auditor of a corporation, the present or former directors, officers, employees or agents of the corporation shall furnish such

(*a*) information and explanations, and

(*b*) access to records, documents, books, accounts and vouchers of the corporation or any of its subsidiaries

as are, in the opinion of the auditor, necessary to enable him to make the examination and report required under section 169 and that the directors, officers, employees or agents are reasonably able to furnish.

[¶23-780]

(2) *Idem.* — On the demand of the auditor of a corporation, the directors of the corporation shall

(*a*) obtain from the present or former directors, officers, employees and agents of any subsidiary of the corporation the information and explanations that the present or former directors, officers, employees and agents are reasonably able to furnish and that are, in the opinion of the auditor, necessary to enable him to make the examination and report required under section 169; and

(*b*) furnish the auditor with the information and explanations so obtained.

[¶23-781]

Sec. 171. Audit committee. — (1) Subject to subsection (2), a corporation described in subsection 102(2) shall, and any other corporation may, have an audit committee composed of not less than three directors of the corporation, a majority of whom are not officers or employees of the corporation or any of its affiliates.

[¶23-782]

(2) *Exemption.* — A corporation may apply to the Director for an order authorizing the corporation to dispense with an audit committee, and the Director may, if he is satisfied that the shareholders will not be prejudiced by such an order, permit the corporation to dispense with an audit committee on such reasonable conditions as he thinks fit.

[¶23-783]

(3) *Duty of committee.* — An audit committee shall review the financial statements of the corporation before such financial statements are approved under section 158.

[¶23-784]

(4) *Auditor's attendance.* — The auditor of a corporation is entitled to receive notice of every meeting of the audit committee and, at the expense of the corporation, to attend and be heard thereat; and, if so requested by a member of the audit committee, shall attend every meeting of the committee held during the term of office of the auditor.

[¶23-785]

(5) *Calling meeting.* — The auditor of a corporation or a member of the audit committee may call a meeting of the committee.

[¶23-786]

(6) *Notice of errors.* — A director or an officer of a corporation shall forthwith notify the audit committee and the auditor of any error or mis-statement of which he becomes aware in a financial statement that the auditor or a former auditor has reported on.

[¶23-787]

(7) *Error in financial statements.* — If the auditor or former auditor of a corporation is notified or becomes aware of an error or mis-statement in a financial statement on which he has reported, and if in his opinion the error or mis-statement is material, he shall inform each director accordingly.

[¶23-788]

(8) *Duty of directors.* — When under subsection (7) the auditor or former auditor informs the directors of an error or mis-statement in a financial statement, the directors shall

(a) prepare and issue revised financial statements; or

(b) otherwise inform the shareholders and if the corporation is one that is required to comply with section 160, it shall inform the Director of the error or mis-statement in the same manner as it informs the shareholders.

[¶23-789]

(9) *Offence.* — Every director or officer of a corporation who knowingly fails to comply with subsection (6) or (8) is guilty of an offence and liable on summary conviction to a fine not exceeding five thousand dollars or to imprisonment for a term not exceeding six months or to both.

Sec. 171(9)   ¶23-789

[¶23-790]

Sec. 172. Qualified privilege (defamation). — Any oral or written statement or report made under this Act by the auditor or former auditor of a corporation has qualified privilege.

Part XV
Fundamental Changes

[¶23-805]

Sec. 173. Amendment of articles. — (1) Subject to sections 176 and 177, the articles of a corporation may by special resolution be amended to

(a) change its name;

(b) change the place in which its registered office is situated;

(c) add, change or remove any restriction on the business or businesses that the corporation may carry on;

(d) change any maximum number of shares that the corporation is authorized to issue;

(e) create new classes of shares;

(f) reduce or increase its stated capital which, for the purposes of the amendment, is deemed to be set out in the articles;

(g) change the designation of all or any of its shares, and add, change or remove any rights, privileges, restrictions and conditions, including rights to accrued dividends, in respect of all or any of its shares, whether issued or unissued;

(h) change the shares of any class or series, whether issued or unissued, into a different number of shares of the same class or series or into the same or a different number of shares of other classes or series;

(i) divide a class of shares, whether issued or unissued, into series and fix the number of shares in each series and the rights, privileges, restrictions and conditions thereof;

(j) authorize the directors to divide any class of unissued shares into series and fix the number of shares in each series and the rights, privileges, restrictions and conditions thereof;

(k) authorize the directors to change the rights, privileges, restrictions and conditions attached to unissued shares of any series;

(l) revoke, diminish or enlarge any authority conferred under paragraphs (j) and (k);

(m) increase or decrease the number of directors or the minimum or maximum number of directors, subject to sections 107 and 112;

(n) add, change or remove restrictions on the issue, transfer or ownership of shares; or

(o) add, change or remove any other provision that is permitted by this Act to be set out in the articles.

[¶23-806]

(2) *Termination.* — The directors of a corporation may, if authorized by the shareholders in the special resolution effecting an amendment under this section, revoke the resolution before it is acted on without further approval of the shareholders.

[¶23-806a]

(3) *Amendment of number name.* — Notwithstanding subsection (1), where a corporation has a designating number as a name, the directors may amend its articles to change that name to a verbal name.

[¶23-807]

Sec. 174. Constraints on shares. — (1) Subject to sections 176 and 177, a corporation any of the issued shares of which are or were part of a distribution to the public and remain outstanding and are held by more than one person may by special resolution amend its articles in accordance with the regulations to constrain

(a) the issue or transfer of shares of any class or series to persons who are not resident Canadians;

(b) the issue or transfer of shares of any class or series to enable the corporation or any of its affiliates or associates to qualify under any prescribed law of Canada or a province

(i) to obtain a licence to carry on any business,

(ii) to become a publisher of a Canadian newspaper or periodical, or

(iii) to acquire shares of a financial intermediary as defined in the regulations; or

(c) the issue, transfer or ownership of shares of any class or series in order to assist the corporation or any of its affiliates or associates to qualify under any prescribed law of Canada or a province to receive licences, permits, grants, payments or other benefits by reason of attaining or maintaining a specified level of Canadian ownership or control, or

(d) the issue, transfer or ownership of shares of any class or series in order to assist the corporation to comply with

(i) section 379 of the *Trust and Loan Companies Act*; or

(ii) section 411 of the *Insurance Companies Act*.

(1991, c. 45, s. 554; c. 47, s. 722(1)–(2).)

[¶23-807a]

(2) *Exception in respect of paragraph (1)(c).* — Paragraph (1)(c) does not permit a constraint on the issue, transfer or ownership of shares of any class or series of which any shares are outstanding unless

(a) in the case of a constraint in respect of a class, the shares of the class, or

(b) in the case of a constraint in respect of a series, the shares of the series

are already subject to a constraint permitted under that paragraph.

[¶23-808]

(3) *Limitation on ownership of shares.* — A corporation may, pursuant to paragraph (1)(c), limit the number of shares of that corporation that may be owned, or prohibit the ownership of shares, by any person whose ownership would adversely affect the ability of the corporation or any of its affiliates or associates to attain or maintain a level of Canadian ownership or control specified in its articles that equals or exceeds a specified level referred to in paragraph (1)(c).

[¶23-809]

(4) *Change or removal of constraint.* — A corporation referred to in subsection (1) may by special resolution amend its articles to change or remove any constraint on the issue, transfer or ownership of its shares.

[¶23-810]

(5) *Termination.* — The directors of a corporation may, if authorized by the shareholders in the special resolution effecting an amendment under subsection (1) or (4), revoke the resolution before it is acted on without further approval of the shareholders.

[¶23-811]

(6) *Regulations.* — Subject to subsections 61(2) and (3), the Governor in Council may make regulations with respect to a corporation that constrains the issue, transfer or ownership of its shares prescribing

(a) the disclosure required of the constraints in documents issued or published by the corporation;

(b) the duties and powers of the directors to refuse to issue or register transfers of shares in accordance with the articles of the corporation;

(c) the limitations on voting rights of any shares held contrary to the articles of the corporation;

(d) the powers of the directors to require disclosure of beneficial ownership of shares of the corporation and the right of the corporation and its directors, employees and agents to rely on such disclosure and the effects of such reliance; and

(e) the rights of any person owning shares of the corporation at the time of an amendment to its articles constraining share issues or transfers.

[¶23-812]

(7) *Validity of acts.* — An issue or a transfer of a share or an act of a corporation is valid notwithstanding any failure to comply with this section or the regulations.

(1991, c. 45, s. 554; c. 47, s. 722(1)–(2).)

[¶23-813]

Sec. 175. Proposal to amend. — (1) Subject to subsection (2), a director or a shareholder who is entitled to vote at an annual meeting of shareholders may, in accordance with section 137, make a proposal to amend the articles.

[¶23-814]

(2) *Notice of amendment.* — Notice of a meeting of shareholders at which a proposal to amend the articles is to be considered shall set out the proposed amendment and, where applicable, shall state that a dissenting shareholder is entitled to be paid the fair value of his shares in accordance with section 190, but failure to make that statement does not invalidate an amendment.

[¶23-815]

Sec. 176. Class vote. — (1) The holders of shares of a class or, subject to subsection (4), of a series are, unless the articles otherwise provide in the case of an amendment referred to in paragraphs (a), (b) and (e), entitled to vote separately as a class or series on a proposal to amend the articles to

(a) increase or decrease any maximum number of authorized shares of such class, or increase any maximum number of authorized shares of a class having rights or privileges equal or superior to the shares of such class;

(b) effect an exchange, reclassification or cancellation of all or part of the shares of such class;

(c) add, change or remove the rights, privileges, restrictions or conditions attached to the shares of such class and, without limiting the generality of the foregoing,

(i) remove or change prejudicially rights to accrued dividends or rights to cumulative dividends,

(ii) add, remove or change prejudicially redemption rights,

(iii) reduce or remove a dividend preference or a liquidation preference, or

(iv) add, remove or change prejudicially conversion privileges, options, voting, transfer or pre-emptive rights, or rights to acquire securities of a corporation, or sinking fund provisions;

(*d*) increase the rights or privileges of any class of shares having rights or privileges equal or superior to the shares of such class;

(*e*) create a new class of shares equal or superior to the shares of such class;

(*f*) make any class of shares having rights or privileges inferior to the shares of such class equal or superior to the shares of such class;

(*g*) effect an exchange or create a right of exchange of all or part of the shares of another class into the shares of such class; or

(*h*) constrain the issue, transfer or ownership of the shares of such class or change or remove such constraint.

[¶23-815a]

(2) *Exception.* — Subsection (1) does not apply in respect of a proposal to amend the articles to add a right or privilege for a holder to convert shares of a class or series into shares of another class or series that is subject to a constraint permitted under paragraph 174(1)(*c*) but is otherwise equal to the class or series first mentioned.

[¶23-815b]

(3) *Deeming provision.* — For the purpose of paragraph (1)(*e*), a new class of shares, the issue, transfer or ownership of which is to be constrained by an amendment to the articles pursuant to paragraph 174(1)(*c*), that is otherwise equal to an existing class of shares shall be deemed not to be equal or superior to the existing class of shares.

[¶23-816]

(4) *Limitation.* — The holders of a series of shares of a class are entitled to vote separately as a series under subsection (1) only if such series is affected by an amendment in a manner different from other shares of the same class.

[¶23-817]

(5) *Right to vote.* — Subsection (1) applies whether or not shares of a class or series otherwise carry the right to vote.

[¶23-818]

(6) *Separate resolutions.* — A proposed amendment to the articles referred to in subsection (1) is adopted when the holders of the shares of each class or series entitled to vote separately thereon as a class or series have approved such amendment by a special resolution.

[¶23-819]

Sec. 177. Delivery of articles. — (1) Subject to any revocation under subsection 173(2) or 174(5), after an amendment has been adopted under section 173, 174 or 176 articles of amendment in prescribed form shall be sent to the Director.

Sec. 177(1)   ¶23-819

[¶23-820]

(2) *Reduction of stated capital.* — If an amendment effects or requires a reduction of stated capital, subsections 38(3) and (4) apply.

[¶23-822]

Sec. 178.　Certificate of amendment. — On receipt of articles of amendment, the Director shall issue a certificate of amendment in accordance with section 262.

[¶23-823]

Sec. 179.　Effect of certificate. — (1) An amendment becomes effective on the date shown in the certificate of amendment and the articles are amended accordingly.

[¶23-824]

(2) *Rights preserved.* — No amendment to the articles affects an existing cause of action or claim or liability to prosecution in favour of or against the corporation or its directors or officers, or any civil, criminal or administrative action or proceeding to which a corporation or its directors or officers is a party.

[¶23-825]

Sec. 180.　Restated articles. — (1) The directors may at any time, and shall when reasonably so directed by the Director, restate the articles of incorporation as amended.

[¶23-826]

(2) *Delivery of articles.* — Restated articles of incorporation in prescribed form shall be sent to the Director.

[¶23-827]

(3) *Restated certificate.* — On receipt of restated articles of incorporation, the Director shall issue a restated certificate of incorporation in accordance with section 262.

[¶23-828]

(4) *Effect of certificate.* — Restated articles of incorporation are effective on the date shown in the restated certificate of incorporation and supersede the original articles of incorporation and all amendments thereto.

[¶23-829]

Sec. 181.　Amalgamation. — Two or more corporations, including holding and subsidiary corporations, may amalgamate and continue as one corporation.

[¶23-830]

Sec. 182.　Amalgamation agreement. — (1) Each corporation proposing to amalgamate shall enter into an agreement setting out the terms and means of effecting the amalgamation and, in particular, setting out

(a) the provisions that are required to be included in articles of incorporation under section 6;

(b) the name and address of each proposed director of the amalgamated corporation;

(c) the manner in which the shares of each amalgamating corporation are to be converted into shares or other securities of the amalgamated corporation;

(d) if any shares of an amalgamating corporation are not to be converted into securities of the amalgamated corporation, the amount of money or securities of any body corporate that the holders of such shares are to receive in addition to or instead of securities of the amalgamated corporation;

(e) the manner of payment of money instead of the issue of fractional shares of the amalgamated corporation or of any other body corporate the securities of which are to be received in the amalgamation;

(f) whether the by-laws of the amalgamated corporation are to be those of one of the amalgamating corporations and, if not, a copy of the proposed by-laws; and

(g) details of any arrangements necessary to perfect the amalgamation and to provide for the subsequent management and operation of the amalgamated corporation.

[¶23-831]

(2) *Cancellation.* — If shares of one of the amalgamating corporations are held by or on behalf of another of the amalgamating corporations, the amalgamation agreement shall provide for the cancellation of such shares when the amalgamation becomes effective without any repayment of capital in respect thereof, and no provision shall be made in the agreement for the conversion of such shares into shares of the amalgamated corporation.

[¶23-832]

Sec. 183. Shareholder approval. — (1) The directors of each amalgamating corporation shall submit the amalgamation agreement for approval to a meeting of the holders of shares of the amalgamating corporation of which they are directors and, subject to subsection (4), to the holders of each class or series of such shares.

[¶23-833]

(2) *Notice of meeting.* — A notice of a meeting of shareholders complying with section 135 shall be sent in accordance with that section to each shareholder of each amalgamating corporation, and shall

(a) include or be accompanied by a copy or summary of the amalgamation agreement; and

(b) state that a dissenting shareholder is entitled to be paid the fair value of his shares in accordance with section 190, but failure to make that statement does not invalidate an amalgamation.

[¶23-834]

(3) *Right to vote.* — Each share of an amalgamating corporation carries the right to vote in respect of an amalgamation whether or not it otherwise carries the right to vote.

[¶23-835]

(4) *Class vote.* — The holders of shares of a class or series of shares of an amalgamating corporation are entitled to vote separately as a class or series in respect of an amalgamation if the amalgamation agreement contains a provision that, if contained in a proposed amendment to the articles, would entitle such holders to vote as a class or series under section 176.

[¶23-836]

(5) *Shareholder approval.* — Subject to subsection (4), an amalgamation agreement is adopted when the shareholders of each amalgamating corporation have approved of the amalgamation by special resolutions.

[¶23-837]

(6) *Termination.* — An amalgamation agreement may provide that at any time before the issue of a certificate of amalgamation the agreement may be terminated by the directors of an amalgamating corporation, notwithstanding approval of the agreement by the shareholders of all or any of the amalgamating corporations.

[¶23-838]

Sec. 184. Vertical short-form amalgamation. — (1) A holding corporation and one or more of its wholly-owned subsidiary corporations may amalgamate and continue as one corporation without complying with sections 182 and 183 if

(a) the amalgamation is approved by a resolution of the directors of each amalgamating corporation; and

(b) the resolutions provide that

(i) the shares of each amalgamating subsidiary corporation shall be cancelled without any repayment of capital in respect thereof,

(ii) except as may be prescribed, the articles of amalgamation shall be the same as the articles of incorporation of the amalgamated holding corporation, and

(iii) no securities shall be issued by the amalgamated corporation in connection with the amalgamation.

[¶23-839]

(2) *Horizontal short-form amalgamation.* — Two or more wholly-owned subsidiary corporations of the same holding body corporate may amalgamate and continue as one corporation without complying with sections 182 and 183 if

(a) the amalgamation is approved by a resolution of the directors of each amalgamating corporation; and

(b) the resolutions provide that

(i) the shares of all but one of the amalgamating subsidiary corporations shall be cancelled without any repayment of capital in respect thereof,

(ii) except as may be prescribed, the articles of amalgamation shall be the same as the articles of incorporation of the amalgamating subsidiary corporation whose shares are not cancelled, and

(iii) the stated capital of the amalgamating subsidiary corporations whose shares are cancelled shall be added to the stated capital of the amalgamating subsidiary corporation whose shares are not cancelled.

[¶23-840]

Sec. 185. Sending of articles. — (1) Subject to subsection 183(6), after an amalgamation has been adopted under section 183 or approved under section 184, articles of amalgamation in prescribed form shall be sent to the Director together with the documents required by sections 19 and 106.

[¶23-841]

(2) *Attached declarations.* — The articles of amalgamation shall have attached thereto a statutory declaration of a director or an officer of each amalgamating corporation that establishes to the satisfaction of the Director that

(a) there are reasonable grounds for believing that

(i) each amalgamating corporation is and the amalgamated corporation will be able to pay its liabilities as they become due, and

(ii) the realizable value of the amalgamated corporation's assets will not be less than the aggregate of its liabilities and stated capital of all classes; and

(b) there are reasonable grounds for believing that

(i) no creditor will be prejudiced by the amalgamation, or

(ii) adequate notice has been given to all known creditors of the amalgamating corporations and no creditor objects to the amalgamation otherwise than on grounds that are frivolous or vexatious.

[¶23-842]

(3) *Adequate notice.* — For the purposes of subsection (2), adequate notice is given if

(a) a notice in writing is sent to each known creditor having a claim against the corporation that exceeds one thousand dollars;

(b) a notice is published once in a newspaper published or distributed in the place where the corporation has its registered office and reasonable notice thereof is given in each province where the corporation carries on business; and

(c) each notice states that the corporation intends to amalgamate with one or more specified corporations in accordance with this Act and that a creditor of the corporation may object to the amalgamation within thirty days from the date of the notice.

[¶23-843]

(4) *Certificate of amalgamation.* — On receipt of articles of amalgamation, the Director shall issue a certificate of amalgamation in accordance with section 262.

[¶23-844]

Sec. 186. Effect of certificate. — On the date shown in a certificate of amalgamation

(a) the amalgamation of the amalgamating corporations and their continuance as one corporation become effective;

(b) the property of each amalgamating corporation continues to be the property of the amalgamated corporation;

(c) the amalgamated corporation continues to be liable for the obligations of each amalgamating corporation;

(d) an existing cause of action, claim or liability to prosecution is unaffected;

(e) a civil, criminal or administrative action or proceeding pending by or against an amalgamating corporation may be continued to be prosecuted by or against the amalgamated corporation;

(f) a conviction against, or ruling, order or judgment in favour of or against, an amalgamating corporation may be enforced by or against the amalgamated corporation; and

(g) the articles of amalgamation are deemed to be the articles of incorporation of the amalgamated corporation and the certificate of amalgamation is deemed to be the certificate of incorporation of the amalgamated corporation.

[¶23-845]

Sec. 187. Continuance (import). — (1) A body corporate incorporated otherwise than by or under an Act of Parliament may, if so authorized by the laws of the jurisdiction where it is incorporated, apply to the Director for a certificate of continuance.

Sec. 187(1)   ¶23-845

[¶23-845a]

(2) *Amendments in articles of continuance.* — A body corporate that applies for continuance under subsection (1) may, without so stating in its articles of continuance, effect by those articles any amendment to its Act of incorporation, articles, letters patent or memorandum or articles of association if the amendment is an amendment a corporation incorporated under this Act may make to its articles.

[¶23-846]

(3) *Articles of continuance.* — Articles of continuance in prescribed form shall be sent to the Director together with the documents required by sections 19 and 106.

[¶23-847]

(4) *Certificate of continuance.* — On receipt of articles of continuance, the Director shall issue a certificate of continuance in accordance with section 262.

[¶23-848]

(5) *Effect of certificate.* — On the date shown in the certificate of continuance

(a) the body corporate becomes a corporation to which this Act applies as if it had been incorporated under this Act;

(b) the articles of continuance are deemed to be the articles of incorporation of the continued corporation; and

(c) the certificate of continuance is deemed to be the certificate of incorporation of the continued corporation.

[¶23-849]

(6) *Copy of certificate.* — The Director shall forthwith send a copy of the certificate of continuance to the appropriate official or public body in the jurisdiction in which continuance under this Act was authorized.

[¶23-850]

(7) *Rights preserved.* — When a body corporate is continued as a corporation under this Act,

(a) the property of the body corporate continues to be the property of the corporation;

(b) the corporation continues to be liable for the obligations of the body corporate;

(c) an existing cause of action, claim or liability to prosecution is unaffected;

(d) a civil, criminal or administrative action or proceeding pending by or against the body corporate may be continued to be prosecuted by or against the corporation; and

(e) a conviction against, or ruling, order or judgment in favour of or against, the body corporate may be enforced by or against the corporation.

[¶23-851]

(8) *Issued shares.* — Subject to subsection 49(8), a share of a body corporate issued before the body corporate was continued under this Act is deemed to have been issued in compliance with this Act and with the provisions of the articles of continuance irrespective of whether the share is fully paid and irrespective of any designation, rights, privileges, restrictions or conditions set out on or referred to in the certificate representing the share; and continuance under this section does not deprive a holder of any right or privilege that he claims under, or relieve him of any liability in respect of, an issued share.

¶23-845a   Sec. 187(2)

[¶23-852]

(9) *Exception in case of convertible shares.* — Where a corporation continued under this Act had, before it was so continued, issued a share certificate in registered form that is convertible to bearer form, the corporation may, if a holder of such a share certificate exercises the conversion privilege attached thereto, issue a share certificate in bearer form for the same number of shares to the holder.

[¶23-853]

(10) *Definition of "share".* — For the purposes of subsections (8) and (9), "share" includes an instrument referred to in subsection 29(1), a share warrant as defined in the *Canada Corporations Act*, chapter C-32 of the Revised Statutes of Canada, 1970, or a like instrument.

[¶23-853a]

(11) *Where continued reference to par value shares permissible.* — Where the Director determines, on the application of a body corporate, that it is not practicable to change a reference to the nominal or par value of shares of a class or series that the body corporate was authorized to issue before it was continued under this Act, the Director may, notwithstanding subsection 24(1), permit the body corporate to continue to refer in its articles to those shares, whether issued or unissued, as shares having a nominal or par value.

[¶23-853b]

(12) *Limitation.* — A corporation shall set out in its articles the maximum number of shares of a class or series referred to in subsection (11) and may not amend its articles to increase that maximum number of shares or to change the nominal or par value of those shares.

[¶23-854]

Sec. 188.   Continuance (export). — (1) Subject to subsections (2) and (10), a corporation may, if it is authorized by the shareholders in accordance with this section, and if it establishes to the satisfaction of the Director that its proposed continuance in another jurisdiction or under the *Bank Act*, the *Trust and Loan Companies Act* or the *Insurance Companies Act* will not adversely affect creditors or shareholders of the corporation, apply to the appropriate official or public body of the other jurisdiction, or to the Minister of Finance, as the case may be, requesting that the corporation be continued as if it had been incorporated under the laws of that other jurisdiction or under the *Bank Act*, the *Trust and Loan Companies Act* or the *Insurance Companies Act*. (1991, c. 45, s. 555; c. 46, s. 596(1); c. 47, s. 723(1)–(2).)

[¶23-855]

(2) *Continuance (export) of investment company.* — A corporation to which the *Investment Companies Act* applies shall not apply for continuance in another jurisdiction without the prior consent of the Minister of Finance.

[¶23-856]

(3) *Notice of meeting.* — A notice of a meeting of shareholders complying with section 135 shall be sent in accordance with that section to each shareholder and shall state that a dissenting shareholder is entitled to be paid the fair value of his shares in accordance with section 190, but failure to make that statement does not invalidate a discontinuance under this Act.

[¶23-857]

(4) *Right to vote.* — Each share of the corporation carries the right to vote in respect of a continuance whether or not it otherwise carries the right to vote.

[¶23-858]

(5) *Shareholder approval.* — An application for continuance becomes authorized when the shareholders voting thereon have approved of the continuance by a special resolution.

[¶23-859]

(6) *Termination.* — The directors of a corporation may, if authorized by the shareholders at the time of approving an application for continuance under this section, abandon the application without further approval of the shareholders.

[¶23-860]

(7) *Discontinuance.* — On receipt of notice satisfactory to the Director that the corporation has been continued under the laws of another jurisdiction or under the *Bank Act*, the *Trust and Loans Companies Act* or the *Insurance Companies Act*, the Director shall file the notice and issue a certificate of discontinuance in accordance with section 262. (1991, c. 45, s. 556; c. 46, s. 596(3); c. 47, s. 723(3)–(4).)

[¶23-860a]

(8) *Notice deemed to be articles.* — For the purposes of section 262, a notice referred to in subsection (7) is deemed to be articles that are in the prescribed form.

[¶23-861]

(9) *Rights preserved.* — This Act ceases to apply to the corporation on the date shown in the certificate of discontinuance.

[¶23-862]

(10) *Prohibition.* — A corporation shall not be continued as a body corporate under the laws of another jurisdiction unless those laws provide in effect that

(a) the property of the corporation continues to be the property of the body corporate;

(b) the body corporate continues to be liable for the obligations of the corporation;

(c) an existing cause of action, claim or liability to prosecution is unaffected;

(d) a civil, criminal or administrative action or proceeding pending by or against the corporation may be continued to be prosecuted by or against the body corporate; and

(e) a conviction against, or ruling, order or judgment in favour of or against the corporation may be enforced by or against the body corporate.

(1991, c. 46, s. 596(1), (3).)

[¶23-863]

Sec. 189. Borrowing powers. — (1) Unless the articles or by-laws of or a unanimous shareholder agreement relating to a corporation otherwise provide, the articles of a corporation are deemed to state that the directors of a corporation may, without authorization of the shareholders,

(a) borrow money upon the credit of the corporation;

(b) issue, reissue, sell or pledge debt obligations of the corporation;

(c) subject to section 44, give a guarantee on behalf of the corporation to secure performance of an obligation of any person; and

(d) mortgage, hypothecate, pledge or otherwise create a security interest in all or any property of the corporation, owned or subsequently acquired, to secure any obligation of the corporation.

[¶23-863a]

(2) *Delegation of borrowing powers.* — Notwithstanding subsection 115(3) and paragraph 121(a), unless the articles or by-laws of or a unanimous shareholder agreement relating to a corporation otherwise provide, the directors may, by resolution, delegate the powers referred to in subsection (1) to a director, a committee of directors or an officer.

[¶23-864]

(3) *Extraordinary sale, lease or exchange.* — A sale, lease or exchange of all or substantially all the property of a corporation other than in the ordinary course of business of the corporation requires the approval of the shareholders in accordance with subsections (4) to (8).

[¶23-865]

(4) *Notice of meeting.* — A notice of a meeting of shareholders complying with section 135 shall be sent in accordance with that section to each shareholder and shall

(a) include or be accompanied by a copy or summary of the agreement of sale, lease or exchange; and

(b) state that a dissenting shareholder is entitled to be paid the fair value of his shares in accordance with section 190, but failure to make that statement does not invalidate a sale, lease or exchange referred to in subsection (3).

[¶23-866]

(5) *Shareholder approval.* — At the meeting referred to in subsection (4) the shareholders may authorize the sale, lease or exchange and may fix or authorize the directors to fix any of the terms and conditions thereof.

[¶23-867]

(6) *Right to vote.* — Each share of the corporation carries the right to vote in respect of a sale, lease or exchange referred to in subsection (3) whether or not it otherwise carries the right to vote.

[¶23-868]

(7) *Class vote.* — The holders of shares of a class or series of shares of the corporation are entitled to vote separately as a class or series in respect of a sale, lease or exchange referred to in subsection (3) only if such class or series is affected by the sale, lease or exchange in a manner different from the shares of another class or series.

[¶23-869]

(8) *Shareholder approval.* — A sale, lease or exchange referred to in subsection (3) is adopted when the holders of each class or series entitled to vote thereon have approved of the sale, lease or exchange by a special resolution.

[¶23-870]

(9) *Termination.* — The directors of a corporation may, if authorized by the shareholders approving a proposed sale, lease or exchange, and subject to the rights of third parties, abandon the sale, lease or exchange without further approval of the shareholders.

[¶23-871]

Sec. 190. **Right to dissent.** — (1) Subject to sections 191 and 241, a holder of shares of any class of a corporation may dissent if the corporation is subject to an order under paragraph 192(4)(*d*) that affects the holder or if the corporation resolves to

(*a*) amend its articles under section 173 or 174 to add, change or remove any provisions restricting or constraining the issue, transfer or ownership of shares of that class;

(*b*) amend its articles under section 173 to add, change or remove any restriction on the business or businesses that the corporation may carry on;

(*c*) amalgamate with another corporation, otherwise than under section 184;

(*d*) be continued under the laws of another jurisdiction under section 188; or

(*c*) sell, lease or exchange all or substantially all its property under subsection 189(3).

[¶23-872]

(2) *Further right.* — A holder of shares of any class or series of shares entitled to vote under section 176 may dissent if the corporation resolves to amend its articles in a manner described in that section.

[¶23-873]

(3) *Payment for shares.* — In addition to any other right he may have, but subject to subsection (26), a shareholder who complies with this section is entitled, when the action approved by the resolution from which he dissents or an order made under subsection 192(4) becomes effective, to be paid by the corporation the fair value of the shares held by him in respect of which he dissents, determined as of the close of business on the day before the resolution was adopted or the order was made.

[¶23-874]

(4) *No partial dissent.* — A dissenting shareholder may only claim under this section with respect to all the shares of a class held by him on behalf of any one beneficial owner and registered in the name of the dissenting shareholder.

[¶23-875]

(5) *Objection.* — A dissenting shareholder shall send to the corporation, at or before any meeting of shareholders at which a resolution referred to in subsection (1) or (2) is to be voted on, a written objection to the resolution, unless the corporation did not give notice to the shareholder of the purpose of the meeting and of his right to dissent.

[¶23-876]

(6) *Notice of resolution.* — The corporation shall, within ten days after the shareholders adopt the resolution, send to each shareholder who has filed the objection referred to in subsection (5) notice that the resolution has been adopted, but such notice is not required to be sent to any shareholder who voted for the resolution or who has withdrawn his objection.

[¶23-877]

(7) *Demand for payment.* — A dissenting shareholder shall, within twenty days after he receives a notice under subsection (6) or, if he does not receive such notice, within twenty days after he learns that the resolution has been adopted, send to the corporation a written notice containing

(*a*) his name and address;

(*b*) the number and class of shares in respect of which he dissents; and

(*c*) a demand for payment of the fair value of such shares.

[¶23-878]

(8) *Share certificate.* — A dissenting shareholder shall, within thirty days after sending a notice under subsection (7), send the certificates representing the shares in respect of which he dissents to the corporation or its transfer agent.

[¶23-879]

(9) *Forfeiture.* — A dissenting shareholder who fails to comply with subsection (8) has no right to make a claim under this section.

[¶23-880]

(10) *Endorsing certificate.* — A corporation or its transfer agent shall endorse on any share certificate received under subsection (8) a notice that the holder is a dissenting shareholder under this section and shall forthwith return the share certificates to the dissenting shareholder.

[¶23-881]

(11) *Suspension of rights.* — On sending a notice under subsection (7), a dissenting shareholder ceases to have any rights as a shareholder other than the right to be paid the fair value of his shares as determined under this section except where

(a) the dissenting shareholder withdraws his notice before the corporation makes an offer under subsection (12),

(b) the corporation fails to make an offer in accordance with subsection (12) and the dissenting shareholder withdraws his notice, or

(c) the directors revoke a resolution to amend the articles under subsection 173(2) or 174(5), terminate an amalgamation agreement under subsection 183(6) or an application for continuance under subsection 188(6), or abandon a sale, lease or exchange under subsection 189(9).

in which case his rights as a shareholder are reinstated as of the date he sent the notice referred to in subsection (7).

[¶23-882]

(12) *Offer to pay.* — A corporation shall, not later than seven days after the later of the day on which the action approved by the resolution is effective or the day the corporation received the notice referred to in subsection (7), send to each dissenting shareholder who has sent such notice

(a) a written offer to pay for his shares in an amount considered by the directors of the corporation to be the fair value thereof, accompanied by a statement showing how the fair value was determined; or

(b) if subsection (26) applies, a notification that it is unable lawfully to pay dissenting shareholders for their shares.

[¶23-883]

(13) *Same terms.* — Every offer made under subsection (12) for shares of the same class or series shall be on the same terms.

[¶23-884]

(14) *Payment.* — Subject to subsection (26), a corporation shall pay for the shares of a dissenting shareholder within ten days after an offer made under subsection (12) has been accepted, but any such offer lapses if the corporation does not receive an acceptance thereof within thirty days after the offer has been made.

[¶23-885]

(15) *Corporation may apply to court.* — Where a corporation fails to make an offer under subsection (12), or if a dissenting shareholder fails to accept an offer, the corporation may, within fifty days after the action approved by the resolution is effective or within such further period as a court may allow, apply to a court to fix a fair value for the shares of any dissenting shareholder.

[¶23-886]

(16) *Shareholder application to court.* — If a corporation fails to apply to a court under subsection (15), a dissenting shareholder may apply to a court for the same purpose within a further period of twenty days or within such further period as a court may allow.

[¶23-887]

(17) *Venue.* — An application under subsection (15) or (16) shall be made to a court having jurisdiction in the place where the corporation has its registered office or in the province where the dissenting shareholder resides if the corporation carries on business in that province.

[¶23-888]

(18) *No security for costs.* — A dissenting shareholder is not required to give security for costs in an application made under subsection (15) or (16).

[¶23-889]

(19) *Parties.* — On an application to a court under subsection (15) or (16),

(a) all dissenting shareholders whose shares have not been purchased by the corporation shall be joined as parties and are bound by the decision of the court; and

(b) the corporation shall notify each affected dissenting shareholder of the date, place and consequences of the application and of his right to appear and be heard in person or by counsel.

[¶23-890]

(20) *Powers of court.* — On an application to a court under subsection (15) or (16), the court may determine whether any other person is a dissenting shareholder who should be joined as a party, and the court shall then fix a fair value for the shares of all dissenting shareholders.

[¶23-891]

(21) *Appraisers.* — A court may in its discretion appoint one or more appraisers to assist the court to fix a fair value for the shares of the dissenting shareholders.

[¶23-892]

(22) *Final order.* — The final order of a court shall be rendered against the corporation in favour of each dissenting shareholder and for the amount of his shares as fixed by the court.

[¶23-893]

(23) *Interest.* — A court may in its discretion allow a reasonable rate of interest on the amount payable to each dissenting shareholder from the date the action approved by the resolution is effective until the date of payment.

[¶23-894]

(24) *Notice that subsection (26) applies.* — If subsection (26) applies, the corporation shall, within ten days after the pronouncement of an order under subsection (22), notify each dissenting shareholder that it is unable lawfully to pay dissenting shareholders for their shares.

[¶23-895]

(25) *Effect where subsection (26) applies.* — If subsection (26) applies, a dissenting shareholder, by written notice delivered to the corporation within thirty days after receiving a notice under subsection (24), may

(a) withdraw his notice of dissent, in which case the corporation is deemed to consent to the withdrawal and the shareholder is reinstated to his full rights as a shareholder; or

(b) retain a status as a claimant against the corporation, to be paid as soon as the corporation is lawfully able to do so or, in a liquidation, to be ranked subordinate to the rights of creditors of the corporation but in priority to its shareholders.

[¶23-896]

(26) *Limitation.* — A corporation shall not make a payment to a dissenting shareholder under this section if there are reasonable grounds for believing that

(a) the corporation is or would after the payment be unable to pay its liabilities as they become due; or

(b) the realizable value of the corporation's assets would thereby be less than the aggregate of its liabilities.

[¶23-897]

Sec. 191. Definition of "reorganization". — (1) In this section, "reorganization" means a court order made under

(a) section 241;

(b) the *Bankruptcy and Insolvency Act* approving a proposal; or

(c) any other Act of Parliament that affects the rights among the corporation, its shareholders and creditors.

(1992, c. 27, s. 90(1)(*h*).)

[¶23-898]

(2) *Powers of court.* — If a corporation is subject to an order referred to in subsection (1), its articles may be amended by such order to effect any change that might lawfully be made by an amendment under section 173.

[¶23-899]

(3) *Further powers.* — If a court makes an order referred to in subsection (1), the court may also

(a) authorize the issue of debt obligations of the corporation, whether or not convertible into shares of any class or having attached any rights or options to acquire shares of any class, and fix the terms thereof; and

(b) appoint directors in place of or in addition to all or any of the directors then in office.

Sec. 191(3)   ¶23-899

[¶23-900]

(4) *Articles of reorganization.* — After an order referred to in subsection (1) has been made, articles of reorganization in prescribed form shall be sent to the Director together with the documents required by sections 19 and 113, if applicable.

[¶23-901]

(5) *Certificate of reorganization.* — On receipt of articles or reorganization, the Director shall issue a certificate of amendment in accordance with section 262.

[¶23-902]

(6) *Effect of certificate.* — A reorganization becomes effective on the date shown in the certificate of amendment and the articles of incorporation are amended accordingly.

(1992, c. 27, s. 90(1)(*h*).)

[¶23-903]

(7) *No dissent.* — A shareholder is not entitled to dissent under section 190 if an amendment to the articles of incorporation is effected under this section.

(1992, c. 27, s. 90(1)(*h*).)

[¶23-905]

Sec. 192. Definition of "arrangement". — (1) In this section, "arrangement" includes

(*a*) an amendment to the articles of a corporation;

(*b*) an amalgamation of two or more corporations;

(*c*) an amalgamation of a body corporate with a corporation that results in an amalgamated corporation subject to this Act;

(*d*) a division of the business carried on by a corporation;

(*e*) a transfer of all or substantially all the property of a corporation to another body corporate in exchange for property, money or securities of the body corporate;

(*f*) an exchange of securities of a corporation held by security holders for property, money or other securities of the corporation or property, money or securities of another body corporate that is not a take-over bid as defined in section 194;

(*g*) a liquidation and dissolution of a corporation; and

(*h*) any combination of the foregoing.

[¶23-906]

(2) *Where corporation insolvent.* — For the purposes of this section, a corporation is insolvent

(*a*) where it is unable to pay its liabilities as they become due; or

(*b*) where the realizable value of the assets of the corporation are less than the aggregate of its liabilities and stated capital of all classes.

[¶23-907]

(3) *Application to court for approval of arrangement.* — Where it is not practicable for a corporation that is not insolvent to effect a fundamental change in the nature of an arrangement under any other provision of this Act, the corporation may apply to a court for an order approving an arrangement proposed by the corporation.

[¶23-908]

(4) *Powers of court.* — In connection with an application under this section, the court may make any interim or final order it thinks fit including, without limiting the generality of the foregoing,

(a) an order determining the notice to be given to any interested person or dispensing with notice to any person other than the Director;

(b) an order appointing counsel, at the expense of the corporation, to represent the interests of the shareholders;

(c) an order requiring a corporation to call, hold and conduct a meeting of holders of securities or options or rights to acquire securities in such manner as the court directs;

(d) an order permitting a shareholder to dissent under section 190;

(e) an order approving an arrangement as proposed by the corporation or as amended in any manner the court may direct.

[¶23-909]

(5) *Notice to Director.* — An applicant under this section shall give the Director notice of the application and the Director is entitled to appear and be heard in person or by counsel.

[¶23-910]

(6) *Articles of arrangement.* — After an order referred to in paragraph (4)(e) has been made, articles of arrangement in prescribed form shall be sent to the Director together with the documents required by sections 19 and 113, if applicable.

[¶23-911]

(7) *Certificate of amendment.* — On receipt of articles of arrangement, the Director shall issue a certificate of amendment in accordance with section 262.

[¶23-912]

(8) *Effect of certificate.* — An arrangement becomes effective on the date shown in the certificate of amendment.

Part XVI
Prospectus Qualification

[¶23-960]

Sec. 193. Distribution document. — A corporation that files or distributes in any jurisdiction a prospectus, statement of material facts, registration statement, securities exchange take-over bid circular or similar document relating to the distribution to the public of the securities of the corporation shall forthwith send to the Director a copy of any such document.

Part XVII
Take-over Bids

[¶24-023]

Sec. 194. Definitions. — In this Part,

"*exempt offer*". — "exempt offer" means an offer

(a) to fewer than fifteen shareholders to purchase shares by way of separate agreements,

(b) to purchase shares through a stock exchange or in the over-the-counter market in such circumstances as may be prescribed,

(c) to purchase shares of a corporation that has fewer than fifteen shareholders, two or more joint holders being counted as one shareholder,

(d) exempted under section 204, or

(e) by a corporation to repurchase its own shares to be held under section 32;

"offer". — "offer" includes an invitation to make an offer;

"offeree". — "offeree" means a person to whom a take-over bid is made;

"offeree corporation". — "offeree corporation" means a corporation whose shares are the object of a take-over bid;

"offeror". — "offeror" means a person other than an agent, who makes a take-over bid, and includes two or more persons who, directly or indirectly,

(a) make take-over bids jointly or in concert, or

(b) intend to exercise jointly or in concert voting rights attached to shares for which a take-over bid is made;

"share". — "share" means a share carrying voting rights under all circumstances or by reason of the occurrence of an event that has occurred and that is continuing, and includes

(a) a security currently convertible into such a share, and

(b) currently exercisable options and rights to acquire such a share or such a convertible security;

"take-over bid". — "take-over bid" means an offer, other than an exempt offer, made by an offeror to shareholders at approximately the same time to acquire shares that, if combined with shares already beneficially owned or controlled, directly or indirectly, by the offeror or an affiliate or associate of the offeror on the date of the take-over bid, would exceed ten per cent of any class of issued shares of an offeree corporation and includes every offer, other than an exempt offer, by an issuer to repurchase its own shares.

[¶24-024]

Sec. 195. Bid for all shares. — Where a take-over bid is for all the shares of any class,

(a) shares deposited pursuant to the take-over bid, if not taken up by the offeror, may be withdrawn by or on behalf of an offeree at any time after sixty days following the date of the takeover bid;

(b) the offeror shall not take up shares deposited pursuant thereto until ten days after the date of the take-over bid; and

(c) the offeror, if he so intends, shall state in the take-over bid circular that he intends to invoke the right under section 206 to acquire the shares of offerees who do not accept the takeover bid and that the offeree is entitled to dissent and to demand the fair value of his shares.

[¶24-025]

Sec. 196. Bid for less than all shares. — (1) Where a take-over bid is for less than all the shares of any class,

(a) the offeror shall not take up shares deposited pursuant thereto until twenty-one days after the date of the take-over bid;

(b) the period of time within which shares may be deposited pursuant to the take-over bid or any extension thereof shall not exceed thirty-five days from the date of the take-over bid; and

(c) if a greater number of shares is deposited pursuant to the take-over bid than the offeror is bound or willing to take up and pay for, the shares taken up by the offeror shall be taken up rateably, disregarding fractions, according to the number of shares deposited by each offeree.

[¶24-026]

(2) *Amendment by bid.* — Where a take over bid for all the shares of any class is converted by amendment or otherwise to a bid for less than all the shares of a class, the take-over bid is deemed to be a take-over bid to which subsection (1) applies.

[¶24-027]

Sec. 197. Every bid for shares. — Whether a take-over bid is for all or less than all the shares of any class,

(a) shares deposited pursuant to the take-over bid may be withdrawn by or on behalf of an offeree at any time within ten days after the date of the take-over bid;

(b) shares deposited pursuant to the take-over bid shall, if the terms stipulated by the offeror and not subsequently waived by him have been complied with, be taken up and paid for within fourteen days after the last day within which shares may be deposited pursuant to the take-over bid;

(c) the period of time within which shares may be deposited pursuant to a take-over bid shall not be less than twenty-one days after the date of the take-over bid;

(d) if the terms of the take-over bid are amended by increasing the consideration offered for the shares, the offeror shall pay the increased consideration to each offeree whose shares are taken up pursuant to the take-over bid whether or not such shares have been taken up by the offeror before the amendment of the take-over bid;

(e) if the offeror intends to purchase shares to which the take-over bid relates in the market during the period of time within which shares may be deposited pursuant to the take-over bid, the offeror shall so state in the take-over bid circular; and

(f) if the offeror purchases shares to which a take-over bid relates other than pursuant to the take-over bid during the period of time within which shares may be deposited pursuant to the take-over bid,

(i) the payment other than pursuant to the take-over bid of an amount for a share that is greater than the amount offered in the take-over bid is deemed to be an amendment of the take-over bid to which paragraph (d) applies,

(ii) the offeror shall immediately notify the offerees of the increased consideration being offered for the shares,

(iii) the shares acquired other than pursuant to the take-over bid shall be counted to determine whether a condition as to minimum acceptance has been fulfilled, and

(iv) the shares acquired other than pursuant to the take-over bid shall not be counted among the shares taken up rateably under paragraph 196(1)(c).

[¶24-028]

Sec. 198. Sending bid. — (1) A take-over bid, including a copy of the take-over bid circular in prescribed form and any amendment of the take-over bid, shall be sent concurrently to each director of the offeree corporation, to each shareholder of the offeree corporation resident in Canada and to the Director.

[¶24-029]

(2) *Date of bid.* — A take-over bid is deemed to be dated as of the date on which it is sent.

[¶24-030]

(3) *Shareholders in Canada.* — For the purposes of this section and section 201, a shareholder of an offeree corporation is deemed to be resident in Canada if his latest address as shown in the securities register of the offeree corporation is an address within Canada.

[¶24-031]

Sec. 199. Arrangements for funds. — Where a take-over bid states that the consideration for the shares deposited pursuant thereto is to be paid in money or partly in money, the offeror shall make adequate arrangements to ensure that funds are available to make the required money payment for such shares.

[¶24-032]

Sec. 200. Share-for-share bids. — Where a take-over bid states that the consideration for the shares of the offeree corporation is to be, in whole or in part, securities of the offeror or any other body corporate, the take-over bid circular shall be in prescribed form.

[¶24-033]

Sec. 201. Directors' circular. — (1) The directors of an offeree corporation shall send a directors' circular in prescribed form to each director of the offeree corporation, to each shareholder of the offeree corporation resident in Canada, to the offeror and to the Director.

[¶24-034]

(2) *Notice.* — Unless the directors of an offeree corporation send a directors' circular under subsection (1) within ten days of the date of the take-over bid, the directors shall forthwith notify the offerees and the Director that a directors' circular will be sent and may recommend that the offerees do not tender their shares pursuant to the take-over bid until they receive the directors' circular.

[¶24-035]

(3) *Contents of notice.* — The notice required by subsection (2) shall be in prescribed form.

[¶24-036]

(4) *Time of notice.* — The directors shall send the directors' circular required by subsection (1) to each offeree and to the Director at least seven days before the date the take-over bid terminates or before the sixtieth day of the take-over bid, whichever is earlier.

[¶24-037]

(5) *Dissent of director.* — Where a director of an offeree corporation is of the opinion that a take-over bid is not advantageous to the shareholders of the offeree corporation or where a director disagrees with any statement in a directors' circular, he is entitled to indicate his opinion or disagreement in the directors' circular required by subsection (1) and, if he indicates his opinion or disagreement, he shall include in that circular a statement setting out the reasons for his opinion or disagreement.

[¶24-038]

Sec. 202. Expert's consent. — (1) A report, opinion or statement of a solicitor, auditor, accountant, engineer, appraiser or other person whose profession lends credibility to a statement made by him shall not be included in a take-over bid circular or a directors' circular unless that person has consented in writing to the use of the report, opinion or statement.

[¶24-039]

(2) *Copy to Director.* — On the demand of the Director, a person referred to in subsection (1) shall forthwith send to the Director a copy of any report, opinion or statement referred to in that subsection that is made by that person together with a copy of his consent.

[¶24-040]

Sec. 203. Approval of take-over bid. — (1) When a take-over bid is made by or on behalf of a body corporate, the directors of the body corporate shall approve the take-over bid and the take-over bid circular, and the approval shall be evidenced on the circular by the signature of one or more directors.

[¶24-041]

(2) *Approval of directors' circular.* — The directors of an offeree corporation shall approve a directors' circular that contains the recommendations of a majority of the directors, and the approval shall be evidenced by the signature of one or more directors.

[¶24-042]

Sec. 204. Exemption order. — (1) Any interested person may apply to a court having jurisdiction in the place where the offeree corporation has its registered office for an order exempting a take-over bid from any of the provisions of this Part, and the court may, if it is satisfied that an exemption would not unfairly prejudice a shareholder of the offeree corporation, make an exemption order on such terms as it thinks fit, which order may have retrospective effect.

[¶24-043]

(2) *Notice to Director.* — An applicant under subsection (1) shall give the Director notice of the hearing of an application under that subsection, and the Director is entitled to appear and be heard in person or by counsel.

[¶24-044]

(3) *Publication.* — The Director shall set out in the periodical referred to in section 129 the particulars of exemptions granted under this section.

[¶24-045]

Sec. 205. Offence. — (1) An offeror who, without reasonable cause, fails to comply with this Part or the regulations is guilty of an offence and liable on summary conviction to a fine not exceeding five thousand dollars or to imprisonment for a term not exceeding six months or to both.

[¶24-046]

(2) *Officers, etc., of bodies corporate.* — Where an offeror who is a body corporate commits an offence under subsection (1), any director or officer of the body corporate who knowingly authorized, permitted or acquiesced in the commission of the offence is a party to and guilty of the offence and is liable on summary conviction to a fine not exceeding five thousand dollars or to imprisonment for a term not exceeding six months or to both, whether or not the body corporate has been prosecuted or convicted.

[¶24-047]

(3) *Order of the court.* — Where in connection with a take-over bid a person does not comply with this Act or the regulations, the Director or any interested person may apply to a court and on such application the court may make any order it thinks fit, including, without limiting the generality of the foregoing,

(a) an order restraining the distribution of a take-over bid circular, a directors' circular or other document used in connection with the take-over bid;

(b) an order, if the take-over bid is to continue, requiring correction of the take-over bid circular, directors' circular or other document and distribution of the corrected document to each offeree;

(c) an order varying the dates and times referred to in sections 195 to 197;

(d) an order requiring any person to comply with this Act or the regulations;

(e) an order compensating an aggrieved person;

(f) an order rescinding a transaction;

(g) an order requiring an offeror to dispose of shares acquired pursuant to the take-over bid;

(h) an order prohibiting an offeror from voting shares acquired pursuant to a take-over bid.

[¶24-048]

(4) *"Definition of interested person".* — For the purposes of subsection (3), "interested person" includes

(a) an offeree whether or not he deposits shares pursuant to a take-over bid;

(b) an offeree corporation;

(c) an offeror; and

(d) a rival offeror.

[¶24-049]

Sec. 206. Definitions. — (1) In this section,

"dissenting offeree". — "dissenting offeree" means, where a take-over bid is made for all the shares of a class of shares, a holder of a share of that class who does not accept the take-over bid and includes a subsequent holder of that share who acquires it from the first mentioned holder;

"take-over bid". — "take-over bid" includes

(a) an offer to purchase shares of a class of shares to which no voting rights are attached if the offer complies with sections 195 to 203,

(b) an offer to purchase shares, including shares to which no voting rights are attached, of a corporation having fewer than fifteen shareholders if the offer is made to all shareholders in the prescribed form and manner.

[¶24-050]

(2) *Right to acquire.* — If within one hundred and twenty days after the date of a take-over bid the bid is accepted by the holders of not less than ninety per cent of the shares of any class of shares to which the take-over bid relates, other than shares held at the date of the take-over bid by or on behalf of the offeror or an affiliate or associate of the offeror, the offeror is entitled, on complying with this section, to acquire the shares held by the dissenting offerees.

[¶24-051]

(3) *Notice.* — An offeror may acquire shares held by a dissenting offeree by sending by registered mail within sixty days after the date of termination of the take-over bid and in any event within one hundred and eighty days after the date of the take-over bid, an offeror's notice to each dissenting offeree and to the Director stating that

(a) the offerees holding more than ninety per cent of the shares to which the bid relates accepted the take-over bid;

(b) the offeror is bound to take up and pay for or has taken up and paid for the shares of the offerees who accepted the take-over bid;

(c) a dissenting offeree is required to elect

(i) to transfer his shares to the offeror on the terms on which the offeror acquired the shares of the offerees who accepted the take-over bid, or

(ii) to demand payment of the fair value of his shares in accordance with subsections (9) to (18) by notifying the offeror within twenty days after he receives the offeror's notice;

(d) a dissenting offeree who does not notify the offeror in accordance with subparagraph (c)(ii) is deemed to have elected to transfer his shares to the offeror on the same terms that the offeror acquired the shares from the offerees who accepted the take-over bid; and

(e) a dissenting offeree must send his shares to which the take-over bid relates to the offeree corporation within twenty days after he receives the offeror's notice.

[¶24-052]

(4) *Notice of adverse claim.* — Concurrently with sending the offeror's notice under subsection (3), the offeror shall send to the offeree corporation a notice of adverse claim in accordance with section 78 with respect to each share held by a dissenting offeree.

[¶24-053]

(5) *Share certificate.* — A dissenting offeree to whom an offeror's notice is sent under subsection (3) shall, within twenty days after he receives that notice, send his share certificates of the class of shares to which the take-over bid relates to the offeree corporation.

[¶24-054]

(6) *Payment.* — Within twenty days after the offeror sends an offeror's notice under subsection (3), the offeror shall pay or transfer to the offeree corporation the amount of money or other consideration that the offeror would have had to pay or transfer to a dissenting offeree if the dissenting offeree had elected to accept the take-over bid under subparagraph (3)(c)(i).

[¶24-055]

(7) *Consideration.* — The offeree corporation is deemed to hold in trust for the dissenting shareholders the money or other consideration it receives under subsection (6), and the offeree corporation shall deposit the money in a separate account in a bank or other body corporate any of whose deposits are insured by the Canada Deposit Insurance Corporation or guaranteed by the Quebec Deposit Insurance Board, and shall place the other consideration in the custody of a bank or such other body corporate.

[¶24-056]

(8) *Duty of offeree corporation.* — Within thirty days after the offeror sends an offeror's notice under subsection (3), the offeree corporation shall

Sec. 206(8) **¶24-056**

(*a*) issue to the offeror a share certificate in respect of the shares that were held by dissenting offerees;

(*b*) give to each dissenting offeree who elects to accept the take-over bid terms under subparagraph (3)(*c*)(i) and who sends his share certificates as required under subsection (5) the money or other consideration to which he is entitled, disregarding fractional shares, which may be paid for in money; and

(*c*) send to each dissenting shareholder who has not sent his share certificates as required under subsection (5) a notice stating that

(i) his shares have been cancelled,

(ii) the offeree corporation or some designated person holds in trust for him the money or other consideration to which he is entitled as payment for or in exchange for his shares, and

(iii) the offeree corporation will, subject to subsections (9) to (18), send that money or other consideration to him forthwith after receiving his shares.

[¶24-057]

(9) *Application to court.* — If a dissenting offeree has elected to demand payment of the fair value of his shares under subparagraph (3)(*c*)(ii), the offeror may, within twenty days after it has paid the money or transferred the other consideration under subsection (6), apply to a court to fix the fair value of the shares of that dissenting offeree.

[¶24-058]

(10) *Idem.* — If an offeror fails to apply to a court under subsection (9), a dissenting offeree may apply to a court for the same purpose within a further period of twenty days.

[¶24-058a]

(11) *Status of dissenter if no court application.* — Where no application is made to a court under subsection (10) within the period set out in that subsection, a dissenting offeree is deemed to have elected to transfer his shares to the offeror on the same terms that the offeror acquired the shares from the offerees who accepted the take-over bid.

[¶24-059]

(12) *Venue.* — An application under subsection (9) or (10) shall be made to a court having jurisdiction in the place where the corporation has its registered office or in the province where the dissenting offeree resides if the corporation carries on business in that province.

[¶24-060]

(13) *No security for costs.* — A dissenting offeree is not required to give security for costs in an application made under subsection (9) or (10).

[¶24-061]

(14) *Parties.* — On an application under subsection (9) or (10)

(*a*) all dissenting offerees referred to in subparagraph (3)(*c*)(ii) whose shares have not been acquired by the offeror shall be joined as parties and are bound by the decision of the court; and

(*b*) the offeror shall notify each affected dissenting offeree of the date, place and consequences of the application and of his right to appear and be heard in person or by counsel.

[¶24-062]

(15) *Powers of court.* — On an application to a court under subsection (9) or (10), the court may determine whether any other person is a dissenting offeree who should be joined as a party, and the court shall then fix a fair value for the shares of all dissenting offerees.

[¶24-063]

(16) *Appraisers.* — A court may in its discretion appoint one or more appraisers to assist the court to fix a fair value for the shares of all dissenting offerees.

[¶24-064]

(17) *Final order.* — The final order of the court shall be made against the offeror in favour of each dissenting offeree and for the amount for his shares as fixed by the court.

[¶24-065]

(18) *Additional powers.* — In connection with proceedings under this section, a court may make any order it thinks fit and, without limiting the generality of the foregoing, it may

(a) fix the amount of money or other consideration that is required to be held in trust under subsection (7);

(b) order that that money or other consideration be held in trust by a person other than the offeree corporation;

(c) allow a reasonable rate of interest on the amount payable to each dissenting offeree from the date he sends or delivers his share certificates under subsection (5) until the date of payment;

(d) order that any money payable to a shareholder who cannot be found be paid to the Receiver General and subsection 227(3) applies in respect thereof.

Part XVIII

Liquidation and Dissolution

[¶24-142]

Sec. 207. Definition of "court". — In this Part, "court" means a court having jurisdiction in the place where the corporation has its registered office.

[¶24-143]

Sec. 208. Application of Part. — (1) This Part does not apply to a corporation that is insolvent within the meaning of the *Bankruptcy Act* or that is a bankrupt within the meaning of that Act.

[¶24-144]

(2) *Staying proceedings.* — Any proceedings taken under this Part to dissolve or to liquidate and dissolve a corporation shall be stayed if the corporation is at any time found, in a proceeding under the *Bankruptcy and Insolvency Act*, to be insolvent within the meaning of that Act. (1992, c. 27, s. 90(1)(h).)

(1992, c. 27, s. 90(1)(h).)

[¶24-145]

Sec. 209. Revival. — (1) Where a body corporate is dissolved under this Part or under section 268 of this Act or section 261 of chapter 33 of the Statutes of Canada,

1974-75-76, any interested person may apply to the Director to have the body corporate revived as a corporation under this Act.

[¶24-146]

(2) *Articles of revival.* — Articles of revival in prescribed form shall be sent to the Director.

[¶24-147]

(3) *Certificate of revival.* — On receipt of articles of revival, the Director shall issue a certificate of revival in accordance with section 262.

[¶24-148]

(4) *Rights preserved.* — A body corporate is revived as a corporation under this Act on the date shown on the certificate of revival, and thereafter the corporation, subject to such reasonable terms as may be imposed by the Director and to the rights acquired by any person after its dissolution, has all the rights and privileges and is liable for the obligations that it would have had if it had not been dissolved.

[¶24-149]

Sec. 210. Dissolution before commencing business. — (1) A corporation that has not issued any shares may be dissolved at any time by resolution of all the directors.

[¶24-150]

(2) *Dissolution if no property.* — A corporation that has no property and no liabilities may be dissolved by special resolution of the shareholders or, where it has issued more than one class of shares, by special resolutions of the holders of each class whether or not they are otherwise entitled to vote.

[¶24-150a]

(3) *Dissolution where property disposed of.* — A corporation that has property or liabilities or both may be dissolved by special resolution of the shareholders or, where it has issued more than one class of shares, by special resolutions of the holders of each class whether or not they are otherwise entitled to vote, if

(a) by the special resolution or resolutions the shareholders authorize the directors to cause the corporation to distribute any property and discharge any liabilities; and

(b) the corporation has distributed any property and discharged any liabilities before it sends articles of dissolution to the Director pursuant to subsection (4).

[¶24-151]

(4) *Articles of dissolution.* — Articles of dissolution in prescribed form shall be sent to the Director.

[¶24-152]

(5) *Certificate of dissolution.* — On receipt of articles of dissolution, the Director shall issue a certificate of dissolution in accordance with section 262.

[¶24-153]

(6) *Effect of certificate.* — The corporation ceases to exist on the date shown in the certificate of dissolution.

Voluntary dissolution *Normally used*

[¶24-154]

Sec. 211. Proposing liquidation and dissolution. — (1) The directors may propose, or a shareholder who is entitled to vote at an annual meeting of shareholders may, in accordance with section 137, make a proposal for, the voluntary liquidation and dissolution of a corporation.

[¶24-155]

(2) *Notice of meeting.* — Notice of any meeting of shareholders at which voluntary liquidation and dissolution is to be proposed shall set out the terms thereof.

[¶24-156]

(3) *Shareholders resolution.* — A corporation may liquidate and dissolve by special resolution of the shareholders or, where the corporation has issued more than one class of shares, by special resolutions of the holders of each class whether or not they are otherwise entitled to vote.

[¶24-157]

(4) *Statement of intent to dissolve.* — A statement of intent to dissolve in prescribed form shall be sent to the Director.

[¶24-158]

(5) *Certificate of intent to dissolve.* — On receipt of a statement of intent to dissolve, the Director shall issue a certificate of intent to dissolve in accordance with section 262.

[¶24-159]

(6) *Effect of certificate.* — On issue of a certificate of intent to dissolve, the corporation shall cease to carry on business except to the extent necessary for the liquidation, but its corporate existence continues until the Director issues a certificate of dissolution.

[¶24-160]

(7) *Liquidation.* — After issue of a certificate of intent to dissolve, the corporation shall

(a) immediately cause notice thereof to be sent to each known creditor of the corporation;

(b) forthwith publish notice thereof once a week for four consecutive weeks in a newspaper published or distributed in the place where the corporation has its registered office and take reasonable steps to give notice thereof in each province in Canada where the corporation was carrying on business at the time it sent the statement of intent to dissolve to the Director;

(c) proceed to collect its property, to dispose of properties that are not to be distributed in kind to its shareholders, to discharge all its obligations and to do all other acts required to liquidate its business; and

(d) after giving the notice required under paragraphs (a) and (b) and adequately providing for the payment or discharge of all its obligations, distribute its remaining property, either in money or in kind, among its shareholders according to their respective rights.

[¶24-161]

(8) *Supervision by court.* — The Director or any interested person may, at any time during the liquidation of a corporation, apply to a court for an order that the liquidation be continued under the supervision of the court as provided in this Part, and on such application the court may so order and make any further order it thinks fit.

Sec. 211(8)   ¶24-161

[¶24-162]

(9) *Notice to Director.* — An applicant under this section shall give the Director notice of the application, and the Director is entitled to appear and be heard in person or by counsel.

[¶24-163]

(10) *Revocation.* — At any time after issue of a certificate of intent to dissolve and before issue of a certificate of dissolution, a certificate of intent to dissolve may be revoked by sending to the Director a statement of revocation of intent to dissolve in prescribed form, if such revocation is approved in the same manner as the resolution under subsection (3).

[¶24-164]

(11) *Certificate of revocation of intent to dissolve.* — On receipt of a statement of revocation of intent to dissolve, the Director shall issue a certificate of revocation of intent to dissolve in accordance with section 262.

[¶24-165]

(12) *Effect of certificate.* — On the date shown in the certificate of revocation of intent to dissolve, the revocation is effective and the corporation may continue to carry on its business or businesses.

[¶24-166]

(13) *Right to dissolve.* — If a certificate of intent to dissolve has not been revoked and the corporation has complied with subsection (7), the corporation shall prepare articles of dissolution.

[¶24-167]

(14) *Articles of dissolution.* — Articles of dissolution in prescribed form shall be sent to the Director.

[¶24-168]

(15) *Certificate of dissolution.* — On receipt of articles of dissolution, the Director shall issue a certificate of dissolution in accordance with section 262.

[¶24-169]

(16) *Effect of certificate.* — The corporation ceases to exist on the date shown in the certificate of dissolution.

[¶24-170]

Sec. 212. Dissolution by Director. — (1) Subject to subsections (2) and (3), where a corporation

    (a) has not commenced business within three years after the date shown in its certificate of incorporation,

    (b) has not carried on its business for three consecutive years, or

    (c) is in default for a period of one year in sending to the Director any fee, notice or document required by this Act,

the Director may dissolve the corporation by issuing a certificate of dissolution under this section or he may apply to a court for an order dissolving the corporation, in which case section 217 applies.

[¶24-171]

(2) *Publication.* — The Director shall not dissolve a corporation under this section until he has

(a) given one hundred and twenty days notice of his decision to dissolve the corporation to the corporation and to each director thereof; and

(b) published notice of his decision to dissolve the corporation in the *Canada Gazette*, in the periodical referred to in section 129 and in a newspaper published or distributed in the place where the corporation has its registered office.

[¶24-172]

(3) *Certificate of dissolution.* — Unless cause to the contrary has been shown or an order has been made by a court under section 246, the Director may, after the expiration of the period referred to in subsection (2), issue a certificate of dissolution in prescribed form.

[¶24-173]

(4) *Effect of certificate.* — The corporation ceases to exist on the date shown in the certificate of dissolution.

[¶24-174]

Sec. 213. Grounds for dissolution. — (1) The Director or any interested person may apply to a court for an order dissolving a corporation if the corporation has

(a) failed for two or more consecutive years to comply with the requirements of this Act with respect to the holding of annual meetings of shareholders;

(b) contravened subsection 16(2) or section 21, 157 or 159; or

(c) procured any certificate under this Act by misrepresentation.

[¶24-175]

(2) *Notice to Director.* — An applicant under this section shall give the Director notice of the application, and the Director is entitled to appear and be heard in person or by counsel.

[¶24-176]

(3) *Dissolution order.* — On an application under this section or section 212, the court may order that the corporation be dissolved or that the corporation be liquidated and dissolved under the supervision of the court, and the court may make any other order it thinks fit.

[¶24-177]

(4) *Certificate.* — On receipt of an order under this section, section 212 or 214, the Director shall

(a) if the order is to dissolve the corporation, issue a certificate of dissolution in prescribed form; or

(b) if the order is to liquidate and dissolve the corporation under the supervision of the court, issue a certificate of intent to dissolve in prescribed form and publish notice of such order in the *Canada Gazette* and in the periodical referred to in section 129.

[¶24-178]

(5) *Effect of certificate.* — The corporation ceases to exist on the date shown in the certificate of dissolution.

[¶24-179]

Sec. 214. Further grounds. — (1) A court may order the liquidation and dissolution of a corporation or any of its affiliated corporations on the application of a shareholder,

(a) if the court is satisfied that in respect of a corporation or any if its affiliates

(i) any act or omission of the corporation or any of its affiliates effects a result,

(ii) the business or affairs of the corporation or any of its affiliates are or have been carried on or conducted in a manner, or

(iii) the powers of the directors of the corporation or any of its affiliates are or have been exercised in a manner

that is oppressive or unfairly prejudicial to or that unfairly disregards the interests of any security holder, creditor, director or officer; or

(b) if the court is satisfied that

(i) a unanimous shareholder agreement entitles a complaining shareholder to demand dissolution of the corporation after the occurrence of a specified event and that event has occurred, or

(ii) it is just and equitable that the corporation should be liquidated and dissolved.

[¶24-180]

(2) *Alternative order.* — On an application under this section, a court may make such order under this section or section 241 as it thinks fit.

[¶24-181]

(3) *Application of s. 242.* — Section 242 applies to an application under this section.

[¶24-182]

Sec. 215. Application for supervision. — (1) An application to a court to supervise a voluntary liquidation and dissolution under subsection 211(8) shall state the reasons, verified by an affidavit of the applicant, why the court should supervise the liquidation and dissolution.

[¶24-183]

(2) *Court supervision.* — If a court makes an order applied for under subsection 211(8), the liquidation and dissolution of the corporation shall continue under the supervision of the court in accordance with this Act.

[¶24-184]

Sec. 216. Application to court. — (1) An application to a court under subsection 214(1) shall state the reasons, verified by an affidavit of the applicant, why the corporation should be liquidated and dissolved.

[¶24-185]

(2) *Show cause order.* — On an application under subsection 214(1), the court may make an order requiring the corporation and any person having an interest in the corporation or claim against it to show cause, at a time and place therein specified, not less than four weeks after the date of the order, why the corporation should not be liquidated and dissolved.

[¶24-186]

(3) *Powers of court.* — On an application under subsection 214(1), the court may order the directors and officers of the corporation to furnish the court with all material information known to or reasonably ascertainable by them, including

(a) financial statements of the corporation;

(b) the name and address of each shareholder of the corporation; and

(c) the name and address of each known creditor or claimant, including any creditor or claimant with unliquidated, future or contingent claims, and any person with whom the corporation has a contract.

[¶24-187]

(4) *Publication.* — A copy of an order made under subsection (2) shall be

(a) published as directed in the order, at least once in each week before the time appointed for the hearing, in a newspaper published or distributed in the place where the corporation has its registered office; and

(b) served on the Director and each person named in the order.

[¶24-188]

(5) *Person responsible.* — Publication and service of an order under this section shall be effected by the corporation or by such other person and in such manner as the court may order.

[¶24-189]

Sec. 217. Powers of court. — In connection with the dissolution or the liquidation and dissolution of a corporation, the court may, if it is satisfied that the corporation is able to pay or adequately provide for the discharge of all its obligations, make any order it thinks fit including, without limiting the generality of the foregoing,

(a) an order to liquidate;

(b) an order appointing a liquidator, with or without security, fixing his remuneration and replacing a liquidator;

(c) an order appointing inspectors or referees, specifying their powers, fixing their remuneration and replacing inspectors or referees;

(d) an order determining the notice to be given to any interested person, or dispensing with notice to any person;

(e) an order determining the validity of any claims made against the corporation;

(f) an order, at any stage of the proceedings, restraining the directors and officers from

(i) exercising any of their powers, or

(ii) collecting or receiving any debt or other property of the corporation, and from paying out or transferring any property of the corporation, except as permitted by the court;

(g) an order determining and enforcing the duty or liability of any present or former director, officer or shareholder

(i) to the corporation, or

(ii) for an obligation of the corporation;

(h) an order approving the payment, satisfaction or compromise of claims against the corporation and the retention of assets for such purpose, and determining the adequacy of provisions for the payment or discharge of obligations of the corporation, whether liquidated, unliquidated, future or contingent;

(i) an order disposing of or destroying the documents and records of the corporation;

(j) on the application of a creditor, the inspectors or the liquidator, an order giving directions on any matter arising in the liquidation;

(*k*) after notice has been given to all interested parties, an order relieving a liquidator from any omission or default on such terms as the court thinks fit and confirming any act of the liquidator;

(*l*) subject to section 223, an order approving any proposed interim or final distribution to shareholders in money or in property;

(*m*) an order disposing of any property belonging to creditors or shareholders who cannot be found;

(*n*) on the application of any director, officer, security holder, creditor or the liquidator,

  (i) an order staying the liquidation on such terms and conditions as the court thinks fit,

  (ii) an order continuing or discontinuing the liquidation proceedings, or

  (iii) an order to the liquidator to restore to the corporation all its remaining property;

(*o*) after the liquidator has rendered his final account to the court, an order dissolving the corporation.

[¶24-190]

Sec. 218.   Effect of order. — The liquidation of a corporation commences when a court makes an order therefor.

[¶24-191]

Sec. 219.   Cessation of business and powers. — (1) If a court makes an order for liquidation of a corporation,

(*a*) the corporation continues in existence but shall cease to carry on business, except the business that is, in the opinion of the liquidator, required for an orderly liquidation; and

(*b*) the powers of the directors and shareholders cease and vest in the liquidator, except as specifically authorized by the court.

[¶24-192]

(2) *Delegation by liquidator.* — The liquidator may delegate any of the powers vested in him by paragraph (1)(*b*) to the directors or shareholders.

[¶24-193]

Sec. 220.   Appointment of liquidator. — (1) When making an order for the liquidation of a corporation or at any time thereafter, the court may appoint any person, including a director, an officer or a shareholder of the corporation or any other body corporate, as liquidator of the corporation.

[¶24-194]

(2) *Vacancy.* — Where an order for the liquidation of a corporation has been made and the office of liquidator is or becomes vacant, the property of the corporation is under the control of the court until the office of liquidator is filled.

[¶24-195]

Sec. 221.   Duties of liquidator. — A liquidator shall

(*a*) forthwith after his appointment give notice thereof to the Director and to each claimant and creditor known to the liquidator;

(*b*) forthwith publish notice in the *Canada Gazette* and in the periodical referred to in section 129 and by insertion once a week for two consecutive weeks in a newspaper published or distributed in the place where the corporation has its registered office and take reasonable steps to give notice thereof in each province where the corporation carries on business, requiring any person

(i) indebted to the corporation to render an account and pay to the liquidator at the time and place specified any amount owing,

(ii) possessing property of the corporation, to deliver it to the liquidator at the time and place specified, and

(iii) having a claim against the corporation, whether liquidated, unliquidated, future or contingent, to present particulars thereof in writing to the liquidator not later than two months after the first publication of the notice;

(c) take into his custody and control the property of the corporation;

(d) open and maintain a trust account for the moneys of the corporation;

(e) keep accounts of the moneys of the corporation received and paid out by him;

(f) maintain separate lists of the shareholders, creditors and other persons having claims against the corporation;

(g) if at any time the liquidator determines that the corporation is unable to pay or adequately provide for the discharge of its obligations, apply to the court for directions;

(h) deliver to the court and to the Director, at least once in every twelve-month period after his appointment or more often as the court may require, financial statements of the corporation in the form required by section 155 or in such other form as the liquidator may think proper or as the court may require; and

(i) after his final accounts are approved by the court, distribute any remaining property of the corporation among the shareholders according to their respective rights.

[¶24-196]

Sec. 222.   Powers of liquidator. — (1) A liquidator may

(a) retain lawyers, accountants, engineers, appraisers and other professional advisers;

(b) bring, defend or take part in any civil, criminal or administrative action or proceeding in the name and on behalf of the corporation;

(c) carry on the business of the corporation as required for an orderly liquidation;

(d) sell by public auction or private sale any property of the corporation;

(e) do all acts and execute any documents in the name and on behalf of the corporation;

(f) borrow money on the security of the property of the corporation;

(g) settle or compromise any claims by or against the corporation; and

(h) do all other things necessary for the liquidation of the corporation and distribution of its property.

[¶24-197]

(2) *Reliance on statements.* — A liquidator is not liable if he relies in good faith on

(a) financial statements of the corporation represented to him by an officer of the corporation or in a written report of the auditor of the corporation to reflect fairly the financial condition of the corporation; or

(b) an opinion, a report or a statement of a lawyer, an accountant, an engineer, an appraiser or other professional adviser retained by the liquidator.

[¶24-198]

(3) *Application for examination.* — If a liquidator has reason to believe that any person has in his possession or under his control, or has concealed, withheld or misappropriated any property of the corporation, he may apply to the court for an order requiring that person to appear before the court at the time and place designated in the order and to be examined.

[¶24-199]

(4) *Power of court.* — If the examination referred to in subsection (3) discloses that a person has concealed, withheld or misappropriated property of the corporation, the court may order that person to restore it or pay compensation to the liquidator.

[¶24-200]

Sec. 223. Costs of liquidation. — (1) A liquidator shall pay the costs of liquidation out of the property of the corporation and shall pay or make adequate provision for all claims against the corporation.

[¶24-201]

(2) *Final account.* — Within one year after his appointment, and after paying or making adequate provision for all claims against the corporation, the liquidator shall apply to the court

(a) for approval of his final accounts and for an order permitting him to distribute in money or in kind the remaining property of the corporation to its shareholders according to their respective rights; or

(b) for an extension of time, setting out the reasons therefor.

[¶24-202]

(3) *Shareholder application.* — If a liquidator fails to make the application required by subsection (2), a shareholder of the corporation may apply to the court for an order for the liquidator to show cause why a final accounting and distribution should not be made.

[¶24-203]

(4) *Publication.* — A liquidator shall give notice of his intention to make an application under subsection (2) to the Director, each inspector appointed under section 217, each shareholder and any person who provided a security or fidelity bond for the liquidation, and he shall publish the notice in a newspaper published or distributed in the place where the corporation has its registered office or as otherwise directed by the court.

[¶24-204]

(5) *Final order.* — If the court approves the final accounts rendered by a liquidator, the court shall make an order

(a) directing the Director to issue a certificate of dissolution;

(b) directing the custody or disposal of the documents and records of the corporation; and

(c) subject to subsection (6), discharging the liquidator.

[¶24-205]

(6) *Delivery of order.* — The liquidator shall forthwith send a certified copy of the order referred to in subsection (5) to the Director.

[¶24-206]

(7) *Certificate of dissolution.* — On receipt of the order referred to in subsection (5), the Director shall issue a certificate of dissolution in accordance with section 262.

[¶24-207]

(8) *Effect of certificate.* — The corporation ceases to exist on the date shown in the certificate of dissolution.

[¶24-208]

Sec. 224. Right to distribution in money. — (1) If in the course of liquidation of a corporation the shareholders resolve or the liquidator proposes to

(a) exchange all or substantially all the property of the corporation for securities of another body corporate that are to be distributed to the shareholders, or

(b) distribute all or part of the property of the corporation to the shareholders in kind,

a shareholder may apply to the court for an order requiring the distribution of the property of the corporation to be in money.

[¶24-209]

(2) *Powers of court.* — On an application under subsection (1), the court may order

(a) all the property of the corporation to be converted into and distributed in money; or

(b) the claims of any shareholder applying under this section to be satisfied by a distribution in money, in which case subsections 190(20) to (22) apply.

[¶24-210]

Sec. 225. Custody of records. — (1) A person who has been granted custody of the documents and records of a dissolved corporation remains liable to produce such documents and records for six years following the date of its dissolution or until the expiration of such other shorter period as may be ordered under subsection 223(5).

[¶24-211]

(2) *Offence.* — A person who, without reasonable cause, contravenes subsection (1) is guilty of an offence and liable on summary conviction to a fine not exceeding five thousand dollars or to imprisonment for a term not exceeding six months or to both.

[¶24-212]

Sec. 226. Definition of "shareholder". — (1) In this section, "shareholder" includes the heirs and legal representatives of a shareholder.

[¶24-213]

(2) *Continuation of actions.* — Notwithstanding the dissolution of a body corporate under this Act,

(a) a civil, criminal or administrative action or proceeding commenced by or against the body corporate before its dissolution may be continued as if the body corporate had not been dissolved;

(b) a civil, criminal or administrative action or proceeding may be brought against the body corporate within two years after its dissolution as if the body corporate had not been dissolved; and

(c) any property that would have been available to satisfy any judgment or order if the body corporate had not been dissolved remains available for such purpose.

[¶24-214]

(3) *Service.* — Service of a document on a corporation after its dissolution may be effected by serving the document on a person shown in the last notice filed under section 106 or 113.

[¶24-214a]

(3.1) *Idem.* — Service of a document on a company to which the *Canada Corporations Act*, chapter C-32 of the Revised Statutes of Canada, 1970, applied that has been dissolved by subsection 261(8) of the *Canada Business Corporations Act*, chapter 33 of the Statutes of Canada, 1974-75-76 and chapter 9 of the Statutes of Canada, 1978-79, may be effected by serving the document on a person shown as a director in the last annual summary filed by the company pursuant to the *Canada Corporations Act*. (1992, c. 1, s. 57.)

[¶24-215]

(4) *Reimbursement.* — Notwithstanding the dissolution of a body corporate under this Act, a shareholder to whom any of its property has been distributed is liable to any person claiming under subsection (2) to the extent of the amount received by that shareholder on such distribution, and an action to enforce such liability may be brought within two years after the date of the dissolution of the body corporate.

[¶24-216]

(5) *Representative action.* — A court may order an action referred to in subsection (4) to be brought against the persons who were shareholders as a class, subject to such conditions as the court thinks fit and, if the plaintiff establishes his claim, the court may refer the proceedings to a referee or other officer of the court who may

(a) add as a party to the proceedings before him each person who was a shareholder found by the plaintiff;

(b) determine, subject to subsection (4), the amount that each person who was a shareholder shall contribute towards satisfaction of the plaintiff's claim; and

(c) direct payment of the amounts so determined.

(1992, c. 1, s. 57.)

[¶24-217]

Sec. 227.   Unknown claimants. — (1) On the dissolution of a body corporate under this Act, the portion of the property distributable to a creditor or shareholder who cannot be found shall be converted into money and paid to the Receiver General.

[¶24-218]

(2) *Constructive satisfaction.* — A payment under subsection (1) is deemed to be in satisfaction of a debt or claim of such creditor or shareholder.

[¶24-219]

(3) *Recovery.* — If at any time a person establishes that he is entitled to any moneys paid to the Receiver General under this Act, the Receiver General shall pay an equivalent amount to him out of the Consolidated Revenue Fund.

[¶24-220]

Sec. 228.   Vesting in Crown. — (1) Subject to subsection 226(2) and section 227, property of a body corporate that has not been disposed of at the date of its dissolution under this Act vests in Her Majesty in right of Canada.

(2) *Return of property on revival.* — If a body corporate is revived as a corporation under section 209, any property, other than money, that vested in Her Majesty pursuant to subsection (1), that has not been disposed of shall be returned to the corporation and there shall be paid to the corporation out of the Consolidated Revenue Fund

(a) an amount equal to any money received by Her Majesty pursuant to subsection (1); and

(b) where property other than money vested in Her Majesty pursuant to subsection (1) and that property has been disposed of, an amount equal to the lesser of

(i) the value of any such property at the date it vested in Her Majesty, and

(ii) the amount realized by Her Majesty from the disposition of that property.

Part XIX
Investigation

Sec. 229.   Investigation. — (1) A security holder or the Director may apply, *ex parte* or on such notice as the court may require, to a court having jurisdiction in the place where the corporation has its registered office for an order directing an investigation to be made of the corporation and any of its affiliated corporations.

(2) *Grounds.* — If, on an application under subsection (1), it appears to the court that

(a) the business of the corporation or any of its affiliates is or has been carried on with intent to defraud any person,

(b) the business or affairs of the corporation or any of its affiliates are or have been carried on or conducted, or the powers of the directors are or have been exercised in a manner that is oppressive or unfairly prejudicial to or that unfairly disregards the interests of a security holder,

(c) the corporation or any of its affiliates was formed for a fraudulent or unlawful purpose or is to be dissolved for a fraudulent or unlawful purpose, or

(d) persons concerned with the formation, business or affairs of the corporation or any of its affiliates have in connection therewith acted fraudulently or dishonestly,

the court may order an investigation to be made of the corporation and any of its affiliated corporations.

(3) *Notice to Director.* — If a security holder makes an application under subsection (1) he shall give the Director reasonable notice thereof and the Director is entitled to appear and be heard in person or by counsel.

(4) *No security for costs.* — An applicant under this section is not required to give security for costs.

(5) *Hearings in camera.* — An *ex parte* application under this section shall be heard *in camera.*

[¶24-274]

(6) *Consent to publish proceedings required.* — No person may publish anything relating to *ex parte* proceedings under this section except with the authorization of the court or the written consent of the corporation being investigated.

[¶24-275]

Sec. 230. Powers of court. — (1) In connection with an investigation under this Part, the court may make any order it thinks fit including, without limiting the generality of the foregoing,

(a) an order to investigate;

(b) an order appointing an inspector, who may be the Director, fixing the remuneration of an inspector, and replacing an inspector;

(c) an order determining the notice to be given to any interested person, or dispensing with notice to any person;

(d) an order authorizing an inspector to enter any premises in which the court is satisfied there might be relevant information, and to examine any thing and make copies of any document or record found on the premises;

(e) an order requiring any person to produce documents or records to the inspector;

(f) an order authorizing an inspector to conduct a hearing, administer oaths, and examine any person on oath, and prescribing rules for the conduct of the hearing;

(g) an order requiring any person to attend a hearing conducted by an inspector and to give evidence on oath;

(h) an order giving directions to an inspector or any interested person on any matter arising in the investigation;

(i) an order requiring an inspector to make an interim or final report to the court;

(j) an order determining whether a report of an inspector should be published and, if so, ordering the Director to publish the report in whole or in part or to send copies to any person the court designates;

(k) an order requiring an inspector to discontinue an investigation;

(l) an order requiring the corporation to pay the cost of the investigation.

[¶24-276]

(2) *Copy of report.* — An inspector shall send to the Director a copy of every report made by the inspector under this Part.

[¶24-277]

Sec. 231. Power of inspector. — (1) An inspector under this Part has the powers set out in the order appointing him.

[¶24-277a]

(2) *Exchange of information.* — In addition to the powers set out in the order appointing him, an inspector appointed to investigate a corporation may furnish to, or exchange information and otherwise cooperate with, any public official in Canada or elsewhere who is authorized to exercise investigatory powers and who is investigating, in respect of the corporation, any allegation of improper conduct that is the same as or similar to the conduct described in subsection 229(2).

[¶24-278]

(3) *Court order.* — An inspector shall on request produce to an interested person a copy of any order made under subsection 230(1).

[¶24-279]

Sec. 232.   Hearing in camera. — (1) Any interested person may apply to the court for an order that a hearing conducted by an inspector under this Part be heard *in camera* and for directions on any matter arising in the investigation.

[¶24-280]

(2) *Right to counsel.* — A person whose conduct is being investigated or who is being examined at a hearing conducted by an inspector under this Part has a right to be represented by counsel.

[¶24-281]

Sec. 233.   Criminating statements. — No person is excused from attending and giving evidence and producing documents and records to an inspector under this Part by reason only that the evidence tends to criminate that person or subject that person to any proceeding or penalty, but no such evidence shall be used or is receivable against that person in any proceeding thereafter instituted against that person under an Act of Parliament, other than a prosecution under section 132 of the *Criminal Code* for perjury in giving the evidence or a prosecution under section 136 of the *Criminal Code* in respect of the evidence. (1985 (1st Supp.), c. 27, s. 187.)

(1985 (1st Supp.), c. 27, s. 187.)

[¶24-282]

Sec. 234.   Absolute privilege (defamation). — Any oral or written statement or report made by an inspector or any other person in an investigation under this Part has absolute privilege.

[¶24-283]

Sec. 235.   Information respecting ownership and control. — (1) If the Director is satisfied that, for the purposes of Part XI, XIII or XVII, or for the purposes of enforcing any regulation made under section 174, there is reason to inquire into the ownership or control of a security of a corporation or any of its affiliates, the Director may require any person that he reasonably believes has or has had an interest in the security or acts or has acted on behalf of a person with such an interest to report to him or to any person he designates

(a) information that such person has or can reasonably be expected to obtain as to present and past interests in the security; and

(b) the names and addresses of the persons so interested and of any person who acts or has acted in relation to the security on behalf of the persons so interested.

[¶24-284]

(2) *Constructive interest in securities.* — For the purposes of subsection (1), a person is deemed to have an interest in a security if

(a) he has a right to vote or to acquire or dispose of the security or any interest therein;

(b) his consent is necessary for the exercise of the rights or privileges of any other person interested in the security; or

(c) any other person interested in the security can be required or is accustomed to exercise rights or privileges attached to the security in accordance with his instructions.

[¶24-285]

(3) *Publication.* — The Director shall publish in the periodical referred to in section 129 the particulars of information obtained by him under this section, if the particulars

(a) are required to be disclosed by this Act or the regulations; and

(b) have not previously been so disclosed.

[¶24-286]

(4) *Offence.* — A person who fails to comply with this section is guilty of an offence and liable on summary conviction to a fine not exceeding five thousand dollars or to imprisonment for a term not exceeding six months or to both.

[¶24-287]

(5) *Officers, etc., of bodies corporate.* — Where a body corporate commits an offence under subsection (4), any director or officer of the body corporate who knowingly authorized, permitted or acquiesced in the commission of the offence is a party to and guilty of the offence and is liable on summary conviction to a fine not exceeding five thousand dollars or to imprisonment for a term not exceeding six months or to both, whether or not the body corporate has been prosecuted or convicted.

[¶24-288]

Sec. 236. Solicitor-client privilege. — Nothing in this Part shall be construed as affecting the privilege that exists in respect of a solicitor and his client.

[¶24-289]

Sec. 237. Inquiries. — The Director may make inquiries of any person relating to compliance with this Act.

Part XX
Remedies, Offences and Punishment

[¶24-319]

Sec. 238. Definitions. — In this Part,

"action". — "action" means an action under this Act;

"complainant". — "complainant" means

(a) a registered holder or beneficial owner, and a former registered holder or beneficial owner, of a security of a corporation or any of its affiliates,

(b) a director or an officer or a former director or officer of a corporation or of any of its affiliates,

(c) the Director, or

(d) any other person who, in the discretion of a court, is a proper person to make an application under this Part.

[¶24-320]

Sec. 239. Commencing derivative action. — (1) Subject to subsection (2), a complainant may apply to a court for leave to bring an action in the name and on behalf of a corporation or any of its subsidiaries, or intervene in an action to which any such body corporate is a party, for the purpose of prosecuting, defending or discontinuing the action on behalf of the body corporate.

[¶24-321]

(2) *Conditions precedent.* — No action may be brought and no intervention in an action may be made under subsection (1) unless the court is satisfied that

(a) the complainant has given reasonable notice to the directors of the corporation or its subsidiary of his intention to apply to the court under subsection (1) if the directors of the corporation or its subsidiary do not bring, diligently prosecute or defend or discontinue the action;

(b) the complainant is acting in good faith; and

(c) it appears to be in the interests of the corporation or its subsidiary that the action be brought, prosecuted, defended or discontinued.

[¶24-322]

Sec. 240. Powers of court. — In connection with an action brought or intervened in under section 239, the court may at any time make any order it thinks fit including, without limiting the generality of the foregoing,

(a) an order authorizing the complainant or any other person to control the conduct of the action;

(b) an order giving directions for the conduct of the action;

(c) an order directing that any amount adjudged payable by a defendant in the action shall be paid, in whole or in part, directly to former and present security holders of the corporation or its subsidiary instead of to the corporation or its subsidiary;

(d) an order requiring the corporation or its subsidiary to pay reasonable legal fees incurred by the complainant in connection with the action.

[¶24-323]

Sec. 241. Application to court re oppression. — (1) A complainant may apply to a court for an order under this section.

[¶24-324]

(2) *Grounds.* — If, on an application under subsection (1), the court is satisfied that in respect of a corporation or any of its affiliates

(a) any act or omission of the corporation or any of its affiliates effects a result,

(b) the business or affairs of the corporation or any of its affiliates are or have been carried on or conducted in a manner, or

(c) the powers of the directors of the corporation or any of its affiliates are or have been exercised in a manner

that is oppressive or unfairly prejudicial to or that unfairly disregards the interests of any security holder, creditor, director or officer, the court may make an order to rectify the matters complained of.

[¶24-325]

(3) *Powers of court.* — In connection with an application under this section, the court may make any interim or final order it thinks fit including, without limiting the generality of the foregoing,

(a) an order restraining the conduct complained of;

(b) an order appointing a receiver or receiver-manager;

(c) an order to regulate a corporation's affairs by amending the articles or by-laws or creating or amending a unanimous shareholder agreement;

(d) an order directing an issue or exchange of securities;

(*e*) an order appointing directors in place of or in addition to all or any of the directors then in office;

(*f*) an order directing a corporation, subject to subsection (6), or any other person, to purchase securities of a security holder;

(*g*) an order directing a corporation, subject to subsection (6), or any other person, to pay to a security holder any part of the moneys paid by him for securities;

(*h*) an order varying or setting aside a transaction or contract to which a corporation is a party and compensating the corporation or any other party to the transaction or contract;

(*i*) an order requiring a corporation, within a time specified by the court, to produce to the court or an interested person financial statements in the form required by section 155 or an accounting in such other form as the court may determine;

(*j*) an order compensating an aggrieved person;

(*k*) an order directing rectification of the registers or other records of a corporation under section 243;

(*l*) an order liquidating and dissolving the corporation;

(*m*) an order directing an investigation under Part XIX to be made;

(*n*) an order requiring the trial of any issue.

[¶24-326]

(4) *Duty of directors.* — If an order made under this section directs amendment of the articles or by-laws of a corporation,

(*a*) the directors shall forthwith comply with subsection 191(4); and

(*b*) no other amendment to the articles or by-laws shall be made without the consent of the court, until a court otherwise orders.

[¶24-327]

(5) *Exclusion.* — A shareholder is not entitled to dissent under section 190 if an amendment to the articles is effected under this section.

[¶24-328]

(6) *Limitation.* — A corporation shall not make a payment to a shareholder under paragraph (3)(*f*) or (*g*) if there are reasonable grounds for believing that

(*a*) the corporation is or would after that payment be unable to pay its liabilities as they become due; or

(*b*) the realizable value of the corporation's assets would thereby be less than the aggregate of its liabilities.

[¶24-329]

(7) *Alternative order.* — An applicant under this section may apply in the alternative for an order under section 214.

[¶24-330]

Sec. 242. Evidence of shareholder approval not decisive. — (1) An application made or an action brought or intervened in under this Part shall not be stayed or dismissed by reason only that it is shown that an alleged breach of a right or duty owed to the corporation or its subsidiary has been or may be approved by the shareholders of such body corporate, but evidence of approval by the shareholders may be taken into account by the court in making an order under section 214, 240 or 241.

[¶24-331]

(2) *Court approval to discontinue.* — An application made or an action brought or intervened in under this Part shall not be stayed, discontinued, settled or dismissed for want of prosecution without the approval of the court given on such terms as the court thinks fit and, if the court determines that the interests of any complainant may be substantially affected by such stay, discontinuance, settlement or dismissal, the court may order any party to the application or action to give notice to the complainant.

[¶24-332]

(3) *No security for costs.* — A complainant is not required to give security for costs in any application made or action brought or intervened in under this Part.

[¶24-333]

(4) *Interim costs.* — In an application made or an action brought or intervened in under this Part, the court may at any time order the corporation or its subsidiary to pay to the complainant interim costs, including legal fees and disbursements, but the complainant may be held accountable for such interim costs on final disposition of the application or action.

[¶24-334]

Sec. 243. Application to court to rectify records. — (1) If the name of a person is alleged to be or to have been wrongly entered or retained in, or wrongly deleted or omitted from, the registers or other records of a corporation, the corporation, a security holder of the corporation or any aggrieved person may apply to a court for an order that the registers or records be rectified.

[¶24-335]

(2) *Notice to Director.* — An applicant under this section shall give the Director notice of the application and the Director is entitled to appear and be heard in person or by counsel.

[¶24-336]

(3) *Powers of court.* — In connection with an application under this section, the court may make any order it thinks fit including, without limiting the generality of the foregoing,

(a) an order requiring the registers or other records of the corporation to be rectified;

(b) an order restraining the corporation from calling or holding a meeting of shareholders or paying a dividend before such rectification;

(c) an order determining the right of a party to the proceedings to have his name entered or retained in, or deleted or omitted from, the registers or records of the corporation, whether the issue arises between two or more security holders or alleged security holders, or between the corporation and any security holders or alleged security holders;

(d) an order compensating a party who has incurred a loss.

[¶24-337]

Sec. 244. Application for directions. — The Director may apply to a court for directions in respect of any matter concerning his duties under this Act, and on such application the court may give such directions and make such further order as it thinks fit.

[¶24-338]

Sec. 245. Notice of refusal by Director. — (1) If the Director refuses to file any articles or other document required by this Act to be filed by him before the articles or other document become effective, he shall, within twenty days after receipt thereof by him or twenty days after he receives any approval that may be required under any other Act, whichever is the later, give written notice of his refusal to the person who sent the articles or document, giving reasons therefor.

[¶24-339]

(2) *Deemed refusal.* — If the Director does not file or give written notice of his refusal to file any articles or document within the time limited therefor in subsection (1), he is deemed for the purposes of section 246 to have refused to file the articles or document.

[¶24-340]

Sec. 246.   Appeal from Director's decision. — A person who feels aggrieved by a decision of the Director

(a) to refuse to file in the form submitted to him any articles or other document required by this Act to be filed by him,

(b) to give a name, to change or revoke a name, or to refuse to reserve, accept, change or revoke a name under section 12,

(c) to refuse to grant an exemption under subsection 2(8), 10(2), 82(3), 127(8), 151(1), section 156, subsection 163(4) or 171(2) or subsection 160(3) and any regulations under that subsection,

(d) to refuse under subsection 187(11) to permit a continued reference to shares having a nominal or par value,

(e) to refuse to issue a certificate of discontinuance under section 188,

(f) to refuse to revive a corporation under section 209, or

(g) to dissolve a corporation under section 212,

may apply to a court for an order requiring the Director to change his decision, and on such application the court may so order and make any further order it thinks fit.

[¶24-341]

Sec. 247.   Restraining or compliance order. — If a corporation or any director, officer, employee, agent, auditor, trustee, receiver, receiver-manager or liquidator of a corporation does not comply with this Act, the regulations, articles, by-laws, or a unanimous shareholder agreement, a complainant or a creditor of the corporation may, in addition to any other right he has, apply to a court for an order directing any such person to comply with, or restraining any such person from acting in breach of, any provisions thereof, and on such application the court may so order and make any further order it thinks fit.

[¶24-342]

Sec. 248.   Summary application to court. — Where this Act states that a person may apply to a court, the application may be made in a summary manner by petition, originating notice of motion, or otherwise as the rules of the court provide, and subject to any order respecting notice to interested parties or costs, or any other order the court thinks fit.

[¶24-343]

Sec. 249.   Appeal. — An appeal lies to the court of appeal from any order made by a court under this Act.

[¶24-344]

Sec. 250. Offences with respect to reports. — (1) A person who makes or assists in making a report, return, notice or other document required by this Act or the regulations to be sent to the Director or to any other person that

(a) contains an untrue statement of a material fact, or

(b) omits to state a material fact required therein or necessary to make a statement contained therein not misleading in the light of the circumstances in which it was made

is guilty of an offence and liable on summary conviction to a fine not exceeding five thousand dollars or to imprisonment for a term not exceeding six months or to both.

[¶24-345]

(2) *Officers, etc., of bodies corporate.* — Where a body corporate commits an offence under subsection (1), any director or officer of the body corporate who knowingly authorized, permitted or acquiesced in the commission of the offense is a party to and guilty of the offence and is liable on summary conviction to a fine not exceeding five thousand dollars or to imprisonment for a term not exceeding six months or to both, whether or not the body corporate has been prosecuted or convicted.

[¶24-346]

(3) *Immunity.* — No person is guilty of an offence under subsection (1) or (2) if the untrue statement or omission was unknown to him and in the exercise of reasonable diligence could not have been known to him.

[¶24-347]

Sec. 251. Offence. — Every person who, without reasonable cause, contravenes a provision of this Act or the regulations for which no punishment is provided is guilty of an offence punishable on summary conviction.

[¶24-348]

Sec. 252. Order to comply. — (1) Where a person is guilty of an offence under this Act or the regulations, any court in which proceedings in respect of the offence are taken may, in addition to any punishment it may impose, order that person to comply with the provisions of this Act or the regulations for the contravention of which he has been convicted.

[¶24-349]

(2) *Limitation period.* — A prosecution for an offence under this Act may be instituted at any time within but not later than two years after the time when the subject-matter of the complaint arose.

[¶24-350]

(3) *Civil remedy not affected.* — No civil remedy for an act or omission is suspended or affected by reason that the act or omission is an offence under this Act.

Part XXI

General

[¶24-392]

Sec. 253. Notice to directors and shareholders. — (1) A notice or document required by this Act, the regulations, the articles or the by-laws to be sent to a shareholder or director of a corporation may be sent by prepaid mail addressed to, or may be delivered personally to,

(a) the shareholder at his latest address as shown in the records of the corporation or its transfer agent; and

(b) the director at his latest address as shown in the records of the corporation or in the last notice filed under section 106 or 113.

[¶24-393]

(2) *Effect of notice.* — A director named in a notice sent by a corporation to the Director under section 106 or 113 and filed by the Director is presumed for the purposes of this Act to be a director of the corporation referred to in the notice.

[¶24-394]

(3) *Deemed receipt.* — A notice or document sent in accordance with subsection (1) to a shareholder or director of a corporation is deemed to be received by him at the time it would be delivered in the ordinary course of mail unless there are reasonable grounds for believing that the shareholder or director did not receive the notice or document at that time or at all.

[¶24-395]

(4) *Undelivered notices.* — If a corporation sends a notice or document to a shareholder in accordance with subsection (1) and the notice or document is returned on three consecutive occasions because the shareholder cannot be found, the corporation is not required to send any further notices or documents to the shareholder until he informs the corporation in writing of his new address.

[¶24-396]

Sec. 254.   Notice to and service upon a corporation. — A notice or document required to be sent to or served upon a corporation may be sent by registered mail to the registered office of the corporation shown in the last notice filed under section 19 and, if so sent, is deemed to be received or served at the time it would be delivered in the ordinary course of mail unless there are reasonable grounds for believing that the corporation did not receive the notice or document at that time or at all.

[¶24-397]

Sec. 255.   Waiver of notice. — Where a notice or document is required by this Act or the regulations to be sent, the sending of the notice or document may be waived or the time for the notice or document may be waived or abridged at any time with the consent in writing of the person entitled thereto.

[¶24-398]

Sec. 256.   Certificate of Director. — (1) Where this Act requires or authorizes the Director to issue a certificate or to certify any fact, the certificate shall be signed by the Director or by a Deputy Director authorized under section 260.

[¶24-399]

(2) *Evidence.* — Except in a proceeding under section 213 to dissolve a corporation, a certificate referred to in subsection (1) or a certified copy thereof, when introduced as evidence in any civil, criminal or administrative action or proceeding, is conclusive proof of the facts so certified without proof of the signature or official character of the person appearing to have signed the certificate.

Sec. 257. Certificate of corporation. — (1) A certificate issued on behalf of a corporation stating any fact that is set out in the articles, the by-laws, a unanimous shareholder agreement, the minutes of the meetings of the directors, a committee of directors or the shareholders, or in a trust indenture or other contract to which the corporation is a party may be signed by a director, an officer or a transfer agent of the corporation.

(2) *Proof.* — When introduced as evidence in any civil, criminal or administrative action or proceeding,

(a) a fact stated in a certificate referred to in subsection (1),

(b) a certified extract from a securities register of a corporation, or

(c) a certified copy of minutes or extract from minutes of a meeting of shareholders, directors or a committee of directors of a corporation,

is, in the absence of evidence to the contrary, proof of the facts so certified without proof of the signature or official character of the person appearing to have signed the certificate.

(3) *Security certificate.* — An entry in a securities register of, or a security certificate issued by, a corporation is, in the absence of evidence to the contrary, proof that the person in whose name the security is registered is owner of the securities described in the register or in the certificate.

Sec. 258. Copies. — Where a notice or document is required to be sent to the Director under this Act, the Director may accept a photostatic or photographic copy thereof.

Sec. 259. Proof required by Director. — (1) The Director may require that a document or a fact stated in a document required by this Act or the regulations to be sent to him shall be verified in accordance with subsection (2).

(2) *Form of proof.* — A document or fact required by this Act or by the Director to be verified may be verified by affidavit or by statutory declaration under the *Canada Evidence Act* before any commissioner for oaths or for taking affidavits.

Sec. 260. Appointment of Director. — The Minister may appoint a Director and one or more Deputy Directors to carry out the duties and exercise the powers of the Director under this Act.

Sec. 261. Regulations. — (1) Subject to subsections (2) and (3), the Governor in Council may make regulations

(a) prescribing any matter required or authorized by this Act to be prescribed;

(b) requiring the payment of a fee in respect of the filing, examination or copying of any document, or in respect of any action that the Director is required or authorized to take under this Act, and prescribing the amount thereof;

(c) prescribing the format and contents of annual returns, notices and other documents required to be sent to the Director or to be issued by him;

(d) prescribing rules with respect to exemptions permitted by this Act; and

(e) prescribing that, for the purpose of paragraph 155(1)(a), the standards as they exist from time to time, of an accounting body named in the regulations shall be followed.

[¶24-408]

(2) *Publication of proposed regulation.* — Subject to subsection (3), the Minister shall publish in the *Canada Gazette* and in the periodical referred to in section 129 at least sixty days before the proposed effective date thereof a copy of every regulation that the Governor in Council proposes to make under this Act and a reasonable opportunity shall be afforded to interested persons to make representations with respect thereto.

[¶24-409]

(3) *Exceptions.* — The Minister is not required to publish a proposed regulation if the proposed regulation

(a) grants an exemption or relieves a restriction;

(b) establishes or amends a fee;

(c) has been published pursuant to subsection (2) whether or not it has been amended as a result of representations made by interested persons as provided in that subsection; or

(d) makes no material substantive change in an existing regulation.

[¶24-410]

Sec. 262. Definition of "statement". — (1) In this section, "statement" means a statement of intent to dissolve and a statement of revocation of intent to dissolve referred to in section 211.

[¶24-411]

(2) *Execution and filing.* — Where this Act requires that articles or a statement relating to a corporation shall be sent to the Director, unless otherwise specifically provided

(a) two copies (in this section called "duplicate originals") of the articles or the statement shall be signed by a director or an officer of the corporation or, in the case of articles of incorporation, by an incorporator; and

(b) on receiving duplicate originals of any articles or statement that are in the prescribed form, any other required documents and the prescribed fees, the Director shall

    (i) endorse on each of the duplicate originals the word "Filed" and the date of the filing,

    (ii) issue in duplicate the appropriate certificate and attach to each certificate one of the duplicate originals of the articles or statement,

    (iii) file a copy of the certificate and attached articles or statement,

    (iv) send to the corporation or its representative the original certificate and attached articles or statement, and

    (v) publish in the *Canada Gazette* or in the periodical referred to in section 129 notice of the issue of the certificate.

[¶24-412]

(3) *Date of certificate.* — A certificate referred to in subsection (2) issued by the Director may be dated as of the day he receives the articles, statement or court order pursuant to which the certificate is issued or as of any later day specified by the court or person who signed the articles or statement.

[¶24-412a]

(4) *Signature.* — A signature required on a certificate referred to in subsection (2) or 263(2) may be printed or otherwise mechanically reproduced thereon.

[¶24-412b]

(5) *Date of certificate.* — Notwithstanding subsection (3), a certificate of discontinuance may be dated as of the day a corporation is continued under the laws of another jurisdiction.

[¶24-413]

Sec. 263.   Annual return. — (1) Every corporation shall, on the prescribed date, send to the Director an annual return in prescribed form and the Director shall file it.

[¶24-414]

(2) *Certificate of compliance.* — The Director may furnish any person with a certificate that a corporation has sent to the Director a document required to be sent to him under this Act.

[¶24-415]

Sec. 264.   Alteration. — The Director may alter a notice or documents, other than an affidavit or statutory declaration, if so authorized by the person who sent the document or by his representative.

[¶24-416]

Sec. 265.   Corrections. — (1) If a certificate containing an error is issued to a corporation by the Director, the directors or shareholders of the corporation shall, on the request of the Director, pass the resolutions and send to him the documents required to comply with this Act, and take such other steps as the Director may reasonably require, and the Director may demand the surrender of the certificate and issue a corrected certificate.

[¶24-417]

(2) *Date of corrected certificate.* — A certificate corrected under subsection (1) shall bear the date of the certificate it replaces.

[¶24-418]

(3) *Notice.* — If a corrected certificate issued under subsection (1) materially amends the terms of the original certificate, the Director shall forthwith give notice of the correction in the *Canada Gazette* or in the periodical referred to in section 129.

[¶24-419]

Sec. 266.   Inspection. — (1) A person who has paid the prescribed fee is entitled during usual business hours to examine a document required by this Act or the regulations to be sent to the Director, except a report sent to him under subsection 230(2), and to make copies of or extracts therefrom.

[¶24-420]

(2) *Copies.* — The Director shall furnish any person with a copy or a certified copy of a document required by this Act or the regulations to be sent to the Director, except a report sent to him under subsection 230(2).

[¶24-421]

Sec. 267.   Records of Director. — (1) Records required by this Act to be prepared and maintained by the Director may be in bound or loose-leaf form or in photographic film form, or may be entered or recorded by any system of mechanical or electronic data processing or by any other information storage device that is capable of reproducing any required information in intelligible written form within a reasonable time.

[¶24-422]

(2) *Obligation to furnish.* — Where records maintained by the Director are prepared and maintained other than in written form

(*a*) the Director shall furnish any copy required to be furnished under subsection 266(2) in intelligible written form; and

(*b*) a report reproduced from those records, if it is certified by the Director, is admissible in evidence to the same extent as the original written records would have been.

[¶24-423]

(3) *Retention of records.* — The Director is not required to produce any document, other than a certificate and attached articles or statement filed under section 262, after six years from the date he receives it.

[¶24-424]

Sec. 268.   Definition of "charter". — (1) In this section, "charter" includes

(*a*) an act of incorporation and any amendments thereto; and

(*b*) letters patent of incorporation and any letters patent supplementary thereto.

[¶24-424a]

(2) *Amendment of charter.* — In connection with a continuance under this Act, the shareholders of a body corporate incorporated or continued by or under an Act of Parliament other than this Act who are entitled to vote at annual meetings of shareholders may, notwithstanding any provision in any other Act of Parliament or any provision in the charter of the body corporate,

(*a*) by special resolution, authorize the directors of the body corporate to apply under section 187 for a certificate of continuance; and

(*b*) by the same resolution, make any amendment to the charter of the body corporate that a corporation incorporated under this Act may make to its articles.

[¶24-424b]

(3) *Change of class rights.* — Notwithstanding subsection (2), the shareholders of a body corporate may not, by a special resolution under that subsection, make any change of the nature referred to in subsection 176(1) that affects a class or series of shares, unless

(*a*) the charter of the body corporate otherwise provides in respect of an amendment of the nature referred to in paragraph 176(1)(*a*), (*b*) or (*e*); or

(*b*) the holders of the class or series of shares approve the change in accordance with section 176.

[¶24-424c]

(4) *Authorizing continuance.* — Subject to subsections (6) and (7), the directors of a body corporate incorporated or continued by or under an Act of Parliament other than this Act may, notwithstanding any provision in any other Act of Parliament or any provision in the charter of the body corporate, apply under section 187 for a certificate of continuance where the articles of continuance do not make any amendment to the charter of the body corporate other than an amendment required to conform to this Act.

[¶24-425]

(5) *No dissent.* — A shareholder is not entitled to dissent under section 190 in respect of an amendment made under subsection (2), (3) or (4).

[¶24-428]

(6) *Discretionary continuance.* — The Governor in Council may, by order, require that a body corporate incorporated by or under an Act of Parliament to which Part I or Part II of the *Canada Corporations Act*, chapter C-32 of the Revised Statutes of Canada, 1970, does not apply, other than a body corporate that carries on the business of

(a) a bank,

(b) a company or society to which the *Insurance Companies Act* applies,

(c) a trust company within the meaning of the *Trust Companies Act*, or

(d) a loan company within the meaning of the *Loan Companies Act*

shall apply for a certificate of continuance under section 187 within such period as may be prescribed. (1991, c. 46, s. 597; c. 47, s. 724(1)–(2).)

[¶24-429]

(7) *Idem.* — A body corporate to which Part IV of the *Canada Corporations Act* applies, other than a body corporate that carries on a business referred to in paragraph (6)(b), (c) or (d), may apply for a certificate of continuance under section 187.

[¶24-430]

(8) *Fees.* — A body corporate that obtains a certificate of continuance under this section is not required to pay any fees otherwise payable under this Act in respect of such continuance.

[¶24-432]

(9) *Idem.* — A body corporate referred to in subsection (6) that does not make an application to obtain a certificate of continuance within the period prescribed is dissolved on the expiration of that period.

[¶24-433]

(10) *Continuance prohibited.* — A body corporate to which Part II or Part III of the *Canada Corporations Act*, chapter C-32 of the Revised Statutes of Canada, 1970, applies or any similar body corporate incorporated otherwise than by or under an Act of Parliament may not apply for a certificate of continuance under section 187.

(1991, c. 46, s. 597; c. 47, s. 724(1)–(2).)

Canada Business Corporations Act Regulations

SOR/79-316, P.C. 1979-1195, gazetted April 25, 1979, effective April 6, 1979, as amended by SOR/79-513, gazetted July 11, 1979; SOR/79-728, dated October 11, 1979; SOR/80-873, dated November 13, 1980; SOR/81-3, gazetted January 4, 1981; SOR/81-189, gazetted March 11, 1981; SOR/81-868, gazetted November 11, 1981; SOR/82-187, gazetted February 10, 1982; SOR/83-511, gazetted June 22, 1983; SOR/83-781, gazetted October 26, 1983; SOR/83-817, gazetted November 9, 1983; SOR/85-384, gazetted May 15, 1985; SOR/86-365 and SOR/86-366, gazetted April 16, 1986; SOR/86-421, gazetted April 30, 1986; SOR/86-983, gazetted October 1, 1986; SOR/87-248, gazetted May 13, 1987; SOR/87-629, gazetted November 11, 1987; SOR/88-63, gazetted January 20, 1988; SOR/88-491, gazetted October 12, 1988; SOR/89-159, gazetted March 29, 1989; SOR/89-323, gazetted July 5, 1989; SOR/91-567, gazetted October 23, 1991.

Short Title

[¶24-500]

Sec. 1.   These Regulations may be cited as the *Canada Business Corporations Regulations*.

Interpretation

[¶24-503]

Sec. 2.   In these Regulations,

"Act" means the *Canada Business Corporations Act*;

"document" means a document required to be sent to the Director under the Act.

Part I

General

Forms

[¶24-506]

Sec. 3.   The periodical referred to in section 129 of the Act shall set out any administrative forms, procedures and policy guidelines established by the Director from time to time for the better administration of the Act.

[¶24-509]

Sec. 4.   (1) The following forms, set out in Schedule I, are the forms of documents required to be sent to the Director or to be issued by the Director under the Act:

(*a*) articles of incorporation — Form 1;

(*b*) certificate of incorporation — Form 2;

(*c*) a notice referred to in subsections 19(2) and (4) of the Act — Form 3;

(*d*) articles of amendment — Form 4;

(*e*) certificate of amendment referred to in sections 13, 27, 178, 191 and 192 of the Act — Form 5;

(*f*) a notice referred to in subsections 106(1) and 113 of the Act — Form 6;

(*g*) restated articles of incorporation — Form 7;

(*h*) restated certificate of incorporation — Form 8;

(*i*) articles of amalgamation — Form 9;

(*j*) certificate of amalgamation — Form 10;

(*k*) articles of continuance — Form 11;

(*l*) certificate of continuance — Form 12;

(*m*) certificate of discontinuance — Form 13;

(*n*) articles of reorganization — Form 14;

(*o*) articles of arrangement — Form 14.1;

(*p*) articles of revival — Form 15:

(*q*) certificate of revival — Form 16;

(*r*) articles of dissolution — Form 17;

(*s*) certificate of dissolution — Form 18;

(*t*) a statement referred to in subsections 211(4) and (10) of the Act — Form 19;

(*u*) certificate of intent to dissolve — Form 20; and

(*v*) certificate of revocation of intent to dissolve — Form 21.

(SOR/89-323, s. 5.)

[¶24-512]

(2) Subject to subsection (3), forms furnished by the Director are not required to be used.

[¶24-515]

(3) The annual return referred to in section 263 of the Act shall be on Form 22, furnished by the Director, and sent to him by the corporation within 60 days next following the anniversary date of incorporation of the corporation, setting out the required information as at that date.

[¶24-518]

(4) If a document sent to the Director pursuant to the Act is not on a form furnished by him, it shall conform as closely as possible to the format of the relevant prescribed form.

(SOR/89-323, s. 5.)

Format of Documents

[¶24-521]

Sec. 5. All documents referred to in subsection 4(1) shall be

(*a*) on good quality white paper approximately 8¹/₂ by 11 inches in size;

(*b*) printed or typewritten; and

(*c*) legible and suitable for microfilming and photocopying.

[¶24-524]

Sec. 6. Where possible, each individual item in a document shall be set out in one or more contiguous, sequentially numbered paragraphs and each such item shall be preceded by an appropriate heading.

[¶24-527]

Sec. 7. (1) Numbers in a document shall be in numerals and not in words.

[¶24-530]

(2) Information in a document shall, where practical, be set out in tabular form.

[¶24-533]

Sec. 8. Abbreviations in a document shall,

(*a*) if formed by the truncation of a word, be followed by a period; and

(*b*) if formed by the deletion of alphabetic characters from the middle of a word, not be followed by a period, but a corporate name may contain alphabetic characters that are not followed by a period.

[¶24-536]

Sec. 9. (1) If an item of information required to be disclosed in a form does not apply, it shall be so indicated by the phrase "not applicable", by the abbreviation "N/A" or by a brief explanatory statement.

[¶24-539]

(2) If information is set out in response to one item in a document, it may be referred to in response to any other item in that document by a cross-reference.

[¶24-542]

Sec. 10. (1) Where

(*a*) any provision required to be set out in a form furnished by the Director is too long to be set out in the space provided in the form, or

(*b*) an agreement or other document is to be incorporated by reference in and to be part of the form,

the person completing the form may, subject to subsection (2), incorporate the provision, agreement or other document in the form by setting out in the space provided in the form the following sentence: "The annexed Schedule 1 (or as the case may be) is incorporated in this form", and by annexing the provision, agreement or other document to the form as that schedule.

[¶24-545]

(2) A separate schedule is required in respect of each item that is incorporated in a form by reference pursuant to subsection (1).

"Resident Canadian" Class of Persons Prescribed

[¶24-548]

Sec. 11. For the purposes of paragraph (*b*) of the definition "resident Canadian" in subsection 2(1) of the Act, the following classes of persons are prescribed:

(*a*) persons who are full-time employees of the Government of Canada or a province, of an agency of any such government or of a federal or provincial crown corporation;

(b) persons who are full-time employees of a body corporate

(i) of which more than 50 per cent of the voting shares are beneficially owned or over which control or direction is exercised by resident Canadians,

(ii) a majority of the directors of which are resident Canadians, or

(iii) that is a subsidiary or a wholly-owned subsidiary of a body corporate described in subparagraph (i) or (ii),

where the principal reason for the residence of the employees outside Canada is to act as such employees;

(c) persons who are full-time students at a university or other educational institution recognized by the educational authorities of a majority of the provinces of Canada and have been resident outside Canada less than 10 consecutive years;

(d) persons who are full-time employees of an international association or organization of which Canada is a member; or

(e) persons who were, at the time of reaching their sixtieth birthday, ordinarily resident in Canada and have been resident outside Canada less than 10 consecutive years. (SOR/81-3)

Part II

Corporate Names

Interpretation

[¶24-551]

Sec. 12. In this Part,

"confusing", in relation to a corporate name, means a corporate name the use of which causes confusion with a trade mark or trade name in the manner described in section 13;

"distinctive", in relation to a trade name, means a trade name that actually distinguishes the business in association with which it is used by its owner from the business of others or that is adapted so as to distinguish them;

"secondary meaning", in relation to a trade name, means a trade name that has been used in Canada or elsewhere by any applicant or his predecessors so as to have become distinctive in Canada as at the date of filing an application for a corporate name;

"trade mark", means a trade mark as defined by the *Trade Marks Act*;

"trade name", means the name under which any business is carried on, whether it is the name of a body corporate, a trust, a partnership, a proprietorship or an individual;

"use", means actual use by a person that carries on business in Canada or elsewhere.

Confusion of Names

[¶24-554]

Sec. 13. A corporate name is confusing with

(a) a trade mark if the use of both the corporate name and the trade mark is likely to lead to the inference that the business carried on or intended to be carried on under the corporate name and the business connected with the trade mark are one business, whether or not the nature of the business of each is generally the same; or

(b) a trade name if the use of both names is likely to lead to the inference that the business carried on or intended to be carried on under the corporate name and the business carried on under the trade name are one business, whether or not the nature of the business of each is generally the same.

Consideration of Whole Name

[¶24-557]

Sec. 14. Subject to section 19, when determining whether a trade name is distinctive, the name as a whole and not only its separate elements shall be considered.

[¶24-560]

Sec. 15. (Repealed by SOR/86-365, s. 1, effective April 1, 1986.)

Prohibited Names

[¶24-563]

Sec. 16. For the purposes of paragraph 12(1)(*a*) of the Act, a corporate name is prohibited where the name contains any of the following:

(*a*) "Air Canada";

(*b*) "Trans Canada Airlines" or "Lignes aériennes Trans Canada";

(*c*) "Canada Standard" or "CS";

(*d*) "Cooperative", "Coopérative", "co-op" or "pool" when it connotes a cooperative venture;

(*e*) "Parliament Hill" or "Colline du Parlement";

(*f*) "Royal Canadian Mounted Police", "Gendarmerie Royale du Canada", "RCMP" or "GRC"; or

(*g*) "United Nations", "Nations Unies", "UN" or "ONU".

[¶24-566]

Sec. 17. For the purposes of paragraph 12(1)(*a*) of the Act, a corporate name is prohibited where the name connotes that the corporation

(*a*) carries on business under royal, vice-regal or governmental patronage, approval or authority, unless the appropriate government department or agency requests the name in writing;

(*b*) is sponsored or controlled by or is affiliated with the Government of Canada, the government of a province, the government of a country other than Canada or a political subdivision or agency of any such government, unless the appropriate government, political subdivision or agency consents in writing to the use of the name;

(*c*) is sponsored or controlled by or is affiliated with a university or an association of accountants, architects, engineers, lawyers, physicians, surgeons or any other professional association recognized by the laws of Canada or a province unless the appropriate university or professional association consents in writing to the use of the name; or

(*d*) carries on the business of a bank, loan company, insurance company, trust company, other financial intermediary or a stock exchange that is regulated by a law of Canada or a province unless the appropriate government department or agency consents in writing to the use of the name.

[¶24-569]

Sec. 18. For the purposes of paragraph 12(1)(a) of the Act, a corporate name is prohibited where the name contains a word or phrase that is obscene or connotes a business that is scandalous, obscene or immoral.

[¶24-572]

Sec. 19. For the purposes of paragraph 12(1)(a) of the Act, a corporate name is prohibited where the name is not distinctive because

(a) it is too general,

(b) it is only descriptive, in any language, of the quality, function or other characteristic of the goods or services in which the corporation deals or intends to deal,

(c) it is primarily or only the name or surname used alone of an individual who is living or has died within 30 years preceding the date of the request to the Director for that name, or

(d) it is primarily or only a geographic name used alone,

unless the person requesting the name establishes that it has, through use, acquired and continues to have secondary meaning at the time of the request.

[¶24-575]

Sec. 20. For the purposes of paragraph 12(1)(a) of the Act, a corporate name is prohibited where the name is confusing having regard to all the circumstances, including

(a) the inherent distinctiveness of the whole or any elements of any trade mark or trade name and the extent to which it has become known;

(b) the length of time the trade mark or trade name has been in use;

(c) the nature of the goods or services associated with a trade mark or the nature of the business carried on under or associated with a trade name, including the likelihood of any competition among businesses using such a trade mark or trade name;

(d) the nature of the trade with which a trade mark or trade name is associated, including the nature of the products or services and the means by which they are offered or distributed;

(e) the degree of resemblance between the proposed corporate name and any trade mark or trade name in appearance or sound or in the ideas suggested by them; and

(f) the territorial area in Canada in which the proposed corporate name or an existing trade name is likely to be used.

[¶24-578]

Sec. 21. For the purposes of paragraph 12(1)(a) of the Act, a corporate name is prohibited where an element of the name is the family name of an individual, whether or not preceded by his given name or initials, unless the individual or his heir or legal representative consents in writing to the use of his name and the individual has or had a material interest in the corporation.

[¶24-581]

Sec. 22. For the purposes of paragraph 12(1)(a) of the Act,

(a) a corporate name is prohibited where its use is likely to lead to the inference , that the business carried on or intended to be carried on under it and the business of a body corporate that is dissolved are one business, whether or not the nature of their businesses is generally the same; and

(b) the name of a revived corporation is prohibited where it is confusing with a name acquired by another corporation between the date of dissolution and revival of the revived corporation.

Deceptively Misdescriptive Names

[¶24-584]

Sec. 23. For the purposes of paragraph 12(1)(a) of the Act, a corporate name is deceptively misdescriptive if it misdescribes, in any language,

(a) the business, goods or services in association with which it is proposed to be used;

(b) the conditions under which the goods or services will be produced or supplied or the persons to be employed in the production or supply of those goods or services; or

(c) the place of origin of those goods or services.

Certain Names Not Prohibited

[¶24-587]

Sec. 24. A corporate name is not prohibited only because it contains alphabetic or numeric characters, initials, punctuation marks or any combination thereof.

[¶24-590]

Sec. 25. A corporate name that is confusing with the name of a body corporate that has not carried on business in the 2 years immediately preceding the date of a request for that corporate name shall not for that reason alone be prohibited if the body corporate that has that name

(a) consents in writing to the use of the name; and

(b) undertakes in writing to dissolve forthwith or to change its name before the corporation proposing to use the name commences to use it.

[¶24-593]

Sec. 26. A corporate name containing a word that is the same as or similar to the distinctive element of an existing trade mark or trade name shall not for that reason alone be prohibited if

(a) the person who has the trade mark or trade name consents in writing to the use of the corporate name; and

(b) the corporate name is not confusing.

[¶24-596]

Sec. 27. (1) A corporate name that is confusing with the name of a body corporate shall not for that reason alone be prohibited if

(a) the request for that corporate name relates to a proposed corporation that is the successor to the business of the body corporate and the body corporate has ceased or will cease to carry on business;

(b) the body corporate undertakes in writing to dissolve forthwith or to change its name before the corporation proposing to use the name commences to carry on business; and

(c) subject to subsection (2), the corporate name sets out in numerals the year of incorporation in parentheses immediately before the word "limited", "limitée", "incorporated", "incorporée", "corporation" or "société commerciale canadienne" or the abbreviation "Ltd.", "Ltée", "Inc.", "Corp." or "S.C.C."

Sec. 27(1)   ¶24-5

[¶24-599]

(2) A corporate name referred to in paragraph (1)(c) after two years of use may be changed to delete the reference to the year of incorporation if the corporate name so changed is not confusing.

[¶24-602]

Sec. 28. (1) When two or more corporations amalgamate, the name of the amalgamated corporation shall not be prohibited if

(a) it is the same as one of the amalgamating corporations;

(b) it is a distinctive combination of the names of the amalgamating corporations and is not otherwise confusing or prohibited; or

(c) it is a distinctive new name that is not confusing.

[¶24-603]

(2) Where a corporation acquires all or substantially all of the property of an affiliated body corporate, the use by the corporation of the name of the affiliated body corporate shall not be prohibited if the body corporate undertakes in writing to dissolve forthwith or to change its name before the corporation adopts the name.

Part III

Insider Trading

First Insider Report

[¶24-605]

Sec. 29. A report required to be sent to the Director by subsections 127(1) and (2) of the Act by an insider who owns or exercises control or direction over any securities of the corporation shall be in Form 24.

Subsequent Insider Report

[¶24-608]

Sec. 30. A report required to be sent to the Director by subsection 127(4) of the Act shall be in Form 25.

Deemed Insider Report

[¶24-611]

Sec. 31. A report required to be sent to the Director by subsection 127(3) of the Act shall be in Form 24 or Form 25 as applicable.

Notice Pursuant to Section 122.1 [128] of the Act

[¶24-613]

Sec. 31.1. For the purposes of section 128 of the Act, a corporation that has 15 or more shareholders, two or more joint shareholders being counted as one shareholder, and that proposes to purchase or otherwise acquire its own shares by means of an exempt offer, as defined in paragraph (b) or (e) of the definition "exempt offer" in section 194 of ᵗhe Act, in the circumstances described in paragraphs 58(c) and (d) of these Regulations, ₐll at least 10 days before the proposed purchase or acquisition send to the Director the notice or advertisement referred to in subparagraph 58(c)(i) or (d)(i) or (ii), whichever is applicable. (SOR/83-817)

Part IV

Proxies and Proxy Solicitation

Form of Proxy

[¶24-614]

Sec. 32. (1) A form of proxy required to be sent to the Director by subsection 150(2) of the Act (hereinafter called "a form of proxy") shall indicate, in bold faced type,

(a) the meeting at which it is to be used; and

(b) whether the proxy is solicited by or on behalf of the management of the corporation.

[¶24-617]

(2) A form of proxy shall contain a designated blank space for a date and shall state that if it is not dated in the space, it is deemed to bear the date on which it is mailed by the person making the solicitation.

[¶24-620]

(3) A form of proxy shall indicate, in bold faced type, that the shareholder may appoint a proxyholder other than any person designated in the form of proxy to attend and act on his behalf at the meeting, and shall contain instructions as to the manner in which the shareholder may do so.

[¶24-623]

(4) If a form of proxy designates a person as proxyholder, it shall provide a means for the shareholder to designate some other person as proxyholder.

[¶24-626]

(5) A form of proxy shall provide a means for the shareholder to specify that the shares registered in his name shall be voted for or against each matter or group of related matters identified in the notice of meeting, a management proxy circular, a dissident's proxy circular or a proposal under section 137 of the Act, other than the appointment of an auditor and the election of directors.

[¶24-629]

(6) A form of proxy may confer authority with respect to matters for which a choice is not provided in accordance with subsection (5) if the form of proxy, the management proxy circular or the dissidents proxy circular states in bold faced type how the proxyholder will vote the shares in respect of each matter or group of related matters.

[¶24-632]

(7) A form of proxy shall provide a means for the shareholder to specify that the shares registered in his name shall be voted or withheld from voting in respect of the appointment of an auditor or the election of directors.

[¶24-635]

(8) A form of proxy, a management proxy circular or a dissident's proxy circular sh~ state that the shares represented by the proxy will be voted or withheld from voting any ballot that may be called for and that, if the shareholder specifies a choice u~

subsection (5) or (7), with respect to any matter to be acted upon, the shares shall be voted accordingly.

[¶24-638]

Sec. 33. A form of proxy may confer discretionary authority in respect of amendments to matters identified in the notice of meeting or other matters that may properly come before the meeting, if

(a) the person by or on whose behalf the solicitation is made is not aware within a reasonable time before the solicitation that the amendments or other matters are to be presented for action at the meeting; and

(b) the form of proxy, the management proxy circular or the dissident's proxy circular states specifically that it confers such discretionary authority.

[¶24-641]

Sec. 34. A form of proxy shall not confer authority to vote in respect of the appointment of an auditor or the election of a director unless a *bona fide* proposed nominee for the appointment or election is named in the form of proxy, a management proxy circular, a dissident's proxy circular or a proposal under section 137 of the Act.

Contents of Management Proxy Circular

[¶24-644]

Sec. 35. A management proxy circular shall contain the following information:

(a) a statement of the right of a shareholder to revoke a proxy under subsection 148(4) of the Act and the method by which he may exercise it;

(b) a statement, in bold faced type, to the effect that the solicitation is made by or on behalf of the management of the corporation;

(c) the name of any director of the corporation who has informed the management in writing that he intends to oppose any action intended to be taken by the management and the action that he intends to oppose;

(d) the method of solicitation, if otherwise than by mail, and if the solicitation is to be made by specially engaged employees or agents, the material features of any contract or arrangement for the solicitation, the parties to the contract or arrangement and the cost or anticipated cost thereof;

(e) the name of the person by whom the cost of the solicitation has been or will be borne, directly or indirectly;

(f) the number of shares of each class of shares of the corporation entitled to be voted at the meeting and the number of votes to which each share of each such class is entitled;

(g) if the corporation has amended its articles under section 174 of the Act to constrain the issue or transfer of its voting shares, the general nature of the constrained share provisions;

(h) if the proceeds of an issue of securities were used for a purpose other than that stated in the document under which the securities were issued, the date of the document, the amount and designation of the securities so issued and details of the use made during the financial period of the proceeds;

(i) details of any financial assistance, in circumstances permitted by subsection 44(1) of the Act or referred to in paragraph 44(2)(e) of the Act, given by a corporation since the beginning of its last completed financial year

(i) to a shareholder of the corporation or any of its affiliates who is not a director, officer or employee thereof, or to an associate of any such shareholder, or

(ii) to any person in connection with a purchase of shares issued or to be issued by the corporation, if the giving of the assistance was material to the corporation or any of its affiliates or to the recipient of the assistance;

(*j*) if indemnification under section 124 of the Act is paid or becomes payable in the financial period,

(i) the amount paid or payable,

(ii) the name and title of the individual indemnified or to be indemnified, and

(iii) the circumstances that gave rise to the indemnity;

(*k*) if insurance referred to in subsection 124(4) of the Act is purchased,

(i) the amount or, where there is a comprehensive liability policy, the approximate amount of premium paid by the corporation in respect of directors as a group and officers as a group,

(ii) the aggregate amount of premium, if any, paid by the individuals in each such group,

(iii) the total amount of insurance purchased for each such group, and

(iv) a summary of any deductibility or co-insurance clause or other provision in the insurance contract that exposes the corporation to liability in addition to the payment of the premiums;

(*l*) details of any action brought or taken under section 239 or 241 of the Act to which the corporation is a party;

(*m*) the name of each person who, to the knowledge of the directors or officers of the corporation, beneficially owns or exercises control or direction over shares carrying more than 10 per cent of the votes attached to shares of the corporation, the approximate number of the shares so owned, controlled or directed by each such person and the percentage of voting shares of the corporation represented by the number of shares so owned, controlled or directed;

(*n*) if a change in the effective control of the corporation has occurred since the beginning of its last financial year, the name of the person who, to the knowledge of the directors or officers of the corporation, acquired control, the date and a description of the transaction in which control was acquired and the percentage of shares entitled to be voted now owned, controlled or directed by the person;

(*o*) the percentage of votes required for approval of any matter that is to be submitted to a vote of shareholders at the meeting other than the election of directors or the appointment of an auditor;

(*p*) if a new auditor is proposed to be appointed, the name of the proposed auditor, the name of each auditor appointed within the preceding 5 years and the date on which each auditor was first appointed;

(*q*) if directors are to be elected, a statement of the right of any class of shareholders to elect a specified number of directors or to cumulate their votes and of any conditions precedent to the exercise thereof;

(*r*) in tabular form, if directors are to be relected, so far as practicable, with respect to each person proposed to be nominated by management for election as a director and each director whose term of office will continue after the meeting,

(i) the name of each person, the time when his term of office or the term of office for which he is a proposed nominee will expire and all othe major positions and offices with the corporation or any of its significant affiliates presently held by him, indicating which of the persons are proposed nominees for election as directors at the meeting,

(ii) the present principal occupation or employment of each such person, givin the name and principal business of any body corporate or other organization which the occupation or employment is carried on and similar information a all principal occupations or employments of each such person within the 5 preceding years, unless he is now a director and was elected to his present term of office by a vote of shareholders at a meeting the notice of which was accompanied by a proxy circular containing that information,

(iii) if any such person is or has been a director of the corporation, the period or periods during which he has so served,

(iv) the approximate number of shares of each class of shares of the corporation and of its holding body corporate beneficially owned or over which control or direction is exercised by each such person, and

(v) if more than 10 per cent of the votes attached to shares of any class of the corporation or of its holding body corporate are beneficially owned or subject to control or direction by any such person and his associates, the approximate number of each class of shares so owned, controlled or directed by the associates and the name of each associate;

(s) the details of any contract, arrangement or understanding between any proposed management nominee and any other person, except the directors and officers of the corporation acting solely in their capacity as such, pursuant to which the nominee is to be elected, including the name of the other person;

(t) if action is to be taken with respect to

(i) the election of directors,

(ii) any bonus, profit sharing or other plan of remuneration, contract or arrangement in which any director or officer of the corporation will participate,

(iii) any pension or retirement plan of the corporation in which any director or officer of the corporation will participate, or

(iv) the granting to any director or officer of the corporation of any option or right to purchase any securities other than rights issued rateably to all shareholders or to all shareholders resident in Canada,

a statement of Executive Remuneration in Form 26;

(u) (Revoked by SOR/86-983, s. 1(2).)

(v) if action is to be taken with respect to any of the matters referred to in subparagraphs (t) (i) to (iv), a statement in respect of

(i) each director and officer of the corporation,

(ii) each proposed management nominee for election as a director of the corporation, and

(iii) each associate of any director, officer or proposed management nominee

who is or has been indebted to the corporation or any of its subsidiaries at any time during the last completed financial year, of the largest aggregate amount of debt outstanding at any time since the beginning of the corporation's last completed financial year, the nature of the debt, details of the transaction in which it was incurred, the amount presently outstanding and the rate of interest paid or charged thereon, but

(iv) an amount owing for purchases subject to usual trade terms, for ordinary travel and expense advances and for other transactions in the ordinary course of business may be omitted in determining the amount of debt, and

(v) information need not be furnished in respect of a person whose aggregate debt did not exceed $10,000 at any time during the period;

(w) the details including, where practicable, the approximate amount of any material interest of

(i) a director or officer of the corporation,

(ii) a proposed management nominee for election as a director of the corporation,

(iii) a shareholder required to be named by paragraph (*m*), and

(iv) an associate or affiliate of any of the foregoing persons

in any transaction since the beginning of the corporation's last completed financial year or in any proposed transaction that has materially affected or will materially affect the corporation or any of its affiliates, but

(v) an interest arising from the ownership of securities of the corporation may be omitted unless the security holder receives a benefit or advantage not shared rateably by all holders of the same class of security or all holders of the same class of security who are resident in Canada,

(vi) any transaction or interest may be omitted where

(A) the rate or charges involved in the transaction are fixed by law or determined by competitive bids,

(B) the interest of the person in the transaction is solely that of a director of another body corporate that is a party to the transaction,

(C) the transaction involves services as a bank or other depository of funds, transfer agent, registrar, trustee under a trust indenture or other similar services, or

(D) the transaction does not involve remuneration for services, and

(I) the interest of the person results from the beneficial ownership of less than 10 per cent of any class of shares of another body corporate that is a party to the transaction,

(II) the transaction is in the ordinary course of business of the corporation or any of its affiliates, and

(III) the amount of the transaction or series of transactions is less than 10 per cent of the total sales or purchases, as the case may be, of the corporation and its affiliates for the last completed financial year, and

(vii) details of transactions not omitted under subparagraphs (v) and (vi) that involve remuneration paid, directly or indirectly, to any of the persons referred to in this paragraph for services in any capacity shall be included, unless the interest of the person arises solely from the beneficial ownership of less than 10 per cent of any class of shares of another body corporate furnishing the services to the corporation or its affiliates;

(*x*) details of each transaction referred to in paragraph (*w*), the name and address of each person whose interest in the transaction is disclosed and the nature of the relationship by reason of which the interest is required to be disclosed;

(*y*) where a transaction referred to in paragraph (*w*) involves the purchase or sale of assets by the corporation or any affiliate otherwise than in the ordinary course of business, the cost of the assets to the purchaser and the cost of the assets to the seller if acquired by the seller within the 2 years prior to the transaction;

(*z*) details of a material underwriting discount or commission with respect to the sale of securities by the corporation where any person referred to in paragraph (*w*) has contracted or will contract with the corporation in respect of an underwriting or is an associate or affiliate of a person that has so contracted or will so contract;

(*aa*) where a person other than the directors or officers of the corporation or any of its affiliates manage the corporation or any of its subsidiaries,

(i) details of the management agreement or arrangement including the name and address of every person who is a party to the agreement or arrangement or who is responsible to perform it,

(ii) the names and addresses of the insiders of a body corporate with which the corporation or any of its subsidiaries has a management agreement or arrangement,

(iii) the amounts paid or payable by the corporation and any of its subsidiaries to a person named pursuant to subparagraph (i) since the beginning of the corporation's last completed financial year,

(iv) details of any debt owed to the corporation or any of its subsidiaries by a person referred to in subparagraphs (i) and (ii) that was outstanding at any time since the beginning of the corporation's last completed financial year, and

(v) details of any transaction or arrangement, other than one referred to in subparagraph (i), with the corporation or any of its subsidiaries since the beginning of the corporation's last completed financial year in which a person referred to in subparagraphs (i) and (ii) has a material interest that would be required to be disclosed by paragraph (*w*),

and for the purposes of this paragraph,

(vi) "details" of debt include the largest aggregate amount of debt outstanding at any time during the period, the nature of the debt, details of the transaction in which it was incurred, the amount presently outstanding and the rate of interest paid or charged thereon,

(vii) an amount owing for purchases, subject to usual trade terms, for ordinary travel and expense advances and for other transactions in the ordinary course of business may he omitted in determining debt, and

(viii) a matter that is not material may be omitted;

(*bb*) details of any material interest of

(i) each person who was a director or officer of the corporation at any time since the beginning of its last completed financial year,

(ii) each proposed management nominee for election as a director of the corporation, and

(iii) each associate of any of the foregoing persons

in any matter to be acted upon at the meeting other than the election of directors or the appointment of an auditor;

(*cc*) if action is to be taken with respect to the authorization or issue of securities, except to exchange the securities for other securities of the corporation,

(i) the designation and number or amount of securities to be authorized or issued,

(ii) a description of the securities, but

(A) if the terms of securities to be authorized cannot be stated because no issue thereof is contemplated in the immediate future and if no further authorization by shareholders for their issue is to be obtained, a statement that the terms of the securities to be authorized, including dividend or interest rates, conversion prices, voting rights, redemption prices, maturity dates and other matters will be determined by the directors, and

(B) if the securities are shares of an listing class, the description required except for a statement of any preemptive rights may be omitted,

(iii) details of the transaction in which the securities are to be issued including the nature and approximate amount of the consideration received or to be received by the corporation, and the purpose for which the consideration has been or is to be used,

(iv) if it is impracticable to furnish the details required under subparagraph (iii), a statement of the reason why it is impracticable, the purpose of the authorization and whether shareholders' approval for the issue of the securities will be sought, and

(v) if the securities are to be issued other than in a general public offering for money or other than rateably to all holders of the same class of securities or all holders of the same class of securities who are resident in Canada, the reasons for the proposed authorization or issue and its effect on the rights of present security holders;

(*dd*) if action is to be taken under section 173 or 174 of the Act to modify the rights, privileges, restrictions or conditions attached to any class of securities of the corporation or to authorize or issue securities in order to exchange them for other securities of the corporation,

    (i) the designation and number or amount of outstanding securities that are to be modified, and, if securities are to be issued in exchange, the designation and number or amount of securities to be exchanged and the basis of the exchange,

    (ii) details of material differences between the outstanding securities and the modified or new securities,

    (iii) the reasons for the proposed modification or exchange and the general effect on the rights of existing security holders,

    (iv) a brief statement of arrears in dividends or of defaults in principal or interest in respect of the outstanding securities that are to be modified or exchanged, and

    (v) all other information material to the proposed modification or exchange;

(*ee*) if action is to be taken with respect to any plan for

    (i) an amalgamation with another corporation otherwise than under section 184 of the Act,

    (ii) a sale, lease or exchange of all or substantially all of the property of the corporation under subsection 189(3) of the Act,

    (iii) a continuance under the laws of another jurisdiction under section 188 of the Act, or

    (iv) the liquidation or dissolution of the corporation,

the material features of the plan including the reasons for it and its general effect on the rights of existing security holders;

(*ff*) if action is to be taken with respect to a plan referred to in subparagraph (*ee*)(i), a statement containing, with respect to the corporation and the other body corporate,

    (i) a brief description of the business,

    (ii) the location and general character of the plants and other important physical properties,

    (iii) a brief description of arrears in dividends or defaults in principal or interest in respect of securities of the corporation or body corporate and of the effect of the plan,

    (iv) the existing and *pro forma* capitalization in tabular form,

    (v) an historical summary of earnings in tabular form for each of the last 5 fiscal years including per share amounts of net earnings, dividends declared for each year and book value per share at the end of the most recent period,

    (vi) a combined *pro forma* summary of earnings in tabular form for each of the last 5 fiscal years, indicating the aggregate and per share earnings for each such year and the *pro forma* book value per share at the end of the most recent period, but if the transaction will establish a new basis of accounting for the assets of the corporation or body corporate, the *pro forma* summary of earnings may be furnished only for the most recent fiscal year and interim period and shall reflect appropriate *pro forma* adjustments resulting from the new basis of accounting,

    (vii) the high and low sale prices for each quarterly period within the previous 2 years for each class of securities of the corporation and of the other body corporate that is traded on a stock exchange and that will be materially affected by the plan, and

(viii) an introductory summary, not exceeding 6 pages in length, of the contents of the proxy circular that highlights the salient features of the transaction, including a summary of the financial information, with appropriate cross-references to the more detailed information in the circular;

(*gg*) if action is to be taken with respect to a matter referred to in paragraph (*ee*), such financial statements of the corporation as would be required to be included in a prospectus under the laws of one of the jurisdictions referred to in paragraph 60(*a*);

(*hh*) if action is to be taken with respect to a matter referred to in paragraph (*ff*), such financial statements of the other body corporate as would be required to be included in a prospectus under the laws of one of the jurisdictions referred to in paragraph 60(*a*);

(*ii*) a statement of the right of a shareholder to dissent under section 190 of the Act with respect to any matter to be acted upon at the meeting and a brief summary of the procedure to be followed;

(*jj*) if action is to be taken with respect to any matter other than the approval of financial statements, the substance of each such matter or group of related matters, to the extent it has not been described pursuant to paragraphs (*a*) to (ii), in sufficient detail to permit shareholders to form a reasoned judgment concerning the matter, and if any such matter is not required to be submitted to a vote of the shareholders, the reasons for so submitting it and the action intended to be taken by management in the event of a negative vote by the shareholders; and

(*kk*) a statement, signed by a director or officer of the corporation, that the contents and the sending of the circular have been approved by the directors.

[¶24-647]

Sec. 36. A management proxy circular that is sent to the Director shall be accompanied by a statement signed by a director or officer that a copy of the circular has been sent to each director, each shareholder entitled to notice of the meeting to which the circular relates and to the auditor of the corporation.

Dissident's Proxy Circular

[¶24-650]

Sec. 37. For the purposes of section 38, "dissident" means any person, other than the management of the corporation or its affiliates and associates, by or on behalf of whom a solicitation is made, and includes a committee or group that solicits proxies, any member of the committee or group, and any person whether or not named as a member who, acting alone or with one or more other persons, directly or indirectly engages in organizing, directing or financing any such committee or group, except

(*a*) a person who contributes not more than $250 and who does not otherwise participate in the solicitation;

(*b*) a bank or other lending institution or a broker or dealer that, in the ordinary course of business, lends money or executes orders for the purchase or sale of shares and that does not otherwise participate in the solicitation;

(*c*) a person who is employed to solicit and whose activities are limited to the performance of his duties in the course of such employment;

(*d*) a person who only sends soliciting material or performs other ministerial or clerical duties;

(*e*) a person employed in the capacity of lawyer, accountant, advertiser, public relations or financial adviser and whose activities are limited to the performance of his duties in the course of such employment; and

(*f*) an officer or director of, or a person employed by, a person by or on behalf of whom a solicitation is made if he does not directly participate in the solicitation.

Contents of Dissident's Proxy Circular

[¶24-653]

Sec. 38.   A dissident's proxy circular shall contain the following information:

(a) the name and address of the corporation to which the solicitation relates;

(b) the information required by paragraphs 35(a), (d) and (e);

(c) details of the identity and background of each dissident, including

   (i) his name and business address,

   (ii) his present principal occupation or employment and the name, principal business and address of any body corporate or other person in which the occupation or employment is carried on,

   (iii) all material occupations, offices or employments during the preceding 5 years, with starting and ending dates of each and the name, principal business and address of the body corporate or other business organization in which each such occupation, office or employment was carried on,

   (iv) whether he is or has been a dissident within the preceding 10 years and, if so, the body corporate involved, the principals and his relationship to them, the subject matter and the outcome of the solicitation, and

   (v) convictions in criminal proceedings during the preceding 10 years for which a pardon has not been granted, other than convictions in respect of violations for which the maximum penalty is a fine of not more than $5,000 or imprisonment for not more than 6 months, or both, and the date and nature of the conviction, the name and location of the court and the sentence imposed;

(d) the circumstances under which each dissident became involved in the solicitation and the nature and extent of his activities as a dissident;

(e) the information required by paragraphs 35(m), (n) and (o), if known to a dissident;

(f) details of the interest of each dissident in the securities of the corporation to which the solicitation relates, including

   (i) the number of each class of shares of the corporation that he owns beneficially or over which he exercises control or direction,

   (ii) the dates on which securities of the corporation were purchased or sold during the preceding 2 years, the amount purchased or sold on each date and the price at which they were purchased or sold,

   (iii) if any part of the purchase price or market value of any of the securities specified in subparagraph (ii) is represented by funds borrowed or otherwise obtained for the purpose of acquiring or holding the securities, the amount of the indebtedness as of the latest practicable date and a brief description of the transaction including the names of the parties, other than a bank, broker or dealer acting in the transaction in the ordinary course of business,

   (iv) whether he is or was within the preceding year a party to a contract, arrangement or understanding with any person in respect of securities of the corporation, including joint ventures, loan or option arrangements, puts or calls, guarantees against loss or guarantees of profit, division of losses or profits or the giving or withholding of proxies and, if so, the names of the parties to, and the details of the contract, arrangement or understanding,

   (v) the number of each class of shares of an affiliate of the corporation that he owns beneficially or over which he exercises control or direction, and

   (vi) the number of each class of shares of the corporation that each associate of the dissident beneficially owns or exercises control or direction over and the name and address of each such associate;

(g) if directors are to be elected, information required by paragraphs 35(*r*), (*s*), (*w*) and (*bb*), in respect of each proposed nominee for election as a director and his associates;

(*h*) the information required by paragraphs 35(*w*) and (*bb*), in respect of each dissident and his associates; and

(*i*) details of any contract, arrangement or understanding, including the names of the parties, between a dissident or his associates and any person with respect to

(i) future employment by the corporation or any of its affiliates, or

(ii) future transactions to which the corporation or any of its affiliates will or may be a party.

(SOR/82-187.)

[¶24-656]

Sec. 39.   If a dissident is a partnership, body corporate, association or other organization, the information required by paragraphs 38(*c*), (*d*), (*f*), (*h*) and (*i*) to be included in a dissident's proxy circular shall be given in respect of each partner, officer and director of and each person who controls the dissident and who is himself not a dissident.

[¶24-659]

Sec. 40.   Information that is not known to a dissident and that cannot be reasonably ascertained by him may be omitted from a dissident's proxy circular, but the circumstances that render the information unavailable shall be disclosed therein.

[¶24-662]

Sec. 41.   (1) A dissident's proxy circular shall contain a statement, signed by a dissident or a person authorized by him, that the contents and the sending of the circular have been approved by the dissident.

[¶24-665]

(2) A dissident's proxy circular that is sent to the Director pursuant to subsection 150(2) of the Act shall be accompanied by a statement signed by a dissident or a person authorized by him to the effect that

(*a*) the circular complies with these Regulations; and

(*b*) a copy of the circular has been sent to each director, each shareholder and to the auditor of the corporation.

Date of Proxy Circular and Information

[¶24-668]

Sec. 42.   A proxy circular shall be dated as of a date not more than 30 days before the date on which it is first sent to a shareholder of the corporation and the information, other than financial statements, required to be contained in it shall be given as of the date of the circular.

Financial Statements in Proxy Circular

[¶24-671]

Sec. 43.   (1) Where financial statements accompany or form part of a management proxy circular, the statements shall be prepared in the manner prescribed for the financial statements in Part V.

[¶24-674]

(2) The financial statements referred to in subsection (1), if not reported upon by the auditor of the corporation, shall be accompanied by a report of the chief financial officer of the corporation stating that the financial statements have not been audited but have been prepared in accordance with Part V.

Part V
Financial Disclosure

General

[¶24-675]

Sec. 44. The financial statements referred to in paragraph 155(1)(a) of the Act shall, except as otherwise provided by this Part, be prepared in accordance with the standards, as they exist from time to time, of the Canadian Institute of Chartered Accountants set out in the C.I.C.A. Handbook.

[¶24-676]

Sec. 45. The auditor's report referred to in section 169 of the Act shall, except as otherwise provided by this Part, be prepared in accordance with the standards of the Canadian Institute of Chartered Accountants set out in the C.I.C.A. Handbook.

Contents of Financial Statements

[¶24-677]

Sec. 46. (1) The financial statements referred to in section 155 of the Act shall include at least

(a) a balance sheet;

(b) a statement of retained earnings;

(c) an income statement; and

(d) a statement of changes in financial position.

[¶24-678]

(2) Financial statements need not be designated by the names set out in paragraphs (1)(a) to (d).

Reporting Classes of Business

[¶24-679]

Sec. 47. (1) In this section, "corporation" means a corporation that carries on a diversified as distinct from an integrated business and that sends its financial statements to the Director pursuant to subsection 160(1) of the Act.

[¶24-679a]

(2) The financial statements of a corporation shall disclose separately or in a schedule thereto a summary of financial information for each class of business the revenue from which is 10 per cent or more of the corporation's total revenues for the period.

[¶24-679b]

(3) The financial statements or schedule referred to in subsection (2) shall contain a note stating that the directors of the corporation have determined its classes of business at a meeting of directors and have recorded them in the minutes of the meeting.

[¶24-679c]

(4) Subject to subsection (5), the classes of business referred to in subsection (2) shall be designated in accordance with the Statistics Canada Standard Industrial Classification Code.

[¶24-679d]

(5) Where the directors of the corporation do not adopt the Statistics Canada Standard Industrial Classification Code to identify the corporation's classes of business, the financial statements or a note hereto shall contain a description of the basis used to determine the corporation's classes of business. (SOR/79-728)

[¶24-679e]

(6) Subsections (1) to (5) do not apply to any corporation that discloses segmented information in accordance with the standards as they exist from time to time of the Canadian Institute of Chartered Accountants set out in the C.I.C.A. Handbook. (SOR/81-3)

Part VI

Exemption from Public Disclosure of Financial Statement

Interpretation

[¶24-684]

Sec. 48. In this Part, "disclosing corporation" means a corporation referred to in section 160 of the Act.

[¶24-687]

Sec. 49. Disclosure of information may be detrimental to a disclosing corporation within the meaning of section 156 of the Act, in addition to any other reason, where the disclosing corporation would be at a disadvantage

(*a*) in its dealings with suppliers, customers or others; or

(*b*) because it deals in only one line of products or services and its competitors

(i) are not required to make similar disclosure, or

(ii) deal in several lines of products or services and disclose information in a form that prevents identification of financial information in respect of any particular product or service.

Prescribed Circumstances for Exemptions
Under Subsection 160(3) or 163(4) of the Act

[¶24-690]

Sec. 50. (1) The Director may, subject to subsections (2) and 3) and on such other reasonable conditions as he thinks fit, exempt a disclosing corporation from the application of subsection 160(2) of the Act if the disclosing corporation is a subsidiary of a holding body corporate incorporated under the laws of (*a*) Canada or a province; or

(*b*) any other jurisdiction, and the business of the disclosing corporation is not economically significant in Canada having regard to its products or services or its share of any market.

[¶24-691]

(2) A disclosing corporation referred to in paragraph (1)(*a*) shall, as a condition of receiving an exemption under subsection (1), send to the Director for public disclosure a summary of its financial statements that are the subject of the application showing the amounts set out therein with respect to

(*a*) current assets,

(*b*) fixed assets,

(*c*) other assets,

(*d*) total assets,

(*e*) current liabilities,

(*f*) long-term liabilities,

(*g*) total liabilities,

(*h*) shareholders' equity,

(*i*) investments in affiliated bodies corporate,

(*j*) loans and advances from affiliated bodies corporate, and

(*k*) percentage of change of gross revenue from the immediately preceding financial period.

[¶24-692]

(3) A disclosing corporation referred to in paragraph (1)(*b*) shall, as a condition of receiving an exemption under subsection (1), send to the Director for public disclosure its financial statements prepared in combined form that include the Canadian operations of the disclosing corporation and its affiliates that carry on business in Canada.

[¶24-693]

(4) The Director may, on such reasonable conditions as he thinks fit, exempt a disclosing corporation from the application of subsection 160(2) of the Act where the corporation is affiliated with another body corporate by reason only that some or all of its shares are held by another person

(*a*) in trust; or

(*b*) subject to an agreement or arrangement under which, upon the fulfilment of a condition or the happening of an event that it is reasonable to expect will be fulfilled or will happen, the affiliation with the other body corporate will terminate.

[¶24-694]

(5) The Director may, on such reasonable conditions as he thinks fit, exempt a disclosing corporation from the application of subsection 160(2) of the Act where the corporation (hereinafter referred to as the "controlled corporation") would be affiliated with another body corporate by reason of being controlled by the other body corporate or by reason of both bodies corporate being controlled by the same person (which body corporate or person so controlling the controlled corporation is hereinafter referred to as the "controller"), and

(*a*) the controlled corporation is a party to an agreement or arrangement under which, upon the fulfilment of a condition or the happening of an event that it is reasonable to expect will be fulfilled or will happen, the controlled corporation will

(i) cease to be controlled by the controller, and

(ii) become controlled by a person with whom the controller deals at arm's length; and

(b) the principal reason for the control of the controlled corporation by the controller is to secure the interests of the controller in respect of

(i) any loan made by the controller, the whole or any part of which is outstanding, or

(ii) any shares issued by the controlled corporation that are held by the controller and that are, under the agreement or arrangement, to be redeemed by the controlled corporation or purchased by a person referred to in subparagraph (a)(ii).

[¶24-695]

(6) The Director may, on such reasonable conditions as he thinks fit, exempt a corporation from appointing an auditor where the corporation

(a) is a wholly-owned subsidiary of a holding body corporate incorporated under the laws of Canada or a province; and

(b) is required to comply with section 160 of the Act. (SOR/80-873)

Part VII
Constrained Share Corporations

Interpretation

[¶24-699]

Sec. 51. In this Part,

"Canadian" means

(a) a resident Canadian,

(b) a partnership of which a majority of the members are resident Canadians and in which interests representing in value more than 50 per cent of the total value of the partnership property are owned by resident Canadians,

(c) a trust established by a resident Canadian

(i) a majority of the trustees of which are resident Canadians, or

(ii) in which beneficial interests representing in value more than 50 per cent of the total value of the trust property are owned by resident Canadians,

(d) Her Majesty in right of Canada or of a province or territory of Canada or a municipal corporation or public board or commission in Canada, or

(e) a body corporate

(i) incorporated under the laws of Canada or a province,

(ii) of which a majority of the directors are resident Canadians, and

(iii) over which persons described in any of paragraphs (a) to (d) or in this paragraph exercise control or direction or of which such persons beneficially own shares or securities currently convertible into shares carrying more than 50 per cent of the voting rights under all circumstances or by reason of the occurrence of an event that has occurred and that is continuing, including currently exercisable options or rights to acquire such shares or convertible securities;

"constrained class" means the class of persons specified in the articles of a constrained share corporation as being ineligible to hold, as a class, more than the maximum aggregate holdings;

"constrained share corporation" means a corporation that has provisions in its articles imposing a constraint;

"constraint" means a restriction on

(a) the issue or transfer of shares of any class or series to persons who are not resident Canadians,

(b) the issue or transfer of shares of any class or series to enable a corporation or any of its affiliates or associates to qualify under a law of Canada or a province referred to in paragraph 57(1)(a)

(i) to obtain a licence to carry on any business,

(ii) to become a publisher of a Canadian newspaper or periodical, or

(iii) to acquire shares of a financial intermediary as defined in paragraph 57(1)(b), or

(c) the issue, transfer or ownership of shares of any class or series in order to assist a corporation or any of its affiliates or associates to qualify under a law of Canada referred to in subsection 57(2) to receive licences, permits, grants, payments or other benefits by reason of attaining or maintaining a specified level of Canadian ownership or control (SOR/83-817, s. 2(3).);

"control" means control in any manner that results in control in fact, whether directly through the ownership of shares or indirectly through a trust, a contract, the ownership of shares of any other body corporate or otherwise;

"maximum aggregate holdings" means the total number of voting shares of a constrained share corporation that may be held by or on behalf of persons in the constrained class and their associates in accordance with the articles of the corporation;

"maximum individual holdings" means the total number of voting shares of a constrained share corporation that may be held by or on behalf of any one person in the constrained class and his associates in accordance with the articles of the corporation;

"voting share" means a share that is subject to a constraint referred to in paragraph (a) or (b) of the definition "constraint" in this section and that carries voting rights under all circumstances or by reason of the occurrence of an event that has occurred and that is continuing and includes a security currently convertible into such a share and a currently exercisable option or right to acquire such a share or such a convertible security.

(SOR/83-817, s. 2(4).)

Disclosure Required

[¶24-702]

Sec. 52. Each of the following documents issued or published by a constrained share corporation shall indicate conspicuously the general nature of its constrained share provisions:

(a) certificate representing a voting share;

(b) management proxy circular; and

(c) prospectus, statement of material facts, registration statement or similar document.

Powers and Duties of Directors

[¶24-705]

Sec. 53. (1) The directors of a constrained share corporation that has provisions in its articles imposing a constraint referred to in paragraph (a) or (b) of the definition "constraint" in section 51 shall refuse to register a transfer of a voting share of the corporation in accordance with the articles if

(a) the total number of voting shares held by or on behalf of persons in the constrained class exceeds the maximum aggregate holdings and the transfer is to a person in the constrained class;

(b) the total number of voting shares held by or on behalf of persons in the constrained class does not exceed the maximum aggregate holdings and the transfer would cause the number of such shares held by persons in the constrained class to exceed the maximum aggregate holdings;

(c) the total number of voting shares held by or on behalf of a person in the constrained class exceeds the maximum individual holdings and the transfer is to that person; or

(d) the total number of voting shares held by or on behalf of a person in the constrained class does not exceed the maximum individual holdings and the transfer would cause the number of such shares held by that person to exceed the maximum individual holdings. (SOR/83-817 s. 3(1).)

[¶24-708]

(2) Notwithstanding subsection (1), the directors of a constrained share corporation that is described in that subsection shall register a transfer of a voting share of the corporation to a person in the constrained class if that person establishes that he was the beneficial owner of that share on the day on which the corporation became a constrained share corporation. (SOR/83-817 s. 3(2).)

[¶24-711]

(3) The directors of a constrained share corporation that is described in subsection (1) shall not issue a voting share of the corporation to a person in the constrained class in circumstances where the directors are required to refuse to register a transfer of such a share by subsection (1). (SOR/83-817 s. 3(2).)

[¶24-714]

(4) For the purposes of subsection (3), the directors may count as issued shares the voting shares that it is currently offering to its shareholders or prospective shareholders.

[¶24-715]

Sec. 53.1. The directors of a constrained share corporation that has provisions in its articles imposing a constraint referred to in paragraph (c) of the definition "constraint" in section 51

(a) shall not issue a share of such corporation to a person

(i) whose ownership of such share would be contrary to such constraint,

(ii) who, in respect of the issue of such share, has been requested by such corporation to furnish it with information referred to in subsection 55.1(7) and has not furnished such information, or

(iii) whose ownership of such share the directors have determined, on the basis of information furnished to such corporation by that person pursuant to a request referred to in subparagraph (ii), may be contrary to such constraint; and

(b) shall refuse to register a transfer of a share of such corporation if the transfer is to a person

(i) whose ownership of such share is contrary to such constraint,

(ii) who, in respect of the registration of such share, has been requested by such corporation to furnish it with information referred to in subsection 55.1(7) and has not furnished such information, or

(iii) whose ownership of such share the directors have determined, on the basis of information furnished to such corporation by that person pursuant to a request referred to in subparagraph (ii), may be contrary to such constraint. (SOR/83-817)

[¶24-715a]

Sec. 53.2. Sections 54 and 55 apply to a constrained share corporation that has provisions in its articles imposing a constraint referred to in paragraph (*a*) or (*b*) of the definition "constraint" in section 51. (SOR/83-817)

Limitation on Voting Rights

[¶24-717]

Sec. 54. (1) Where on the day on which a corporation becomes a constrained share corporation the total number of voting shares of the corporation held by or on behalf of a person in the constrained class exceeds the maximum individual holdings, that person or his nominee may, in person or by proxy, exercise the voting rights attached to the lesser of the voting shares so held on that day or on any subsequent day.

[¶24-720]

(2) After the total number of shares held by or on behalf of the person referred to in subsection (1) is reduced below the maximum individual holdings, he or his nominee may, in person or by proxy, exercise the voting rights attached to shares so held.

[¶24-723]

Sec. 55. (1) Except as provided in subsection 54(1), where the total number of voting shares of a constrained share corporation held by or on behalf of a person in the constrained class exceeds the maximum individual holdings, no person shall, in person or by proxy, exercise the voting rights attached to the shares held by or on behalf of the person in the constrained class.

[¶24-726]

(2) Where it appears from the share register of a constrained share corporation that the total number of voting shares held by a shareholder is less than the maximum individual holdings, a proxyholder for that shareholder may vote those shares, unless the proxyholder has knowledge that the shares beneficially owned by the shareholder exceed the maximum individual holdings.

[¶24-729]

(3) Where, after the day on which a corporation becomes a constrained share corporation, a corporation or trust that was not a person in the constrained class becomes a person in the constrained class, the corporation or trust shall not exercise the voting rights attached to any shares it holds in the constrained share corporation while it is a person in the constrained class.

Sale of Constrained Shares

[¶24-730]

Sec. 55.1. (1) For the purposes of subsection 46(1) of the Act, before a constrained share corporation concludes that shares of the corporation are owned contrary to a constraint referred to in paragraph (*c*) of the definition "constraint" in section 51 or the directors of the corporation determine that shares of the corporation may be owned contrary to such constraint, the corporation shall send by registered mail a written notice in accordance with subsection (5) to the person shown in the securities register of the corporation as the holder of the shares. (SOR/83-817)

[¶24-730a]

(2) For the purposes of subsection 46(1) of the Act, in determining that shares of a constrained share corporation may be owned contrary to a constraint referred to in paragraph (c) of the definition "constraint" in section 51, the directors of the corporation shall

(a) ascertain whether or not the corporation has received a reply to a request for information referred to in subsection (7) respecting such shares and consider the reply, if any, thereto; and

(b) examine and consider any other records of the corporation containing information that would indicate whether such shares are owned contrary to such constraint. (SOR/83-817)

[¶24-730b]

(3) For the purposes of subsection 46(1) of the Act, where a constrained share corporation has sent a notice referred to in subsection (1) to a person shown in the securities register of the corporation as the holder of shares and

(a) the corporation has concluded that shares in respect of which the notice was sent are owned contrary to a constraint referred to in paragraph (c) of the definition "constraint" in section 51, or

(b) the directors of the corporation have determined in accordance with subsection (2) that shares in respect of which the notice was sent may be owned contrary to such constraint,

and the corporation intends to sell all or some of the shares pursuant to subsection 46(1) of the Act, the corporation shall, not less than 90 days but not more than 150 days after the sending of such notice, send to that person by registered mail a further written notice in accordance with subsection (6) respecting the shares that the corporation intends to sell. (SOR/83-817)

[¶24-730c]

(4) Where a corporation sends a notice under subsection (1) or (3), the corporation shall, at the time the notice is sent, enter or cause to be entered in the securities register of the corporation the particulars of such notice including the date on which it was sent. (SOR/83-817)

[¶24-730d]

(5) The notice referred to in subsection (1) shall contain

(a) the name and address of the holder of the shares as shown in the securities register of the corporation;

(b) a statement identifying the certificate representing the shares by certificate number or otherwise;

(c) a statement indicating that all or some of the shares may be sold by the corporation pursuant to subsection 46(1) of the Act if such shares are owned, or the directors of the corporation determine in accordance with subsection (2) that such shares may be owned, contrary to a constraint referred to in paragraph (c) of the definition "constraint" in section 51;

(d) a statement indicating that the corporation may conclude that all or some of the shares are owned contrary to a constraint referred to in paragraph (c) of the definition "constraint" in section 51;

(e) a statement indicating that the directors of the corporation may determine in accordance with subsection (2) that all or some of the shares may be owned contrary to a constraint referred to in paragraph (c) of the definition "constraint" in section 51 and that for the purpose of making such determination the directors of the corporation will

(i) consider the reply, if any, to a request for information referred to in subsection (7) respecting such shares, and

(ii) examine and consider any other records of the corporation containing information that would indicate whether such shares are owned contrary to such constraint;

(*f*) a statement indicating that no share in respect of which the notice is sent may be sold pursuant to subsection 46(1) of the Act if a transfer of such share is registered in the securities register of the corporation after the notice was sent unless the corporation again complies with the requirements set out in this Part respecting the sale of such share;

(*g*) a statement indicating that no share in respect of which the notice is sent may be sold pursuant to subsection 46(1) of the Act unless not less than 60 days but not more than 150 days have elapsed from the day on which a notice referred to in subsection (3) is sent to the holder of such share;

(*h*) a statement indicating the earliest date and the latest date on which the corporation may sell the shares, having regard to the requirements set out in section 55.3;

(*i*) a statement indicating that the shares may be sold on any stock exchange where shares of the corporation are listed and posted for trading or, where shares of the corporation are not listed and posted for trading on any stock exchange, in such other manner as the directors of the corporation determine to be appropriate;

(*j*) a statement indicating that, if not all the shares of the holder represented by a certificate are sold pursuant to subsection 46(1) of the Act, a certificate representing the shares that are not sold will be issued upon surrender for cancellation of the certificate representing the shares sold; and

(*k*) a statement indicating that, forthwith upon the sale of the shares pursuant to subsection 46(1) of the Act, the corporation will

(i) register the transfer or a notice of the sale of such shares or cause the transfer or a notice of the sale of such shares to be registered in the securities register of the corporation, and

(ii) send a notice of such sale in accordance with paragraph 55.4(1)(*b*) to the person shown in the securities register of the corporation as the holder of such shares at the time of sale. (SOR/83-817)

[¶24-730e]

(6) The notice referred to in subsection (3) shall contain

(*a*) the name and address of the holder of the shares as shown in the securities register of the corporation;

(*b*) a statement identifying the certificate representing the shares by certificate number or otherwise;

(*c*) a statement indicating that all or some of the shares may be sold by the corporation pursuant to subsection 46(1) of the Act if such shares are owned, or the directors of the corporation determine in accordance with subsection (2) that such shares may be owned, contrary to a constraint referred to in paragraph (*c*) of the definition "constraint" in section 51;

(*d*) a statement indicating that the corporation has concluded that the shares are owned, or that the directors of the corporation have determined in accordance with subsection (2) that the shares may be owned, contrary to a constraint referred to in paragraph (*c*) of the definition "constraint" in section 51 and indicating the reason why the corporation so concluded or the directors so determined, as the case may be;

(*e*) a statement indicating that the corporation intends to sell all or a specified number of the shares pursuant to subsection 46(1) of the Act;

Sec. 55.1(6)   ¶24-730e

(*f*) a statement indicating that if before the sale the corporation changes its conclusion that the shares are owned, or the directors of the corporation change their determination made in accordance with subsection (2) that the shares may be owned, contrary to a constraint referred to in paragraph (*c*) of the definition "constraint" in section 51 or there is a change in the reason for such conclusion or determination, the corporation will send a notice in accordance with subsection 55.2(1) to the person shown in the securities register of the corporation as the holder of the shares;

(*g*) a statement advising that, unless the person shown in the securities register of the corporation as the holder of the shares receives a notice referred to in paragraph (*f*), such person and all other interested persons should not assume

(i) that the corporation has changed its conclusion that the shares are owned, or the directors of the corporation have changed their determination made in accordance with subsection (2) that the shares may be owned, contrary to a constraint referred to in paragraph (*c*) of the definition "constraint" in section 51,

(ii) that there has been a change in the reason for such conclusion or determination, or

(iii) that the corporation no longer intends to sell the shares pursuant to subsection 46(1) of the Act:

(*h*) a statement indicating that no share in respect of which the notice is sent may be sold pursuant to subsection 46(1) of the Act if a transfer of such share is registered in the securities register of the corporation after the notice referred to in subsection (1) was sent unless the corporation again complies with the requirements set out in this Part respecting the sale of such share;

(*i*) a statement indicating that no share in respect of which the notice is sent may be sold pursuant to subsection 46(1) of the Act unless not less than 60 days but not more than 150 days have elapsed from the day on which the notice was sent to the holder of such share; and

(*j*) a statement indicating each of the matters referred to in paragraphs (5)(*h*) to (*k*). (SOR/83-817)

[¶24-730f]

(7) The notice referred to in subsection (1) shall be accompanied by a request for such information, including a request for the completion of such forms, as would indicate whether the shares are owned contrary to a constraint referred to in paragraph (*c*) of the definition "constraint" in section 51. (SOR/83-817)

[¶24-730g]

(8) The notice referred to in subsection (3) shall be accompanied by a request for information referred to in subsection (7) unless the corporation has received the requested information before the notice is sent. (SOR/83-817)

[¶24-730h]

(9) A request for information referred to in subsection (7) shall be accompanied by instructions for the furnishing of the information and the completion of the forms referred to in that subsection and by a sufficient number of copies of the forms. (SOR/83-817)

[¶24-730i]

Sec. 55.2. (1) Where a constrained share corporation that has provisions in its articles imposing a constraint referred to in paragraph (*c*) of the definition "constraint" in section 51 (*a*) has sent a notice referred to in subsection 55.1(3) to a person shown in the securities register of the corporation as the holder of shares, and

(*b*) has not sold, pursuant to subsection 46(1) of the Act, a share in respect of which the notice was sent,

and the corporation changes its conclusion that the share is owned, or the directors of the corporation change their determination made in accordance with subsection 55.1(2) that the share may be owned, contrary to such constraint, or there is a change in the reason for such conclusion or determination, the corporation shall forthwith send by registered mail to that person a notice of such change of conclusion or determination including the reason therefor or a notice of such change in the reason for such conclusion or determination, as the case may be. (SOR/83-817)

[¶24-730j]

(2) Where a corporation sends a notice under subsection (1), the corporation shall, at the time the notice is sent, enter or cause to be entered in the securities register of the corporation the particulars of such notice including the date on which it was sent. (SOR/83-817)

[¶24-730k]

Sec. 55.3. (1) No share shall be sold by a constrained share corporation pursuant to subsection 46(1) of the Act unless

(*a*) the corporation has sent the notices referred to in subsections 55.1(1) and (3) to the person shown in the securities register of the corporation as the holder of the share;

(*b*) not less than 150 days but not more than 300 days have elapsed from the day on which the notice referred to in subsection 55.1(1) was sent to the holder of the share;

(*c*) not less than 60 days but not more than 150 days have elapsed from the day on which the notice referred to in subsection 55.1(3) was sent to the holder of the share;

(*d*) the corporation has concluded that the share is owned, or the directors of the corporation have determined in accordance with subsection 55.1(2) that the share may be owned, contrary to a constraint referred to in paragraph (*c*) of the definition "constraint" in section 51 and, at the time of sale, the corporation has no reasonable grounds on which to change its conclusion or the directors of the corporation have no reasonable grounds on which to change their determination, as the case may be;

(*e*) the sale takes place

(i) on any stock exchange where shares of the corporation are listed and posted for trading, or

(ii) where shares of the corporation are not listed and posted for trading on any stock exchange, in such other manner as the directors of the corporation determine to be appropriate; and

(*f*) the corporation sells the share with a view to obtaining the best sale price available in the circumstances at the time of sale. (SOR/83-817)

[¶24-730l]

(2) No share in respect of which a notice is sent in accordance with subsection 55.1(1) shall be sold by a constrained share corporation pursuant to subsection 46(1) of the Act if a transfer of such share is registered in the securities register of the corporation after the notice was sent unless the corporation again complies with the requirements set out in this Part respecting the sale of such share. (SOR/83-817)

[¶24-730m]

Sec. 55.4. (1) Forthwith upon a sale of shares by a constrained share corporation pursuant to subsection 46(1) of the Act, the corporation shall

(a) register the transfer or a notice of the sale of such shares or cause the transfer or a notice of the sale of such shares to be registered in the securities register of the corporation; and

(b) send a notice of such sale to the person shown in the securities register of the corporation as the holder of the shares at the time of the sale.

[¶24-730n]

(2) The notice referred to in paragraph (1)(b) shall

(a) state the number of shares sold;

(b) identify the certificate representing the shares sold, by certificate number or otherwise;

(c) state the date and manner of sale;

(d) state the manner in which the person entitled to receive the net proceeds of the sale pursuant to subsection 46(3) of the Act may obtain such proceeds;

(e) state that the corporation concluded that the shares were owned, or that the directors determined in accordance with subsection 55.1(2) that the shares may be owned, contrary to a constraint referred to in paragraph (c) of the definition "constraint" in section 51 and state the reason why the corporation so concluded or the directors so determined, as the case may be; and

(f) contain a statement, if not all of the shares of the holder represented by a certificate were sold, that not all of such shares were sold and that a certificate representing the shares that were not sold will be issued upon surrender for cancellation of the certificate representing the shares sold. (SOR/83-817)

[¶24-730o]

Sec. 55.5. For the purposes of subsection 47(1) of the Act, the proceeds of a sale by a constrained share corporation under subsection 46(1) of the Act shall be deposited in an interest bearing account with a bank in Canada to which the *Bank Act* applies or a trust company in Canada to which the *Trust Companies Act* applies or invested in any investment authorized under subsection 63(1) of the *Canadian and British Insurance Companies Act*. (SOR/83-817 s. 6.)

[¶24-730p]

Sec. 55.6. Section 56 applies to a constrained share corporation that has provisions in its articles imposing a constraint referred to in paragraph (a) or (b) of the definition "constraint" in section 51. (SOR/83-817 s. 6.)

Disclosure of Beneficial Ownership

[¶24-732]

Sec. 56. (1) Subject to section 103 of the Act, the directors of a constrained share corporation may make, amend or repeal any by-laws required to administer the constrained share provisions set out in the articles of the corporation, including by-laws

(a) to require any person in whose name shares of the corporation are registered to furnish a statutory declaration under the *Canada Evidence Act* declaring whether

(i) the shareholder is the beneficial owner of the shares of the corporation or holds them for a beneficial owner,

(ii) the shareholder is an associate of any other shareholder, and

(iii) the shareholder or beneficial owner is a Canadian,

and declaring any further facts that the directors consider relevant;

(*b*) to require any person seeking to have a transfer of a voting share registered in his name or to have a voting share issued to him to furnish a declaration similar to the declaration a shareholder may be required to furnish under paragraph (*a*); and

(*c*) to determine the circumstances in which any declarations are required their form and the times when they are to be furnished.

[¶24-735]

(2) Where a person is required to furnish a declaration pursuant to a by-law made under subsection (1), the directors may refuse to register a transfer of a voting share in his name or to issue a voting share to him until that person has furnished the declaration.

[¶24-738]

(3) In administering the constrained share provisions set out in the articles of a constrained share corporation, the directors of the corporation may rely upon

(*a*) a statement made in a declaration referred to in subsection (1) or (2); and

(*b*) the knowledge of a director, officer, employee or agent of the corporation.

[¶24-741]

(4) Where the directors are required to determine the total number of voting shares of a constrained share corporation held by or on behalf of persons other than Canadians, the directors may rely upon the sum of

(*a*) the voting shares held by every shareholder whose latest address as shown in the share register is outside Canada; and

(*b*) the voting shares held by every shareholder whose latest address as shown in the share register is in Canada but who, to the knowledge of a director, officer, employee or agent of the corporation is not a Canadian.

[¶24-744]

(5) For the purposes of subsection (4), the directors may rely upon the share register of the constrained share corporation as of any date after the day on which the corporation became a constrained share corporation but that date shall not be more than four months before the day on which the determination is made.

References and Definitions for the Purposes of Section 174 of the Act

[¶24-747]

Sec. 57. (1) For the purposes of paragraph 174(1)(*b*) of the Act,

(*a*) the following laws of Canada or a province are prescribed:

(i) the *Air Regulations* under the *Aeronautics Act*,

(ii) Repealed by SOR/88-491, gazetted October 12, 1988.

(iii) the *Canada Oil and Gas Land Regulations* and Canada Oil and Gas Drilling Production Regulations under the *Territorial Lands Act* and *Public Lands Grants Act*,

(iv) the *Broadcasting Act*,

(v) the *Northern Mineral Exploration Assistance Regulations* under the *Appropriation Acts*,

    (vi) section 19 of the *Income Tax Act*,

    (vii) the *Investment Companies Act*,

    (viii) any other law of Canada or of a province with similar requirements in relation to Canadian ownership,

    (ix) the *Securities Act* (Ontario) and any regulations made thereunder,

    (x) the *Securities Act* (Quebec) and any regulations made thereunder,

    (xi) the *National Transportation Act*, 1987 and any regulations made thereunder; and

  (b) "financial intermediary" includes a bank, trust company, loan company, insurance company, investment company and a body corporate carrying on business as a securities broker, dealer or underwriter. (SOR/88-63)

[¶24-750]

(2) For the purposes of subsections 32(1), 46(1) and 49(10) and paragraph 174(1)(c) of the Act, the following laws of Canada are prescribed:

  (a) the *Canada Oil and Gas Act* and any regulations made thereunder; and

  (b) the *Petroleum Incentives Program Act* and any regulations made thereunder.

Part VIII
Take-over Bids

Exempt Offer Circumstances Prescribed

[¶24-753]

Sec. 58. For the purposes of paragraph (b) of the definition "exempt offer" in section 194 of the Act, an offer to purchase shares through a stock exchange or in the over-the-counter market is an exempt offer in the following circumstances, namely, where the offer constitutes

  (a) a redemption of redeemable shares under section 36 of the Act;

  (b) an offer, other than an offer by a corporation to purchase its own shares, made in accordance with the by-laws, regulations, rules or policies governing the stock exchange or the over-the-counter market unless

    (i) a premium over the most recent bid price is offered and a public announcement of the offer is made by or on behalf of the person making the offer,

    (ii) a broker acting for the person making the offer performs services beyond the customary broker's functions or receives more than the customary broker's commissions, or

    (iii) the person making the offer or a person acting for that person solicits or arranges for the solicitation of orders to sell shares of the offeree corporation;

  (c) an offer to purchase shares, including an offer by a corporation to purchase its own shares in connection with which a practice specified in subparagraphs (b)(i) to (iii) is used, through a stock exchange in Canada made in accordance with the by-laws and rules of the exchange and for which a notice of a stock exchange take-over bid has been accepted by the exchange if

    (i) an advertisement containing the information required by the by-laws and rules of the exchange and the information required in the take-over bid circular pursuant to sections 59 to 65, as applicable, is published in clearly readable type in at least one major daily newspaper in each province of Canada in which shareholders reside, or, if fewer than one hundred shareholders reside in a province, a copy of that advertisement is sent to each shareholder in that province, and

(ii) a copy of every document sent to a stock exchange or published in a newspaper is sent concurrently to the Director; and

(*d*) an offer by a corporation to purchase its own shares through a stock exchange or in the over-the-counter market if none of the practices specified in subparagraphs (*b*)(i) to (iii) is used in connection with the offer and

(i) a notice containing the date on which any time period mentioned in the offer begins or ends and the information required by paragraph 59(*d*) and paragraphs 63(1) (*a*), (*g*), (*h*), (*i*) and (*s*) is sent to each shareholder of the corporation resident in Canada and to the Director at least ten days before any shares are so purchased,

(ii) an advertisement containing the information specified in subparagraph (i) is published in clearly readable type in at least one major daily newspaper in each province of Canada in which shareholders reside, at least ten days before any shares are so purchased, or, if fewer than one hundred shareholders reside in a province, a copy of that advertisement is sent to each shareholder in that province at least ten days before any shares are so purchased and in either case a copy of the advertisement is sent concurrently to the Director, or

(iii) where the offer is made on or after October 26, 1987, the offer is made in accordance with the by-laws, rules, policies and practices of the stock exchange.

[¶24-754]

Sec. 58.1.   An offer to purchase shares referred to in paragraph (*b*) of the definition "take-over bid" in subsection 206(1) of the Act shall be made in accordance with sections 193 to 203 of the Act. (SOR/79-513, s. 3, effective June 29, 1979.)

Take-Over Bid Circular
Under Subsection 198(1) of the Act

[¶24-756]

Sec. 59.   A take-over bid circular referred to in subsection 198(1) of the Act shall contain the following information:

(*a*) the identity and business background of the offeror;

(*b*) a statement of the withdrawal rights of offerees under paragraphs 195(*a*) and 197(*a*) of the Act and the dates before which and after which offerees who deposit their shares may exercise those rights;

(*c*) the date on which any other time period mentioned in the circular begins or ends;

(*d*) the details of the method and time of payment of the money or other consideration to be paid for the shares of the offeree corporation;

(*e*) where the obligation of the offeror to take up and pay for shares under a take-over bid is conditional upon a minimum number of shares being deposited, the details of the condition;

(*f*) the number, without duplication, and designation of any securities of the offeree corporation beneficially owned or over which control or direction is exercised by

(i) the offeror,

(ii) an associate or affiliate of the offeror,

(iii) each director and each officer of the offeror and their respective associates, and

(iv) any person known to the directors or officers of the offeror who beneficially owns or exercises control or direction over shares of the offeror carrying more than 10 per cent of the votes attached to shares of the offeror, or, if none are so owned, controlled or directed, a statement to that effect;

(g) where known to the offeror or the directors or officers of the offeror, the number and designation of any shares of the offeree corporation traded by a person referred to in paragraph (f) during the 6 months preceding the date of the take-over bid, including the purchase or sale price and the date of each transaction;

(h) details of any contract, arrangement or understanding, formal or informal, between the offeror and

(i) any shareholder of the offeree corporation with respect to the take-over bid, and

(ii) any person with respect to any shares of the offeree corporation in relation to the bid;

(i) where the shares of the offeree corporation are to be paid for wholly or partly in money, details of any arrangements that have been made by the offeror to ensure that the required funds are available to take up and pay for the shares of the offeree corporation deposited pursuant to the take-over bid;

(j) details of any contract or arrangement made or proposed to be made between the offeror and any of the directors or officers of the offeree corporation, including details of any payment of other benefit proposed to be made or given by way of compensation in respect of loss of office or in respect of their remaining in or retiring from office if the take-over bid is successful;

(k) details of any business relationship between the offeror and the offeree corporation that is material to either of them;

(l) if a purpose of the take-over bid is to acquire effective control of the business of the offeree corporation, any plans or proposals that the offeror has to liquidate the offeree corporation, to sell, lease or exchange all or substantially all its assets or to amalgamate it with any other body corporate, or to make any other major change in its business, corporate structure, management or personnel;

(m) if the offeror intends to purchase shares of the offeree corporation other than pursuant to the take-over bid, a statement of his intention to do so and a summary of the provisions of paragraph 197 of the Act;

(n) if the offeror intends to invoke the right referred to in subsection 206 of the Act to acquire the shares of offerees who do not accept the take-over bid,

(i) a statement of that intention, and

(ii) a statement of the right of an offeree to dissent and to demand the fair value of his shares and the method by which it may be exercised;

(o) where reasonably ascertainable, a summary showing, in reasonable detail for the 6 months preceding the date of the take-over bid, the volume of trading and price range of the shares sought to be acquired pursuant to the take-over bid;

(p) particulars of any information known to the offeror that indicates any material change in the financial position or prospects of the offeree corporation since the date of the most recent publicly filed interim or annual financial statements of the offeree corporation; and

(q) all other material facts known to the offeror.

Take-Over Bid Circular Under
Section 200 of the Act

[¶24-759]

Sec. 60. Where a take-over bid states that the consideration for the shares of the offeree corporation is to be, in whole or in part, securities of the offeror or any other body corporate, the take-over bid circular shall contain, in addition to the information required by section 59, (*a*) the information required to be included in the take-over bid circular under the laws of

(i) Alberta,

(ii) British Columbia,

(iii) Manitoba,

(iv) Ontario,

(v) Quebec,

(vi) Saskatchewan, or

(viii) the United States, if the bid is made in the United States;

(*b*) the financial statements of the offeror on a *pro forma* basis as of the date of the offeror's financial statement giving effect to the take-over bid based on the information in the most recent publicly filed financial statements of the offeree corporation;

(*c*) a description of the financial statement of the offeree corporation relied upon and of the basis of preparation of the *pro forma* financial statements; and

(*d*) basic and fully diluted earnings per share figures prepared in accordance with Part V based upon the *pro forma* financial statements.

[¶24-762]

Sec. 61. A take-over bid circular referred to in section 60 shall contain an introductory summary of its contents, not exceeding 6 pages in length, that highlights the salient features of the take-over bid, including a summary of the financial information, with appropriate cross-references to the more detailed information in the circular.

Where Offeror Has Effective Control

[¶24-765]

Sec. 62. (1) If an offeror exercises effective control over the offeree corporation when a take-over bid is made, the take-over bid circular, in addition to the information required by sections 59 to 61 may contain

(*a*) the information required to be included in a directors' circular under section 68 that has not already been set out in that take-over bid circular; and

(*b*) a statement indicating whether the remuneration of the directors of the offeror and of the offeree corporation will be affected if the take-over bid is successful and, if so, details of the effect.

[¶24-768]

(2) A take-over bid circular that complies with the requirements of subsection (1) is the directors' circular required by subsection 201(1) of the Act.

Where Repurchase of Own Shares Involved

[¶24-771]

Sec. 63. (1) Where a take-over bid is made by a corporation to repurchase its own shares, the take-over bid circular shall contain, instead of the information required under section 59, the following information:

(*a*) the identity of the offeror;

(*b*) the information required by paragraphs 59(*b*) to (*e*), (*h*) to (*j*) and (*m*), and paragraphs 68(*i*) to (*k*), (*q*) and (*r*);

(*c*) where reasonably ascertainable, a summary showing, in reasonable detail for the 12 months preceding the date of the take-over bid, the volume of trading and price range of the shares sought to be acquired pursuant to the take-over bid;

(*d*) the number, without duplication, and designation of any securities of the corporation beneficially owned or over which control or direction is exercised by

(i) each director and each officer of the corporation and their respective associates,

(ii) any person known to the directors or officers who beneficially owns or exercises control or direction over shares of the corporation carrying more than 10 per cent of the votes attached to shares of the corporation, and

(iii) an associate or affiliate of the corporation,

or, if none are so owned, controlled or directed, a statement to that effect;

(*e*) where known to the directors or officers of the corporation, the number and designation of any shares of the corporation traded by a person referred to in paragraph (*d*) during the 12 months preceding the date of the take-over bid, including the purchase or sale price and the date of each transaction;

(*f*) the number and designation of any shares of the corporation traded by the corporation during the 12 months preceding the date of the take-over bid, including the purchase or sale price, the date and the purpose of each transaction;

(*g*) where known to the directors or officers of the corporation, whether any person referred to in paragraph (*d*) accepted or intends to accept the offer in respect of any shares of the corporation;

(*h*) details of the effects of the take-over bid on the corporation, the persons referred to in paragraph (*d*) and the offerees;

(*i*) the purpose of the take-over bid, including any plans or proposals to liquidate the corporation, to sell, lease or exchange all or substantially all of its assets or to amalgamate it with any other body corporate, or to make any major change in its business, corporate structure, management or personnel;

(*j*) financial statements of the corporation prepared for public filing subsequent to the date of its most recent publicly filed financial statements and not previously sent to shareholders;

(*k*) the information required to be included in a directors' circular by paragraphs 68(*o*) and (*p*);

(*l*) the information required to be included in a take-over bid circular by paragraph 60(*d*);

(*m*) a summary of any appraisal, known to the directors or officers of the corporation, regarding the corporation, its material assets or securities within the 2 years preceding the date of the take-over bid;

(*n*) if shares of the class subject to the take-over bid were offered to the public by the corporation during the 5 years preceding the date of the take-over bid, the offering price per share, and the aggregate proceeds received by the corporation;

(*o*) the frequency and amount of dividends with respect to shares of the corporation during the 2 years preceding the date of the take-over bid, any restrictions on the corporation's ability to pay dividends and any plan or intention to declare a dividend or to alter the dividend policy of the corporation;

(*p*) a general description of the consequences of the take-over bid to the corporation and the offerees under the *Income Tax Act*;

(*q*) if offerees are to be solicited otherwise than by mail, the identity of all persons employed or retained by the corporation for that purpose, the material features of any contract or arrangement for the solicitation, the parties to the contract or arrangement and the cost or anticipated cost thereof;

(r) a statement of the expenses incurred or to be incurred in connection with the take-over bid; and

(s) all other material facts known to the directors or officers of the corporation.

[¶24-774]

(2) A take-over bid circular that complies with the requirements of subsection (1) is the directors' circular required by subsection 201(1) of the Act.

Statement of Directors' Approval

[¶24-777]

Sec. 64. Where the offeror is a body corporate, a take-over bid circular shall contain a statement, signed by one or more directors, that the contents and the sending of the circular have been approved by the directors of the offeror.

Experts' Consent

[¶24-780]

Sec. 65. Where a report, opinion or statement of a person referred to in subsection 202(1) of the Act is included in a take-over bid circular, his consent in writing shall be reproduced in the circular.

Certificate Required

[¶24-783]

Sec. 66. A copy of a take-over bid circular sent to the Director pursuant to subsection 198(1) of the Act shall be accompanied by a certificate signed by the offeror or, if the offeror is a body corporate, by a certificate signed by a director, officer or agent of the offeror, certifying that a copy of the circular has been sent to each director and to each shareholder of the offeree corporation resident in Canada.

Amendment to Take-Over Bid

[¶24-786]

Sec. 67. (1) Sections 59 to 66 apply to an amendment of the terms of a take-over bid circular, including a notice under subparagraph 197(f)(ii) of the Act, but it is not necessary to repeat in an amendment of a take-over bid circular any information contained in the circular that continues to be accurate.

[¶24-789]

(2) An amendment to a take-over bid circular shall correct any material statement in the take-over bid circular that is discovered to be misleading or that has become misleading by reason of events subsequent to the date of the circular.

Contents of Directors' Circular

[¶24-792]

Sec. 68. A directors' circular referred to in subsection 201(1) of the Act shall contain the following information:

(a) the number, without duplication, and designation of any securities of the offeree corporation beneficially owned or over which control or direction is exercised

(i) by each director and each officer of the offeree corporation and their associates, and

(ii) where known to the directors or officers, by each person who beneficially owns or exercises control or direction over shares of the offeree corporation carrying more than 10 per cent of the votes attached to shares of the offeree corporation,

or, if none are so owned, controlled or directed, a statement to that effect;

(b) where the offeror is a body corporate the number, without duplication, and designation of any securities of the offeror beneficially owned or over which control or direction is exercised

(i) by each director and each officer of the offeree corporation and their associates, and

(ii) where known to the directors or officers, by each person who beneficially owns or exercises control or direction over shares of the offeree corporation carrying more than 10 per cent of the votes attached to shares of the offeree corporation,

or, if none are so owned, controlled or directed, a statement to that effect;

(c) where known to the directors or officers of the offeree corporation, the number and designation of any shares of the offeree corporation or of the offeror traded by a person referred to in paragraph (a) or (b) during the 6 months preceding the date of the takeover bid, including the purchase or sale price and the date of each transaction;

(d) where the offeror is a body corporate, the number and designation of any securities of the offeror beneficially owned or over which control or direction is exercised by the offeree corporation;

(e) the number and designation of any shares of the offeree corporation or of the offeror traded by the offeree corporation during the 6 months preceding the date of the take-over bid, including the purchase or sale price, the date and the purpose of each such transaction;

(f) where the directors

(i) make a recommendation in relation to the take-over bid, a statement of the recommendation and the reasons for the recommendation, or

(ii) do not recommend acceptance or rejection of a take-over bid, the reasons for their failure to make a recommendation and, if a reason is a division among the directors, the nature of the division;

(g) whether

(i) a director or officer of the offeree corporation or an associate of such director or officer, or

(ii) where known to the directors or officers, any person who beneficially owns or exercises control or direction over shares of the offeree corporation carrying more than 10 per cent of the votes attached to shares of the offeree corporation,

has accepted or intends to accept the offer in respect of any shares of the offeree corporation;

(h) whether

(i) a director or officer of the offeree corporation or an associate of a director or officer, or

(ii) where known to the directors or officers, any person who beneficially owns or exercises control or direction over shares of the offeree corporation carrying more than 10 per cent of the votes attached to shares of the offeree corporation,

has any interest in any material contract to which the offeror is a party and, if so, details of the nature and extent of the interest;

(i) details of all service contracts of directors and officers of the offeree corporation or any of its affiliates with more than a 12 month period remaining or, if there are no such contracts, a statement of that fact;

(*j*) if a contract referred to in paragraph (*i*) has been entered into or amended within the 6 months preceding the date of the take-over bid, the details of the contract replaced or amended;

(*k*) details of any contract or arrangement made or proposed to be made between the offeror and any of the directors or officers of the offeree corporation, including details of any payment or other benefit proposed to be made or given by way of compensation in respect of loss of office or in respect of their remaining in or retiring from office if the take-over bid is successful;

(*l*) where known to the directors or officers of the offeree corporation, the details of any special contract, arrangement or understanding, formal or informal, made or proposed to be made between the offeror and any shareholder of the offeree corporation with respect to the take-over bid;

(*m*) where reasonably ascertainable, a summary showing, in reasonable detail for the 6 months preceding the date of the take-over bid, the volume of trading and the price range of the shares sought to be acquired pursuant to the take-over bid if such information is not disclosed in the take-over bid circular or if, in the opinion of the directors of the offeree corporation, such information is not adequately disclosed therein;

(*n*) financial statements of the offeree corporation prepared for public filing subsequent to the date of its most recent publicly filed financial statements and not previously sent to shareholders;

(*o*) where the information contained in the most recent financial statements of the offeree corporation is materially misleading because of events subsequent to its preparation, a statement of the material events necessary to correct any such misleading representations;

(*p*) details of any information known to any director or officer of the offeree corporation concerning any material change in the prospects of the offeree corporation since the date of the last financial statements of the offeree corporation;

(*q*) where a director or officer of the offeree corporation intends to purchase shares of the offeree corporation during a take-over bid or where he knows of the existence of such an intention on the part of any person, a statement of the intention and the purpose of such purchases, or if no such intention is known to exist, a statement to that effect;

(*r*) a statement made by a director of an offeree corporation under subsection 201(5) of the Act; and

(*s*) all other material facts known to the directors or officers of the offeree corporation.

Notice of Directors' Circular

[¶24-795]

Sec. 69. (1) A notice referred to in subsection 201(2) of the Act shall contain,

(*a*) if practicable, the information required by section 68 and, if any matter required to be disclosed has not been determined, a statement to that effect; and

(*b*) a statement that a directors' circular will follow and the date by which the directors' circular is required to be sent in accordance with subsection 201(4) of the Act.

[¶24-798]

(2) It is not necessary to repeat in a directors' circular that follows a notice under subsection 201(2) of the Act any information contained in the notice.

[¶24-801]

(3) A directors' circular shall correct any material statement in a notice under subsection 201(2) of the Act that is discovered to be misleading or that has become misleading by reason of events subsequent to the date of the notice.

Report to Accompany Financial Statements

[¶24-804]

Sec. 70. (1) Where financial statements accompany or form part of a directors' circular, the statements shall be prepared in the manner prescribed for the financial statements in Part V.

[¶24-807]

(2) The financial statements referred to in subsection (1), if not reported upon by the auditor of the corporation, shall be accompanied by a report of the chief financial officer of the corporation stating that the financial statements have not been audited but have been prepared in accordance with Part V.

Statement of Directors' Approval

[¶24-810]

Sec. 71. A directors' circular and a notice under subsection 201(2) of the Act shall contain a statement, signed by one or more directors, that the contents and the sending of the circular have been approved by the directors of the offeree corporation.

Experts' Consent

[¶24-813]

Sec. 72. Where a report, opinion or statement of a person referred to in subsection 202(1) of the Act is included in a directors' circular, his consent in writing shall be reproduced in the circular.

Certificate Required

[¶24-816]

Sec. 73. A copy of a directors' circular sent to the Director pursuant to subsection 201(1) of the Act shall be accompanied by a certificate signed by a director of the offeree corporation certifying that a copy of the circular has been sent to the offeror, to each director and to each shareholder of the offeree corporation resident in Canada.

Part IX

Rules of Procedure for Applications for Exemptions

Application

[¶24-819]

Sec. 74. This Part applies to every application for an exemption under subsection 2(8), 10(2), 82(3), 127(8), 151(1), section 156, subsection 160(3), 163(4), 171(2) or 187(11) of the Act.

Form for Application

[¶24-822]

Sec. 75. An application for an exemption shall be made to the Director in Form 27.

Time of Filing Applications

[¶24-825]

Sec. 76. (1) An application for an exemption under

(a) subsection 2(8) of the Act may be made at any time;

(b) subsections 10(2) and 187(11) of the Act shall be before the date of issue of the certificate of continuance referred to in subsection 187(4) of the Act;

(c) subsection 82(3) of the Act shall be made at least 30 days before the corporation is required to comply with Part VII [Part VIII] of the Act;

(d) subsection 127(8) of the Act shall be made at least 10 days before the insider is required to send the insider report referred to in section 127 of the Act;

(e) subsection 151(1) of the Act shall be made before the date of the notice referred to in subsection 149(1) of the Act;

(f) section 156 or subsection 160(3) of the Act shall be made at least 60 days before the documents in respect of which the exemption is requested are to be sent to the Director;

(g) subsection 163(3) of the Act may be made at any time; and

(h) subsection 171(2) of the Act may be made at any time.

[¶24-828]

(2) Notwithstanding subsection (1), the Director may on such reasonable conditions as he thinks fit, extend the time for making an application for an exemption.

Notice by Director of Decision

[¶24-831]

Sec. 77. The Director shall, within 30 days after receipt of an application for an exemption, grant the exemption requested or send to the applicant written notice of his refusal together with reasons therefor.

General

[¶24-834]

Sec. 78. The Director may request that an applicant for an exemption furnish him with further information or that any other person furnish him with information in writing that is relevant to the application.

[¶24-837]

Sec. 79. The Director shall furnish the applicant for an exemption with a copy of any information received from any other person under section 78 and shall allow the applicant a reasonable opportunity to respond in writing.

[¶24-840]

Sec. 80. Where an applicant for an exemption or a person from whom the Director has requested information under section 78 does not provide the information within a time specified by the Director, the Director may deal with the application without regard to the information.

[¶24-843]

Sec. 81. If the Director does not grant an exemption or send written notice of his refusal within the time specified in section 77, the applicant may exercise his rights under section 246 of the Act as if the Director had refused the exemption.

Part X
Prescribed Fees

[¶24-846]

Sec. 82. (1) The fee in respect of the filing, examination or copying of any document or in respect of any action that the Director is required or authorized to take under the Act shall be the fee set out in Schedule II and, except in the case of the fee payable under subitem 1(c) or (d) of that Schedule, shall be paid to the Director on the filing, examination or copying of the document or before the Director takes the action in respect of which the fee is payable. (SOR/81-3; SOR/81-868)

[¶24-849]

(2) No fee is payable for the issuance by the Director of

(a) a certificate of amendment issued pursuant to section 178 of the Act, if the only purpose of the amendment is to add an English or French version to a corporation's name, or to replace a corporate name that the Director has directed be changed pursuant to subsection 12(2) or (4) of the Act;

(b) a certificate of dissolution issued pursuant to subsection 210(5) or 211(15) of the Act;

(c) a certificate of intent to dissolve issued pursuant to subsection 211(5) of the Act; or

(d) a certificate of discontinuance issued pursuant to subsection 188(7) of the Act. (SOR/91-567, P.C. 1991-1904, s. 1.)

[¶24-850]

(3) No fee is payable by a department or agency of the Government of Canada or the government of a province for

(a) searches; or

(b) copies of documents under section 266 of the Act.

(SOR/81-3)

List of Forms

[¶24-852]

Form No.		Page
1.	Articles of incorporation	182
2.	Certificate of incorporation	184
3.	Notice of registered office or notice of change of registered office	185
4.	Articles of amendment	187
5.	Certificate of amendment	189
6.	Notice of directors or notice of change of directors	190
7.	Restated articles of incorporation	192
8.	Restated certificate of incorporation	194
9.	Articles of amalgamation	195
10.	Certificate of amalgamation	197
11.	Articles of continuance	198
12.	Certificate of continuance	200
13.	Certificate of discontinuance	201
14.	Articles of reorganization	202
14.1.	Articles of arrangement	204
15.	Articles of revival	206
16.	Certificate of revival	208
17.	Articles of dissolution	209
18.	Certificate of dissolution	211
19.	Statement of intent to dissolve or statement of revocation of intent to dissolve	212
20.	Certificate of intent to dissolve	214
21.	Certificate of revocation of intent to dissolve	215
22.	Annual return	216
23.	Revoked by SOR/86-365, s. 9, gazetted April 16, 1986	
*24.	Insider report	218
26.	Statement of executive remuneration	220
27.	Application for exemption	222

* Forms 24 and 25 revoked and replaced with single Form 24. Effective September 20, 1990. (SOR/90-660).

Schedule I

[¶24-853]

Form 1. Articles of incorporation

Canada Business Corporations Act	Loi régissant les sociétés par actions de régime fédéral	" FORM 1 ARTICLES OF INCORPORATION (SECTION 6)	FORMULE 1 STATUTS CONSTITUTIFS (ARTICLE 6)

1 — Name of corporation

Dénomination de la société

2 — The place in Canada where the registered office is to be situated

Lieu au Canada où doit être situé le siège social

3 — The classes and any maximum number of shares that the corporation is authorized to issue

Catégories et tout nombre maximal d'actions que la société est autorisée à émettre

4 — Restrictions, if any, on share transfers

Restrictions sur le transfert des actions, s'il y a lieu

5 — Number (or minimum and maximum number) of directors

Nombre (ou nombre minimal et maximal) d'administrateurs

6 — Restrictions, if any, on business the corporation may carry on

Limites imposées à l'activité commerciale de la société, s'il y a lieu

7 — Other provisions, if any

Autres dispositions, s'il y a lieu

8 — Incorporators — Fondateurs

Name(s) — Nom(s)	Address (include postal code) Adresse (inclure le code postal)	Signature

FOR DEPARTMENTAL USE ONLY — À L'USAGE DU MINISTÈRE SEULEMENT
Corporation No. — Nº de la société

Filed — Déposée

CCA 1385 (03-89) 46

Canada Business Corporations Act

Articles of Incorporation
FORM 1
INSTRUCTIONS

Format
Documents required to be sent to the Director pursuant to the *Canada Business Corporations Act* (CBCA) must conform to sections 5 to 10 of the *Canada Business Corporations Regulations.*

Item 1
Set out the proposed corporate name that complies with sections 10 and 12 of the Act. Articles of incorporation must be accompanied by a Canada-biased NUANS search report dated not more than ninety (90) days prior to the receipt of the articles by the Director. On request, a number name may be assigned under subsection 11(2) of the Act, without a search.

Item 2
Set out the name of the place and province within Canada where the registered office is to be situated. A specific street address is not required.

Item 3
Set out the details required by paragraph 6(1)(c) of the Act, including details of the rights, privileges, restrictions and conditions attached to each class of shares. All shares must be without nominal or par value and must comply with the provisions of Part V of the Act.

Item 4
If restrictions are to be placed on the right to transfer shares of the corporation, set out a statement to this effect and the nature of such restrictions.

Item 5
State the number of directors. If cumulative voting is permitted, the number of directors must be invariable; otherwise it is permissible to specify a minimum and maximum number of directors.

Item 6
If restrictions are to be placed on the business the corporation may carry on, set out the restrictions.

Item 7
Set out any provisions, permitted by the Act or Regulations to be set out in the by-laws of the corporation, that are to form part of the articles, including any pre-emptive rights or cumulative voting provisions.

Item 8
Each incorporator must state his or her name and residential address, and affix his or her signature. If an incorporator is a body corporate, that name shall be the name of the body corporate, the address shall be that of its registered office, and the articles shall be signed by a person authorized by the body corporate.

Other Documents
The articles must be accompanied by a Notice of Registered Office (Form 3), and a Notice of Directors (Form 6). Note that a Form 6 must be sent to the Director within fifteen (15) days of any change after directors in accordance with subsection 113(1) of the Act.

Other Notices
If a proposed corporation is to engage in
(a) the construction or operation of a pipeline for the transmission of oil or gas as defined in the *National Energy Board Act,*
(b) the construction or operation of a commodity pipeline as defined in the *National Transportation Act, 1987,*
(c) the business of an investment company within the meaning of the *Investment Companies Act,*
the incorporator shall inform the minister of the department or agency that regulates such business.

The information you provide in this document is collected under the authority of the *Canada Business Corporations Act* and will be stored in personal information bank number CCA/P-PU-093. Personal information that you provide is protected under the provisions of the *Privacy Act.* However, public disclosure pursuant to section 266 of the *Canada Business Corporations Act* is permitted under the *Privacy Act.*

Completed documents in duplicate and fees payable to the Receiver General for Canada are to be sent to:

The Director, Canada Business Corporations Act
Place du Portage
Hull, Quebec, Canada
K1A 0C9

Loi régissant les sociétés par actions de régime fédéral

Statuts constitutifs
FORMULE 1
INSTRUCTIONS

Présentation
Tous les documents dont l'envoi au directeur est exigé par la *Loi régissant les sociétés par actions de régime fédéral* doivent être conformes aux articles 5 à 10 du *Règlement sur les sociétés par actions de régime fédéral.*

Rubrique 1
Indiquer une dénomination sociale qui satisfait aux exigences des articles 10 et 12 de la Loi. Les statuts constitutifs doivent être accompagnés d'un rapport de recherche NUANS couvrant le Canada, dont la date remonte à quatre-vingt-dix (90) jours ou moins avant la date de réception des statuts par le directeur. Si un numéro matricule est demandé en guise de dénomination sociale, il peut être assigné, sans recherche préalable, en vertu du paragraphe 11(2) de la Loi.

Rubrique 2
Indiquer le nom de l'endroit et de la province au Canada où le siège social doit être situé. Une adresse précise n'est pas requise.

Rubrique 3
Indiquer les détails requis par l'alinéa 6(1)c) de la Loi, y compris les détails des droits, privilèges, restrictions et conditions attachés à chaque catégorie d'actions. Toutes les actions doivent être sans valeur nominale ni sans valeur au pair et doivent être conformes aux dispositions de la partie V de la Loi.

Rubrique 4
Si le droit de transfert des actions de la société doit être restreint, inclure une déclaration à cet effet et indiquer la nature de ces restrictions.

Rubrique 5
Indiquer le nombre d'administrateurs. Si un vote cumulatif est prévu, ce nombre doit être fixe; autrement, il est permis de spécifier un nombre minimal et maximal d'administrateurs.

Rubrique 6
Si des limites doivent être imposées à l'activité commerciale de la société, les indiquer.

Rubrique 7
Indiquer les dispositions que la Loi ou le règlement permet d'énoncer dans les règlements administratifs de la société et qui doivent faire partie des statuts, y compris les dispositions relatives au vote cumulatif ou aux droits de préemption.

Rubrique 8
Chaque fondateur doit donner son nom, son adresse domiciliaire et apposer sa signature. Si un fondateur est une personne morale, le nom doit être celui de la personne morale, l'adresse doit être celle de son siège social, et les statuts doivent être signés par une personne autorisée par la personne morale.

Autres documents
Les statuts doivent être accompagnés d'un avis de désignation du lieu du siège social (formule 3) et d'une liste des administrateurs (formule 6). Une formule 6 doit être envoyée au directeur dans les quinze (15) jours suivant tout changement dans la composition du conseil d'administration conformément au paragraphe 113(1) de la Loi.

Autres avis
Si la société projetée doit effectuer :
a) la construction ou l'exploitation d'un pipeline pour le transport du pétrole ou du gaz, défini dans la *Loi sur l'Office national de l'énergie,*
b) la construction ou l'exploitation d'un productoduc défini dans la *Loi de 1987 sur les transports nationaux,*
c) le commerce d'une société d'investissement au sens de la *Loi sur les sociétés d'investissement,*
les fondateurs doivent informer le ministre responsable du ministère ou l'agence qui réglemente ces entreprises.

Les renseignements que vous fournissez dans ce document sont recueillis en vertu de la *Loi régissant les sociétés par actions de régime fédéral,* et seront emmagasinés dans le fichier de renseignements personnels MCC/P-PU-093. Les renseignements personnels que vous fournissez sont protégés par les dispositions de la *Loi sur la protection des renseignements personnels.* Cependant, la divulgation au public selon les termes de l'article 266 de la *Loi régissant les sociétés par actions de régime fédéral* est permise en vertu de la *Loi sur la protection des renseignements personnels.*

Les documents remplis en double et les droits payables au receveur général pour Canada doivent être envoyés au :

Directeur, Loi régissant les sociétés par actions de régime fédéral
Place du Portage
Hull (Québec) Canada
K1A 0C9

Form 2. Certificate of incorporation

FORM 2

**Certificate
of Incorporation**

**Canada Business
Corporations Act**

FORMULE 2

**Certificat
de constitution**

**Loi régissant les sociétés
par actions de régime fédéral**

Name of corporation – Dénomination de la société

Corporation number – Numéro de la société

I hereby certify that the above-
named corporation, the articles of
incorporation of which are attached,
was incorporated under the *Canada
Business Corporations Act.*

Je certifie que la société
susmentionnée, dont les statuts
constitutifs sont joints, a été
constituée en société en vertu de la
*Loi régissant les sociétés par
actions de régime fédéral.*

Director – Directeur

Date of Incorporation – Date de constitution

CCA-1398 (02-89) 46

Form 3. Notice of registered office or notice of change of registered office

		FORM 3 NOTICE OF REGISTERED OFFICE OR NOTICE OF CHANGE OF REGISTERED OFFICE (SECTION 19)	FORMULE 3 AVIS DE DÉSIGNATION OU DE CHANGEMENT DU SIÈGE SOCIAL (ARTICLE 19)
Canada Business Corporations Act	Loi régissant les sociétés par actions de régime fédéral		

1 — Name of corporation – Dénomination de la société

2 — Corporation No. — N° de la société

3 — Place in Canada where the registered office is situated   Lieu au Canada où est situé le siège social

4 — Address of registered office   Adresse du siège social

CAUTION: Address of registered office must be within place specified in articles, otherwise an amendment is required (Form 4) in addition to this form
AVIS : L'adresse du siège social doit se situer à l'intérieur des limites du lieu indiqué dans les statuts. Sinon, une modification est requise (formule 4)

5 — Effective date of change   Date d'entrée en vigueur du changement

6 — Previous address of registered office   Adresse précédente du siège social

Date	Signature	Title – Titre
CCA 1386 (06-88)		Filed – Déposée

Canada Business Corporations Act

**Notice of Registered Office or
Notice of Change of Registered Office**
FORM 3
INSTRUCTIONS

Loi régissant les sociétés par actions de régime fédéral

**Avis de désignation ou
de changement du siège social**
FORMULE 3
INSTRUCTIONS

Format
Documents required to be sent to the Director must be in a clear and legible form.

Complete items 1, 3 and 4 for new corporations.
Complete items 1 through 6 for changes.

Item 1
Set out the full legal name of the corporation.

Item 2
Complete only in the case of change of registered office.

Item 3
Set out the place in Canada where the registered office is situated as indicated in the articles of the corporation.

Item 4
Set out in full the address at which the registered office is to be situated or to which it is to be changed.

Item 5
State the date when the change of registered office is to take effect.

Item 6
Set out the previous address of the registered office, if any.

Signature
A director or authorized officer of the corporation shall sign the notice. If a new corporation, an incorporator shall sign the notice.

Completed document is to be sent to:

The Director, Canada Business Corporations Act
Place du Portage
Hull, Quebec, Canada
K1A 0C9

Présentation
Tous les documents dont l'envoi au directeur est exigé doivent être clairs et lisibles.

Remplir les rubriques 1, 3 et 4 pour les nouvelles sociétés.
Remplir les rubriques 1 à 6 si des changements sont survenus.

Rubrique 1
Indiquer la dénomination officielle complète de la société.

Rubrique 2
À remplir seulement dans le cas d'un avis de changement du siège social.

Rubrique 3
Indiquer le lieu au Canada où se situe le siège social, tel qu'il est indiqué dans les statuts de la société.

Rubrique 4
Indiquer l'adresse complète du siège social ou celle où il doit désormais être situé.

Rubrique 5
Indiquer la date à laquelle le changement du siège social doit prendre effet.

Rubrique 6
Indiquer l'adresse précédente du siège social, le cas échéant.

Signature
Un administrateur ou un dirigeant autorisé de la société doit signer l'avis. S'il s'agit d'une nouvelle société, un fondateur doit signer l'avis.

Le document rempli doit être envoyé au :

Directeur, Loi régissant les sociétés par actions de régime fédéral
Place du Portage
Hull (Québec) Canada
K1A 0C9

Form 4. Articles of amendment

| Canada Business Corporations Act Loi régissant les sociétés par actions de régime fédéral | FORM 4 ARTICLES OF AMENDMENT (SECTION 27 OR 177) | FORMULE 4 CLAUSES MODIFICATRICES (ARTICLES 27 OU 177) |

1 — Name of corporation — Dénomination de la société

2 — Corporation No. — N° de la société

3 — The articles of the above-named corporation are amended as follows: Les statuts de la société mentionnée ci-dessus sont modifiés de la façon suivante :

| Date | Signature | Title — Titre |

CCA 1387 (02-89) 46

FOR DEPARTMENTAL USE ONLY - À L'USAGE DU MINISTÈRE SEULEMENT
Filed – Déposée

Form 4   ¶24-853

Canada Business Corporations Act

Articles of Amendment
FORM 4
INSTRUCTIONS

Loi régissant les sociétés par actions de régime fédéral

Clauses modificatrices
FORMULE 4
INSTRUCTIONS

Format
Documents required to be sent to the Director pursuant to the *Canada Business Corporations Act* must conform to sections 5 to 10 of the *Canada Business Corporations Regulations.*

General
(1) Any change in the articles of the corporation must be made in accordance with sections 27 or 177 of the Act. If an amendment involves a change of corporate name, the new name must comply with sections 10 and 12 of the Act. Articles of amendment must be accompanied by a Canada-biased NUANS search report dated not more than ninety (90) days prior to the receipt of the articles by the Director. On request, a number name may be assigned under subsection 11(2) of the Act, without a search.

(2) Each amendment must correspond to the paragraph and subparagraph references of the articles being amended.

(3) A director or authorized officer of the corporation shall sign the articles.

Other Notices
If applicable, the articles must be accompanied by a Notice of Change of Registered Office (Form 3) and Notice of Change of Directors (Form 6).

Completed documents in duplicate and fees payable to the Receiver General are to be sent to:

The Director, Canada Business Corporations Act
Place du Portage
Hull, Quebec, Canada
K1A 0C9

Présentation
Tous les documents dont l'envoi au directeur est exigé par la *Loi régissant les sociétés par actions de régime fédéral* doivent être conformes aux articles 5 à 10 du *Règlement sur les sociétés par actions de régime fédéral.*

Généralités
(1) Toute modification apportée aux statuts de la société doit satisfaire aux exigences des articles 27 ou 177 de la Loi. Dans les cas où la modification comporte un changement de dénomination sociale, la nouvelle dénomination sociale doit satisfaire aux exigences des articles 10 et 12 de la Loi. Les clauses modificatrices doivent être accompagnées d'un rapport de recherche NUANS couvrant le Canada, dont la date remonte à quatre-vingt-dix (90) jours ou moins avant la date de réception par le directeur des clauses modificatrices. Si un numéro matricule est demandé en guise de dénomination sociale, il peut être assigné, sans recherche préalable, en vertu du paragraphe 11(2) de la Loi.

(2) Chaque modification doit correspondre aux renvois des alinéas et sous-alinéas des statuts modifiés.

(3) Un administrateur ou un dirigeant autorisé de la société doit signer les clauses.

Autres avis
S'il y a lieu, les clauses doivent être accompagnées de l'avis de changement du siège social (formule 3) ou de l'avis de changement des administrateurs (formule 6).

Les documents remplis en double et les droits payables au receveur général doivent être envoyés au :

Directeur, Loi régissant les sociétés par actions de régime fédéral
Place du Portage
Hull (Québec) Canada
K1A 0C9

Form 5. Certificate of amendment

FORM 5

**Certificate
of Amendment**

**Canada Business
Corporations Act**

FORMULE 5

**Certificat
de modification**

**Loi régissant les sociétés
par actions de régime fédéral**

Name of corporation - Dénomination de la société   Corporation number - Numéro de la société

I hereby certify that the articles of the
above-named corporation were
amended

Je certifie que les statuts de la société
susmentionnée ont été modifiés

(a) under section 13 of the *Canada Business
Corporations Act* in accordance with the
attached notice;

☐

a) en vertu de l'article 13 de la *Loi régissant
les sociétés par actions de régime fédéral*,
conformement à l'avis ci-joint

(b) under section 27 of the *Canada Business
Corporations Act* as set out in the attached
articles of amendment designating a series
of shares;

☐

b) en vertu de l'article 27 de la *Loi régissant
les sociétés par actions de régime fédéral*,
tel qu'il est indiqué dans les clauses
modificatrices ci-jointes désignant une série
d'actions.

(c) under section 179 of the *Canada
Business Corporations Act* as set out in the
attached articles of amendment;

☐

c) en vertu de l'article 179 de la *Loi
régissant les sociétés par actions de régime
fédéral*, tel qu'il est indiqué dans les clauses
modificatrices ci-jointes.

(d) under section 191 of the *Canada Business
Corporations Act* as set out in the attached
articles of reorganization;

☐

d) en vertu de l'article 191 de la *Loi
régissant les sociétés par actions de régime
fédéral*, tel qu'il est indiqué dans les clauses
de réorganisation ci-jointes.

(e) under section 192 of the *Canada
Business Corporations Act* as set out in the
attached articles of arrangement.

☐

e) en vertu de l'article 192 de la *Loi
régissant les sociétés par actions de régime
fédéral*, tel qu'il est indiqué dans les clauses
d'arrangement ci-jointes

Director - Directeur   Date of Amendment - Date de modification

CCA-1399 (02-89) 46

Form 6.   Notice of directors or notice of change of directors

Canada Business Corporations Act Loi régissant les sociétés par actions de régime fédéral	FORM 6 NOTICE OF DIRECTORS OR NOTICE OF CHANGE OF DIRECTORS (SECTIONS 106 and 113)	FORMULE 6 LISTE DES ADMINISTRATEURS OU AVIS DE CHANGEMENT DES ADMINISTRATEURS (ARTICLES 106 et 113)

1 — Name of corporation — Dénomination de la société

2 — Corporation No. — N° de la société

3 — The following persons became directors of this corporation   Les personnes suivantes sont devenues administrateurs de la présente société

Name Nom	Effective date Date d'entrée en vigueur :	Residential address — Adresse domiciliaire	Occupation	Resident Canadian — Y/N Résident canadien — O/N

4 — The following persons ceased to be directors of this corporation   Les personnes suivantes ont cessé d'être administrateurs de la présente société

Name Nom	Effective date Date d'entrée en vigueur :	Residential address — Adresse domiciliaire

5 — The directors of this corporation now are   Les administrateurs de la présente société sont maintenant

Name — Nom	Residential address — Adresse domiciliaire	Occupation	Resident Canadian — Y/N Résident canadien — O/N

Date	Signature	Title — Titre
CCA 1388 (06-88)		Field — Déposée

**Notice of Directors or
Notice of Change of Directors
FORM 6
INSTRUCTIONS**

Format
Documents required to be sent to the Director must be in a clear and legible form.
Complete items 1 and 5 for new corporations.
Complete items 1 through 5 for changes.

Item 1
Set out the full legal name of the corporation.

Item 2
Always set out the corporation number when filing a Notice of Change of Directors (Form 6).

Items 3, 4 and 5
With respect to each director,
(a) set out first given name, initial and family name;
(b) set out full residential address (not business address), including postal code;
(c) specify occupation clearly – e.g. manager, geologist, lawyer; and
(d) refer to the definition of "resident Canadian" in the *Canada Business Corporations Act* and *Canada Business Corporations Regulations*.

Signature
A director or authorized officer of the corporation shall sign the Notice.
If a new corporation, an incorporator shall sign the Notice.

Completed documents in duplicate are to be sent to:

The Director, Canada Business Corporations Act
Place du Portage
Hull, Quebec, Canada
K1A 0C9

The information you provide in this document is collected under the authority of the *Canada Business Corporations Act* and will be stored in personal information bank number CCA/P-PU-093. Personal information that you provide is protected under the provisions of the *Privacy Act*. However, public disclosure pursuant to section 266 of the *Canada Business Corporations Act* is permitted under the *Privacy Act*.

Loi régissant les sociétés par actions de régime fédéral

**Liste des administrateurs ou
Avis de changement des administrateurs
FORMULE 6
INSTRUCTIONS**

Présentation
Tous les documents dont l'envoi au directeur est exigé doivent être clairs et lisibles.
Remplir les rubriques 1 et 5 pour les nouvelles sociétés.
Remplir les rubriques 1 à 5 si des changements sont survenus.

Rubrique 1
Indiquer la dénomination officielle complète de la société.

Rubrique 2
Indiquer toujours le numéro de la société lors de l'envoi d'un avis de changement des administrateurs.

Rubrique 3, 4 et 5
En ce qui concerne chaque administrateur
a) indiquer son prénom, ses initiales et son nom de famille;
b) donner l'adresse complète de son domicile (non son adresse d'affaires) en incluant le code postal;
c) spécifier clairement son occupation – par exemple: gérant géologique, avocat;
d) consulter la définition de "résident canadien" dans la Loi et le *Règlement sur les sociétés par actions de régime fédéral*.

Signature
Un administrateur ou un dirigeant autorisé de la société doit signer l'avis.
S'il s'agit d'une nouvelle société, un fondateur doit signer l'avis.

Les documents remplis en double doivent être envoyés au :

Directeur, Loi régissant les sociétés par actions de régime fédéral
Place du Portage
Hull (Québec) Canada
K1A 0C9

Les renseignements que vous fournissez dans ce document sont recueillis en vertu de la *Loi régissant les sociétés par actions de régime fédéral*, et seront emmagasinés dans le fichier de renseignements personnels MCC/P-PU-093. Les renseignements personnels que vous fournissez sont protégés par les dispositions de la *Loi sur la protection des renseignements personnels*. Cependant, la divulgation au public selon les termes de l'article 266 de la *Loi régissant les sociétés par actions de régime fédéral* est permise en vertu de la *Loi sur la protection des renseignements personnels*.

Form 7. Restated articles of incorporation

		FORM 7 RESTATED ARTICLES OF INCORPORATION (SECTION 180)	FORMULE 7 STATUTS CONSTITUTIFS MIS À JOUR (ARTICLE 180)
Canada Business Corporations Act	Loi régissant les sociétés par actions de régime fédéral		

1 — Name of corporation — Dénomination de la société

Corporation No. — N° de la société

2 — The place in Canada where the registered office is situated

Lieu au Canada où est situé le siège social

3 — The classes and any maximum number of shares that the corporation is authorized to issue

Catégories et tout nombre maximal d'actions que la société est autorisée à émettre

4 — Restrictions, if any, on share transfers

Restrictions sur le transfert des actions, s'il y a lieu

5 — Number (or minimum and maximum number) of directors

Nombre (ou nombre minimal et maximal) d'administrateurs

6 — Restrictions, if any, on business the corporation may carry on

Limites imposées à l'activité commerciale de la société, s'il y a lieu

7 — Other provsions, if any

Autres dispositions, s'il y a lieu

The foregoing restated articles of incorporation correctly set out, without substantive change, the corresponding provisions of the articles of incorporation as amended and supersede the original articles of incorporation.

Cette mise à jour des statuts constitutifs démontre exactement, sans changement substantiel, les dispositions correspondantes des statuts constitutifs modifiés qui remplacent les statuts constitutifs originaux.

Signature

Date
D - J   M   Y - A

Title — Titre

FOR DEPARTMENTAL USE ONLY —
À L'USAGE DU MINISTÈRE SEULEMENT

Filed — Déposée

CCA 1389 (02-89) 46

Canada Business Corporations Act

Restated Articles of Incorporation
FORM 7
INSTRUCTIONS

Format
Documents required to be sent to the Director pursuant to the *Canada Business Corporations Act* must conform to sections 5 to 10 of the *Canada Business Corporations Regulations.*

General
Restated articles of incorporation shall set out without substantive change the Articles of Incorporation as previously amended.

Item 1
Set out the full legal name of the corporation and the corporation number.

Item 2
Set out the name of the place and province within Canada where the registered office is to be situated. A specific street address is not required

Item 3
Set out the details required by paragraph 6(1)(c) of the Act, including details of the rights, privileges, restrictions and conditions attached to each class of shares. All shares must be without nominal or par value and must comply with the provisions of Part V of the Act.

Item 4
If restrictions are to be placed on the right to transfer shares of the corporation, set out a statement to this effect and the nature of such restrictions.

Item 5
State the number of directors. If cumulative voting is permitted, the number of directors must be invariable; otherwise it is permissible to specify a minimum and maximum number of directors.

Item 6
If restrictions are to be placed on the business the corporation may carry on, set out the restrictions.

Item 7
Set out any provisions permitted by the Act or Regulations to be set out in the by-laws of the corporation that are to form part of the articles, including any pre-emptive rights or cumulative voting provisions.

Signature
A director or authorized officer of the corporation shall sign the restated articles

Completed documents in duplicate and fees payable to the Receiver General are to be sent to:

The Director, Canada Business Corporations Act
Place du Portage
Hull, Quebec, Canada
K1A 0C9

Loi régissant les sociétés par actions de régime fédéral

Statuts constitutifs mis à jour
FORMULE 7
INSTRUCTIONS

Présentation
Tous les documents dont l'envoi au directeur est exigé par la *Loi régissant les sociétés par actions de régime fédéral* doivent être conformes aux articles 5 à 10 du *Règlement sur les sociétés par actions de régime fédéral.*

Généralités
Les statuts mis à jour doivent indiquer sans modification substantielle les statuts constitutifs modifiés au préalable.

Rubrique 1
Indiquer la dénomination officielle complète de la société et son numéro

Rubrique 2
Indiquer le nom de l'endroit et de la province au Canada où le siège social doit être situé. Une adresse précise n'est pas requise.

Rubrique 3
Indiquer les détails requis par l'alinéa 6(1)c) de la Loi, y compris les détails des droits, privilèges, restrictions et conditions assortis à chaque catégorie d'actions. Toutes les actions doivent être sans valeur nominale ou sans valeur au pair et doivent être conformes aux dispositions de la partie V de la Loi.

Rubrique 4
Si le droit de transfert des actions de la société doit être restreint, inclure une déclaration à cet effet et indiquer la nature de ces restrictions.

Rubrique 5
Indiquer le nombre d'administrateurs. Si un vote cumulatif est prévu, ce nombre doit être fixe; autrement, il est permis de spécifier un nombre minimal et maximal d'administrateurs.

Rubrique 6
Si des limites doivent être imposées à l'activité commerciale de la société, les indiquer.

Rubrique 7
Indiquer les dispositions que la Loi ou le règlement permet d'énoncer dans les règlements administratifs de la société et qui doivent faire partie des statuts, y compris les dispositions relatives au vote cumulatif ou aux droits de préemption.

Signature
Un administrateur ou un dirigeant autorisé de la société doit signer les statuts mis à jour.

Les documents remplis en double et les droits payables au receveur général doivent être envoyés au :

Directeur, Loi régissant les sociétés par actions de régime fédéral
Place du Portage
Hull (Québec) Canada
K1A 0C9

Form 8. Restated certificate of incorporation

FORM 8

**Restated Certificate
of Incorporation**

Canada Business
Corporations Act

FORMULE 8

**Certificat de
constitution à jour**

Loi régissant les sociétés
par actions de régime fédéral

Name of corporation – Dénomination de la société   Corporation number – Numéro de la société

I hereby certify that the articles
of incorporation of the above-
named corporation were restated
under section 180 of the *Canada
Business Corporations Act* as set
out in the attached restated articles
of incorporation.

Je certifie que les statuts constitutifs
de la société susmentionnée ont été
mis à jour en vertu de l'article 180
de la *Loi régissant les sociétés par
actions de régime fédéral*, tel qu'il
est indiqué dans les statuts mis à
jour ci-joints.

Director – Directeur

Effective Date of Restatement –
Date d'entrée en vigueur de la mise à jour

CCA-1400 (02-89) 46

Form 9. Articles of amalgamation

		FORM 9 ARTICLES OF AMALGAMATION (SECTION 185)	FORMULE 9 STATUTS DE FUSION (ARTICLE 185)
Canada Business Corporations Act	Loi régissant les sociétés par actions de régime fédéral		

1 — Name of amalgamated corporation

Dénomination de la société issue de la fusion

2 — The place in Canada where the registered office is to be situated

Lieu au Canada où doit être situé le siège social

3 — The classes and any maximum number of shares that the corporation is authorized to issue

Catégories et tout nombre maximal d'actions que la société est autorisée à émettre

4 — Restrictions, if any, on share transfers

Restrictions sur le transfert des actions, s'il y a lieu

5 — Number (or minimum and maximum number) of directors

Nombre (ou nombre minimal et maximal) d'administrateurs

6 — Restrictions, if any, on business the corporation may carry on

Limites imposées à l'activité commerciale de la société, s'il y a lieu

7 — Other provisions, if any

Autres dispositions, s'il y a lieu

8 — The amalgamation has been approved pursuant to that section or subsection of the Act which is indicated as follows:

8 — La fusion a été approuvée en accord avec l'article ou le paragraphe de la Loi indiqué ci-après.

☐ 183

☐ 184(1)

☐ 184(2)

9 - Name of the amalgamating corporations Dénomination des sociétés fusionnantes	Corporation No. N° de la société	Signature	Date	Title Titre

FOR DEPARTMENTAL USE ONLY — A L'USAGE DU MINISTÈRE SEULEMENT
Corporation No. — N° de la société

Filed — Déposée

CCA 1390 (02-89) 46

Form 9   ¶24-853

Canadian Business Corporations Act

Articles of Amalgamation
FORM 9
INSTRUCTIONS

Format
Documents required to be sent to the Director pursuant to the *Canada Business Corporations Act* must conform to sections 5 to 10 of the *Canada Business Corporations Regulations.*

Item 1
Set out the proposed name for the amalgamated corporation that complies with sections 10 and 12 of the Act. If this name is not the same as one of the amalgamating corporations, articles of amalgamation must be accompanied by a Canada-biased NUANS search report dated not more than ninety (90) days prior to the receipt of the articles by the Director. On request, a number name may be assigned under subsection 11(2) of the Act, without a search.

Item 2
Set out the name of the place and province within Canada where the registered office is to be situated. A specific street address is not required.

Item 3
Set out the details required by paragraph 6(1)(c) of the Act, including details of the rights, privileges, restrictions and conditions attached to each class or series of shares. All shares must be without nominal or par value and must comply with the provisions of Part V of the Act.

Item 4
If restrictions are to be placed on the right to transfer shares of the corporation, set out a statement to this effect and the nature of such restrictions.

Item 5
Set out the number of directors. If cumulative voting is permitted, the number of directors must be invariable; otherwise it is permissible to specify a minimum and maximum number of directors.

Item 6
If restrictions are to be placed on the business the corporation may carry on, set out the restrictions.

Item 7
Set out any provisions, permitted by the Act or Regulations to be set out in the by-laws of the corporation, that are to form part of the articles, including any pre-emptive rights or cumulative voting provisions.

Item 8
Indicate whether the amalgamation is under section 183 or subsection 184(1) or (2) of the Act.

Other Notices and Documents
(1) The articles must be accompanied by a Notice of Registered Office (Form 3), a Notice of Directors (Form 6) and a statutory declaration of a director or authorized officer of each amalgamating corporation in accordance with subsection 185(2) of the Act.
(2) All amalgamating corporations should ensure that all filing requirements contained in the Act have been met.

Completed documents in duplicate and fees payable to the Receiver General, are to be sent to:

The Director, Canada Business Corporations Act
Place du Portage
Hull, Quebec, Canada
K1A 0C9

Loi régissant les sociétés par actions de régime fédéral

Statuts de fusion
FORMULE 9
INSTRUCTIONS

Présentation
Tous les documents dont l'envoi au directeur est exigé par la *Loi régissant les sociétés par actions de régime fédéral* doivent être conformes aux articles 5 à 10 du *Règlement sur les sociétés par actions de régime fédéral.*

Rubrique 1
Indiquer la dénomination de la société issue de la fusion, laquelle doit satisfaire aux exigences des articles 10 et 12 de la Loi. Si cette dénomination diffère de celle de l'une des sociétés fusionnantes, les statuts de fusion doivent être accompagnés d'un rapport de recherche NUANS couvrant le Canada, dont la date remonte à quatre-vingt-dix (90) jours ou moins avant la date de réception des statuts par le directeur. Si un numéro matricule est demandé en guise de dénomination sociale, il peut être assigné, sans recherche préalable, en vertu du paragraphe 11(2) de la Loi.

Rubrique 2
Indiquer le nom de l'endroit et de la province au Canada où le siège social doit être situé. Une adresse précise n'est pas requise.

Rubrique 3
Indiquer les détails requis par l'alinéa 6(1)c) de la Loi, y compris les détails des droits, privilèges, restrictions et conditions assortis à chaque catégorie ou série d'actions. Toutes les actions doivent être sans valeur nominale ou sans valeur au pair et doivent être conformes aux dispositions de la partie V de la Loi.

Rubrique 4
Si le droit de transfert des actions de la société doit être restreint, inclure une déclaration à cet effet et indiquer la nature de ces restrictions.

Rubrique 5
Indiquer le nombre des administrateurs. Si un vote cumulatif est prévu, ce nombre doit être fixe; autrement, il est permis de spécifier un nombre minimal et maximal d'administrateurs.

Rubrique 6
Si des limites doivent être imposées à l'activité commerciale de la société, les indiquer.

Rubrique 7
Indiquer les dispositions que la Loi ou le règlement permet d'énoncer dans les règlements administratifs de la société et qui doivent faire partie des statuts, y compris les dispositions relatives au vote cumulatif ou aux droits de préemption.

Rubrique 8
Indiquer si la fusion est faite en vertu de l'article 183 ou des paragraphes 184(1) ou (2) de la Loi.

Autres avis et documents
(1) Les statuts doivent être accompagnés d'un avis de désignation du siège social (formule 3), d'une liste des administrateurs (formule 6) et d'une déclaration solennelle d'un administrateur ou d'un dirigeant autorisé de chaque société fusionnante conformément au paragraphe 185(2) de la Loi.
(2) Les sociétés fusionnantes doivent s'assurer que toutes les exigences de dépôt contenues dans la loi ont été remplies.

Les documents remplis en double et les droits payables au receveur général doivent être envoyés au :

Directeur, Loi régissant les sociétés par actions de régime fédéral
Place du Portage
Hull (Québec) Canada
K1A 0C9

Form 10.   Certificate of amalgamation

FORM 10

**Certificate
of Amalgamation**

**Canada Business
Corporations Act**

FORMULE 10

**Certificat
de fusion**

**Loi régissant les sociétés
par actions de régime fédéral**

Name of corporation – Dénomination de la société

Corporation number – Numéro de la société

I hereby certify that the above-named corporation resulted from an amalgamation, under section 185 of the *Canada Business Corporations Act*, of the corporations set out in the attached articles of amalgamation.

Je certifie que la société susmentionnée est issue d'une fusion, en vertu de l'article 185 de la *Loi régissant les sociétés par actions de régime fédéral*, des sociétés dont les dénominations apparaissent dans les statuts de fusion ci-joints.

Director – Directeur

Date of Amalgamation – Date de fusion

CCA-1401 (03-89) 46

Form 11.　Articles of continuance

Canada Business Corporations Act	Loi régissant les sociétés par actions de régime fédéral	FORM 11 ARTICLES OF CONTINUANCE (SECTION 187)	FORMULE 11 CLAUSES DE PROROGATION (ARTICLE 187)

1 — Name of corporation　　　　　　　　　　　Dénomination de la société

2 — The place in Canada where the registered office is to be situated　　Lieu au Canada où doit être situé le siège social

3 — The classes and any maximum of shares that the corporation is authorized to issue　　Catégories et tout nombre maximal d'actions que la société est autorisée à émettre

4 — Restrictions, if any, on share transfers　　Restrictions sur le transfert des actions, s'il y a lieu

5 — Number (or minimum and maximum number) of directors　　Nombre (ou nombre minimal et maximal) d'administrateurs

6 — Restrictions, if any, on business the corporation may carry on　　Limites imposées à l'activité commerciale de la société, s'il y a lieu

7 — (1) If change of name effected, previous name　　(1) S'il y a changement de dénomination, dénomination antérieure

(2) Details of incorporation　　(2) Détails de la constitution

8 — Other provisions, if any　　Autres dispositions, s'il y a lieu

Date	Signature	Title — Titre

FOR DEPARTMENTAL USE ONLY — À L'USAGE DU MINISTÈRE SEULEMENT
Corporation No. — N° de la société　　　　　Filed — Déposée

CCA 1391 (02-89) 46

Canada Business Corporations Act

Articles of Continuance
FORM 11
INSTRUCTIONS

Format
Documents required to be sent to the Director pursuant to the *Canada Business Corporations Act* must conform to sections 5 to 10 of the *Canada Business Corporations Regulations*.

Item 1
Set out the full legal name of the corporation that complies with sections 10 and 12 of the Act. Articles of continuance must be accompanied by a Canada-biased NUANS search report dated not more than ninety (90) days prior to the receipt of the articles by the Director. On request, a number name may be assigned under subsection 11(2) of the Act, without a search.

Item 2
Set out the name of the place and province within Canada where the registered office is to be situated. A specific street address is not required.

Item 3
Set out the details required by paragraph 6(1)(c) of the Act. Unless an exemption is obtained under subsection 187(11) of the Act, all shares must be without nominal or par value and must comply with Part V of the Act. Nominal or par value shares issued by a body corporate before continuance comply with the Act by virtue of subsections 24(2) and 187(8) and (9) of the Act. In the case of the application of subsection 187(11) of the Act, set out the maximum number of shares of a class or series as required by subsection 187(12) of the Act.

Item 4
If restrictions are to be placed on the right to transfer shares of the corporation, set out a statement to this effect and the nature of such restrictions.

Item 5
Set out the number of directors. If cumulative voting is permitted, the number of directors must be invariable; otherwise it is permissible to specify a minimum and maximum number of directors.

Item 6
If restrictions are to be placed on the business the corporation may carry on, set out the restrictions.

Item 7
(1) Set out the previous name of the body corporate if a change of name is effected on continuance.
(2) Set out the date of incorporation of the body corporate. If the body corporate has been subject to any previous continuance, set out the details of each such continuance, i.e. the date of continuance, any change of name at the time of continuance and the name and provision of the statute under which it was effected.

Item 8
Set out any provisions, permitted by the Act or Regulations to be set out in the by-laws of the corporation, that are to form part of the articles, including any pre-emptive rights or cumulative voting provisions.

Signature
A director or authorized officer of the body corporate shall sign the articles.

Other Documents
If the continuance is under subsection 187(1) of the Act, the articles of continuance must be accompanied by
(a) proof of authorization under the laws of the jurisdiction where the body corporate is incorporated;
(b) a Notice of Registered Office (Form 3) and a Notice of Directors (Form 6); and
(c) a list of the provinces in which the corporation is registered as an extra-provincial corporation.

Completed documents in duplicate and fees payable to the Receiver General are to be sent to:

The Director, Canada Business Corporations Act
Place du Portage
Hull, Quebec, Canada
K1A 0C9

Loi régissant les sociétés par actions de régime fédéral

Clauses de prorogation
FORMULE 11
INSTRUCTIONS

Présentation
Tous les documents dont l'envoi au directeur est exigé par la *Loi régissant les sociétés par actions de régime fédéral* doivent être conformes aux articles 5 à 10 du *Règlement sur les sociétés par actions de régime fédéral.*

Rubrique 1
Indiquer la dénomination officielle complète de la société, laquelle doit satisfaire aux exigences des articles 10 et 12 de la Loi. Les clauses de prorogation doivent être accompagnées d'un rapport de recherche NUANS couvrant le Canada, dont la date remonte à quatre-vingt-dix (90) jours ou moins avant la date de réception par le directeur des clauses de prorogation. Si un numéro matricule est demandé en guise de dénomination sociale, il peut être assigné, sans recherche préalable, en vertu du paragraphe 11(2) de la Loi.

Rubrique 2
Indiquer le nom de l'endroit et de la province au Canada où le siège social doit être situé. Une adresse précise n'est pas requise.

Rubrique 3
Indiquer les détails requis par l'alinéa 6(1)c) de la Loi. Sauf dans les cas où une dispense est accordée en vertu du paragraphe 187(11) de la Loi, toutes les actions doivent être sans valeur nominale ou sans valeur au pair et doivent se conformer à la partie V de la Loi. Les actions avec valeur au pair ou nominales émises par une personne morale avant sa prorogation sont conformes à la Loi en vertu des paragraphes 24(2) et 187(8) et (9) de la Loi. Si le paragraphe 187(11) de la Loi s'applique, indiquer le nombre maximal des actions d'une série ou catégorie requis par le paragraphe 187(12) de la Loi.

Rubrique 4
Si le droit de transfert des actions de la société doit être restreint, inclure une déclaration à cet effet et indiquer la nature de ces restrictions.

Rubrique 5
Indiquer le nombre des administrateurs. Si un vote cumulatif est prévu, ce nombre doit être fixe; autrement, il est permis de spécifier un nombre minimal et maximal d'administrateurs.

Rubrique 6
Si des limites doivent être imposées à l'activité commerciale de la société, les indiquer.

Rubrique 7
(1) Indiquer la dénomination antérieure de la personne morale si un changement de dénomination est effectué lors de la prorogation.
(2) Indiquer la date de constitution de la personne morale. Si la personne morale a fait l'objet de toute prorogation antérieure, indiquer les détails de chacune d'elles, soit la date de prorogation, tout changement de dénomination lors de la prorogation, ainsi que le nom et la disposition du texte de loi en vertu duquel elle a été opérée.

Rubrique 8
Indiquer les dispositions que la Loi ou le règlement permet d'énoncer dans les règlements administratifs de la société et qui doivent faire partie des statuts en incluant les dispositions relatives au vote cumulatif ou aux droits de préemption.

Signature
Un administrateur ou un dirigeant autorisé de la personne morale doit signer les clauses.

Autres documents
Si la prorogation est effectuée en vertu du paragraphe 187(1) de la Loi, les clauses de prorogation doivent être accompagnées :
a) d'une preuve de l'autorisation en vertu de la Loi sous le régime de laquelle la personne morale est constituée ;
b) d'un avis de désignation du siège social (formule 3) et d'une liste des administrateurs (formule 6);
c) d'une liste des provinces où la société est enregistrée à titre de corporation extra-provinciale.

Les documents remplis en double et les droits payables au receveur général doivent être envoyés au :

Directeur, Loi régissant les sociétés par actions de régime fédéral
Place du Portage
Hull (Québec) Canada
K1A 0C9

Form 12. Certificate of continuance

FORM 12

**Certificate
of Continuance**

Canada Business
Corporations Act

FORMULE 12

**Certificat
de prorogation**

Loi régissant les sociétés
par actions de régime fédéral

Name of corporation – Dénomination de la société | Corporation number – Numéro de la société

I hereby certify that the above-named corporation was continued under section 187 of the *Canada Business Corporations Act*, as set out in the attached articles of continuance.

Je certifie que la société susmentionnée a été prorogée en vertu de l'article 187 de la *Loi régissant les sociétés par actions de régime fédéral*, tel qu'il est indiqué dans les clauses de prorogation ci-jointes.

Director – Directeur

Date of Continuance – Date de la prorogation

CCA-1402 (03-89) 46

Form 13. Certificate of discontinuance

FORM 13

**Certificate
of Discontinuance**

**Canada Business
Corporations Act**

FORMULE 13

**Certificat
de changement de régime**

**Loi régissant les sociétés
par actions de régime fédéral**

Name of corporation – Dénomination de la société

Corporation number – Numéro de la société

I hereby certify that the above-
named corporation was discontinued under section 188 of the
Canada Business Corporations Act
and continued under the laws of
another jurisdiction as specified in
the attached notice.

Je certifie que la société
susmentionnée a changé de régime
en vertu de l'article 188 de la *Loi
régissant les sociétés par actions
de régime fédéral* et a été prorogée
sous le régime d'une autre autorité
législative, laquelle est spécifiée
dans l'avis ci-joint.

Director – Directeur

Date of Discontinuance –
Date du changement de régime

CCA-1403 (02-89) 46

Form 14. Articles of reorganization

Canada Business Corporations Act	Loi régissant les sociétés par actions de régime fédéral	FORM 14 ARTICLES OF REORGANIZATION (SECTION 191)	FORMULE 14 CLAUSES DE RÉORGANISATION (ARTICLE 191)

1 — Name of corporation – Dénomination de la société

2 — Corporation No. — N° de la société

3 — In accordance with the order for reorganization, the articles of incorporation are amended as follows:

Conformément à l'ordonnance de réorganisation, les statuts constitutifs sont modifiés comme suit :

Date	Signature	Title – Titre
		FOR DEPARTMENTAL USE ONLY — À L'USAGE DU MINISTÈRE SEULEMENT Filed – Déposée

CCA 1392 (02-89) 46

Canada Business Corporations Act

Articles of Reorganization
FORM 14
INSTRUCTIONS

Format
Documents required to be sent to the Director pursuant to the *Canada Business Corporations Act* must conform to sections 5 to 10 of the *Canada Business Corporations Regulations*.

General
(1) Set out the amendments to the articles of incorporation in accordance with the court order pursuant to section 191 of the Act. If an amendment involves a change of corporate name, the new name must comply with sections 10 and 12 of the Act. Articles of reorganization must be accompanied by a Canada-biased NUANS search report dated not more than ninety (90) days prior to the receipt of the articles by the Director. On request, a number name may be assigned under subsection 11(2) of the Act, without a search.

(2) Any amendment shall conform to and correspond to the paragraph and subparagraph references of the existing articles.

Signature
A director or officer authorized by the corporation or the court shall sign the articles.

Other Documents
The articles must be accompanied by
(a) a copy of the court order; and
(b) if applicable, a Notice of Change of Registered Office (Form 3) and Notice of Change of Directors (Form 6).

Completed documents in duplicate and fees payable to the Receiver General are to be sent to:

The Director, Canada Business Corporations Act
Place du Portage
Hull, Quebec, Canada
K1A 0C9

Loi régissant les sociétés par actions de régime fédéral

Clauses de réorganisation
FORMULE 14
INSTRUCTIONS

Présentation
Tous les documents dont l'envoi au directeur est exigé par la *Loi régissant les sociétés par actions de régime fédéral* doivent être conformes aux articles 5 à 10 du *Règlement sur les sociétés par actions de régime fédéral*.

Généralités
(1) Indiquer les modifications apportées aux statuts constitutifs en vertu de l'ordonnance rendue par le tribunal conformément à l'article 191 de la Loi. Dans les cas où les modifications comportent un changement de dénomination sociale, la nouvelle dénomination doit satisfaire aux exigences des articles 10 et 12 de la Loi. Les clauses de réorganisation doivent être accompagnées d'un rapport de recherche NUANS couvrant le Canada, dont la date remonte à quatre-vingt-dix (90) jours ou moins avant la date de réception par le directeur des clauses de réorganisation. Si un numéro matricule est demandé en guise de dénomination sociale, il peut être assigné, sans recherche préalable, en vertu du paragraphe 11(2) de la Loi.

(2) Toute modification doit être conforme et correspondre aux renvois des alinéas et sous-alinéas des statuts existants.

Signature
Un administrateur ou un dirigeant autorisé par la société ou le tribunal doit signer les clauses.

Autres documents
Les clauses doivent être accompagnées :
a) d'un exemplaire de l'ordonnance du tribunal ;
b) s'il y a lieu, d'un avis de changement du siège social (formule 3) et d'un avis de changement des administrateurs (formule 6).

Les documents remplis en double et les droits payables au receveur général doivent être envoyés au :

Directeur, Loi régissant les sociétés par actions de régime fédéral
Place du Portage
Hull (Québec) Canada
K1A 0C9

Form 14.1. Articles of arrangement

Canada Business Corporations Act	Loi régissant les sociétés par actions de régime fédéral	FORM 14.1 ARTICLES OF ARRANGEMENT (SECTION 192)	FORMULE 14.1 CLAUSES D'ARRANGEMENT (ARTICLE 192)

1 — Name of applicant corporation(s) — Dénomination de la(des) requérante(s)

2 — Corporation No(s). — N°(s) de la(des) société(s)

3 — Name of the corporation(s) the articles of which are amended, if applicable
Dénomination de la(des) société(s) dont les statuts sont modifiés, le cas échéant

4 — Corporation No(s). — N°(s) de la(des) société(s)

5 — Name of the corporation(s) created by amalgamation, if applicable
Dénomination de la(des) société(s) issue(s) de la(des) fusion(s), le cas échéant

6 — Corporation No(s). — N°(s) de la(des) société(s)

7 — Name of the dissolved corporation(s), if applicable
Dénomination de la(des) société(s) dissoute(s), le cas échéant

8 — Corporation No(s). — N°(s) de la(des) société(s)

9 — Name of other bodies corporate involved, if applicable
Dénomination des autres personnes morales en cause, le cas échéant

10 — Corporation No(s). or jurisdiction of incorporation — N°(s) de la(des) société(s)/ ou loi sous le régime de laquelle elle est constituée

11 — In accordance with the order approving the arrangement,   Conformément aux termes de l'ordonnance approuvant l'arrangement,

(a) the articles of the above-named corporation(s) are amended in accordance with the attached plan of arrangement

☐ les statuts de la(des) société(s) susmentionnée(s) sont modifiés en conformité avec le plan d'arrangement ci-joint :

(b) the following bodies corporate are amalgamated in accordance with the attached plan of arrangement

☐ les personnes morales suivantes sont fusionnées conformément au plan d'arrangement ci-joint :

(c) the above-named corporation(s) is(are) liquidated and dissolved in accordance with the attached plan of arrangement

☐ la(les) société(s) susmentionnée(s) est(sont) liquidée(s) et dissoute(s) conformément au plan d'arrangement ci-joint

(d) the plan of arrangement attached hereto, involving the above-named body(ies), corporate is hereby effected

☐ le plan d'arrangement ci-joint portant sur la(les) personne(s) morale(s) susmentionnée(s) prend effet

Date	Signature	Title — Titre

CCA-1780 (06-88)

FOR DEPARTMENTAL USE ONLY — À L'USAGE DU MINISTÈRE SEULEMENT
Field — Déposée

Canada Business Corporations Act

Articles of Arrangement
FORM 14.1
INSTRUCTIONS

Loi régissant les sociétés par actions de régime fédéral

Clauses d'arrangement
FORMULE 14.1
INSTRUCTIONS

Format
Documents required to be sent to the Director pursuant to the *Canada Business Corporations Act* must conform to sections 5 to 10 of the *Canada Business Corporations Regulations.*

Items 2, 4, 6, 8 and 10
Insert corporate number only for corporations incorporated pursuant to the *Canada Business Corporations Act.*

Item 11
Check the appropriate box or boxes
In respect of (b), list the names of all bodies corporate involved in the amalgamation creating the corporation(s) specified in item 5.

In respect of (b), all the information required by Form 9 (Articles of Amalgamation) should appear clearly in the annexed plan of arrangement or a schedule to these articles.

Signature
A director or authorized officer of the corporation or the court shall sign the articles.

Other Documents
The articles must be accompanied by
(a) a copy of the court order; and
(b) if applicable, a Notice of Change of Registered Office (Form 3) and Notice of Change of Directors (Form 6) and a Canada-biased NUANS search report dated not more than ninety (90) days prior to the receipt of the articles by the Director.

Completed documents in duplicate and fees payable to the Receiver General are to be sent to:

The Director, Canada Business Corporations Act
Place du Portage
Hull, Quebec, Canada
K1A 0C9

Présentation
Tous les documents dont l'envoi au directeur est exigé par la *Loi régissant les sociétés par actions de régime fédéral* doivent être conformes aux articles 5 à 10 du *Règlement sur les sociétés par actions de régime fédéral.*

Rubriques 2, 4, 6, 8 et 10
Inscrire le numéro de la société dans les seuls cas où les sociétés sont constituées en vertu de la *Loi régissant les sociétés par actions de régime fédéral.*

Rubrique 11
Cocher la ou les cases appropriées
Sous le point b), énumérer les dénominations de toutes les personnes morales en cause dans la fusion créant la(ies) société(s) spécifiée(s) à la rubrique 5.

Sous le point b), tous les renseignements requis à la formule 9 (statuts de fusion) doivent apparaître clairement dans le plan d'arrangement ci-joint ou dans une annexe à ces statuts.

Signature
Un administrateur ou un dirigeant autorisé par la(ies) société(s) ou le tribunal doit signer les clauses.

Autres documents
Les clauses doivent être accompagnées
a) d'un exemplaire de l'ordonnance du tribunal.
b) le cas échéant, d'un avis de changement du siège social (formule 3) et d'un avis de changement des administrateurs (formule 6) et d'un rapport de recherche NUANS couvrant le Canada. dont la date remonte a quatre-vingt-dix (90) jours ou moins avant la date de réception par le directeur des clauses d'arrangement

Les documents remplis en double et les droits payables au receveur général doivent être envoyés au :

Directeur, Loi régissant les sociétés par actions de régime fédéral
Place du Portage
Hull (Québec) Canada
K1A 0C9

Form 15.   Articles of revival

Canada Business Corporations Act Loi régissant les sociétés par actions de régime fédéral	FORM 15 ARTICLES OF REVIVAL (SECTION 209)	FORMULE 15 CLAUSES DE RECONSTITUTION (ARTICLE 209)

1 — Name of body corporate	Nom de la personne morale	2 – Corporation No. – N° de la société

3 – The place in Canada where the registered office is to be situated   Lieu au Canada où doit être situé le siège social

4 – The classes and any maximum number of shares that the corporation is authorized to issue   Catégories et tout nombre maximal d'actions que la société est autorisée à émettre

5 – Restrictions, if any, on share transfers   Restrictions sur le transfert des actions, s'il y a lieu

6 – Number (or minimum and maximum number) of directors   Nombre (ou nombre minimal et maximal) d'administrateurs

7 – Restrictions, if any, on business the corporation may carry on   Limites imposées à l'activité commerciale de la société, s'il y a lieu

8 – (1) If change of name effected, previous name   (1) S'il y a changement de dénomination, dénomination antérieure

   (2) Details of incorporation   (2) Détails de la constitution

9 – Other provisions, if any   Autres dispositions, s'il y a lieu

10 – Reasons for dissolution   Raisons de la dissolution

11 – Interest of applicant in revival of body corporate (i.e. shareholder, creditor, etc.)   Intérêt du demandeur dans la reconstitution de la personne morale (par ex. actionnaire, créancier, etc.)

12 – Name of applicant in full – Nom complet du demandeur	13 – Address of applicant – Adresse du demandeur
Signature of applicant – Signature du demandeur	Date
FOR DEPARTMENTAL USE ONLY – À L'USAGE DU MINISTÈRE SEULEMENT Corporation No. — N° de la société	Filed — Déposée

CCA 1393 (02-89) 46

¶24-853   **Form 15**

Canada Business Corporations Act

Articles of Revival
FORM 15
INSTRUCTIONS

Loi régissant les sociétés par actions de régime fédéral

Clauses de reconstitution
FORMULE 15
INSTRUCTIONS

Item 1
Set out the full legal name of the body corporate which complies with sections 10 and 12 of the Act. Articles of revival must be accompanied by a Canada-biased NUANS search report dated not more than ninety (90) days prior to the receipt of the articles by the Director. Upon request, a number may be assigned under subsection 11(2) of the Act, without a search.

Rubrique 1
Indiquer le nom officiel complet de la personne morale, laquelle doit satisfaire aux exigences des articles 10 et 12 de la Loi. Les clauses de reconstitution doivent être accompagnées d'un rapport de recherche NUANS couvrant le Canada, dont la date remonte à quatre-vingt-dix (90) jours ou moins avant la date de réception par le directeur des clauses de reconstitution. Si un numéro matricule est demandé en guise de dénomination sociale, il peut être assigné, sans recherche préalable, en vertu du paragraphe 11(2) de la Loi.

Item 2
If applicable, set out the corporation number.

Rubrique 2
S'il y a lieu, indiquer le numéro de la société.

Item 3
Set out the name of the place and province within Canada where the registered office is to be situated. A specific street address is not required.

Rubrique 3
Indiquer le nom de l'endroit et de la province au Canada où le siège social doit être situé. Une adresse précise n'est pas requise.

Item 4
Set out the share structure of the body corporate exactly as it was before dissolution, except that any shares previously with nominal or par value must now be without nominal or par value.

Rubrique 4
Indiquer la structure exacte du capital de la personne morale avant la dissolution, sauf que toute action préalablement avec valeur nominale ou au pair doit dorénavant être sans valeur nominale ou au pair.

Item 5
No new restrictions may be placed on the right to transfer shares of the revived corporation.

Rubrique 5
Aucune nouvelle limite ne doit être imposée sur le droit de transfert des actions de la société reconstituée.

Item 6
The number of directors must be the same as the number of directors of the dissolved body corporate.

Rubrique 6
Le nombre des administrateurs doit être le même que celui de la personne morale dissoute.

Item 7
Any restrictions to be placed on the business of the revived corporation must be identical to such restrictions or objects of the body corporate before its dissolution.

Rubrique 7
Toute limite concernant l'activité commerciale de la société reconstituée doit être identique aux limites ou aux objets de la personne morale avant sa dissolution.

Item 8
(1) Set out the previous name of the body corporate if a change of name is effected on revival.
(2) Set out the date of incorporation of the body corporate. If the body corporate has been subject to any previous continuance or amalgamation, set out the details of each such continuance or amalgamation, i.e., the date, any change of name and the name and provision of the statute under which it was effected.

Rubrique 8
(1) Indiquer la dénomination antérieure de la personne morale si un changement de dénomination est effectué lors de la reconstitution.
(2) Indiquer la date de constitution de la personne morale. Si la personne morale a fait l'objet d'une prorogation ou d'une fusion antérieure, indiquer les détails de chaque prorogation ou fusion, soit la date, tout changement de dénomination, ainsi que le nom et la disposition du texte de loi en vertu duquel elle a été opérée.

Item 9
No provisions may be added that were not included in the charter of the body corporate.

Rubrique 9
Aucune disposition ne peut être ajoutée à moins qu'elle ne soit déjà énoncée dans la charte de la personne morale.

Item 10
State the reasons why the body corporate was dissolved, including specific references when applicable to the statutory provisions under which it was dissolved.

Rubrique 10
Donner les raisons pour lesquelles la personne morale a été dissoute, notamment, le renvoi précis à la disposition statutaire en vertu de laquelle elle a été dissoute, s'il y a lieu.

Item 11
State details of the applicant's interest in the body corporate and why the applicant seeks to have the body corporate revived.

Rubrique 11
Donner les détails de l'intérêt du demandeur dans la personne morale et indiquer pourquoi il demande la reconstitution de la personne morale.

Item 12
Set out the first given name, initial and family name of the applicant.

Rubrique 12
Indiquer le prénom, les initiales et le nom de famille du demandeur.

Item 13
Set out the business or residential address of the applicant.

Rubrique 13
Indiquer l'adresse d'affaires ou domiciliaire du demandeur.

Other Documents
The articles must be accompanied by a Notice of Registered Office (Form 3) and a Notice of Directors (Form 6).

Autres documents
Les clauses doivent être accompagnées d'un avis de désignation du siège social (formule 3) et d'une liste des administrateurs (formule 6).

The information you provide in this document is collected under the authority of the *Canada Business Corporations Act* and will be stored in personal information bank number CCA/P-PU-093. Personal information that you provide is protected under the provisions of the *Privacy Act*. However, public disclosure pursuant to section 266 of the *Canada Business Corporations Act* is permitted under the *Privacy Act*.

Les renseignements que vous fournissez dans ce document sont recueillis en vertu de la *Loi régissant les sociétés par actions de régime fédéral*, et seront emmagasinés dans le fichier de renseignements personnels MCC/P-PU-093. Les renseignements personnels que vous fournissez sont protégés par les dispositions de la *Loi sur la protection des renseignements personnels*. Cependant, la divulgation au public selon les termes de l'article 266 de la *Loi régissant les sociétés par actions de régime fédéral* est permise en vertu de la *Loi sur la protection des renseignements personnels*.

Completed documents in duplicate and fees payable to the Receiver General, are to be sent to:

The Director, Canada Business Corporations Act
Place du Portage
Hull, Quebec, Canada
K1A 0C9

Les documents remplis en double et les droits payables au receveur général doivent être envoyés au :

Directeur, Loi régissant les sociétés par actions de régime fédéral
Place du Portage
Hull (Québec) Canada
K1A 0C9

Form 16.   Certificate of revival

FORM 16

**Certificate
of Revival**

Canada Business
Corporations Act

FORMULE 16

**Certificat
de reconstitution**

Loi régissant les sociétés
par actions de régime fédéral

Name of corporation – Dénomination de la société   Corporation number – Numéro de la société

I hereby certify that the above-
named corporation was revived
under section 209 of the *Canada
Business Corporations Act* as set
out in the attached articles of
revival.

Je certifie que la société
susmentionnée a été reconstituée
en vertu de l'article 209 de la *Loi
régissant les sociétés par actions
de régime fédéral*, tel qu'il est
indiqué dans les clauses de
reconstitution ci-jointes.

Director – Directeur   Date of Revival – Date de reconstitution

CCA-1404 (02-89) 46

Form 17. Articles of dissolution

Canada Business Corporations Act Loi régissant les sociétés par actions de régime fédéral	FORM 17 ARTICLES OF DISSOLUTION (SECTIONS 210 AND 211)	FORMULE 17 CLAUSES DE DISSOLUTION (ARTICLES 210 ET 211)

1 – Name of corporation – Dénomination de la société	2 – Corporation No. – N° de la société

3 – The corporation is not   La société n'est pas

bankrupt or insolvent within the meaning of the *Bankruptcy Act* ☐ insolvable ou en faillite au sens de la *Loi sur la faillite*

4 – The corporation has   La société

not issued any shares under subsection 210(1) of the *Canada Business Corporations Act,* ☐ n'a émis aucune action selon le paragraphe 210(1) de la *Loi régissant les sociétés par actions de régime fédéral.*

no property and no liabilities under subsection 210(2) of the Act, ☐ n'a ni biens et ni dettes selon le paragraphe 210(2) de la Loi,

discharged its liabilities and distributed its property in accordance with subsection 210(3) of the Act, or ☐ a effectué un règlement de dettes et réparti ses biens conformément au paragraphe 210(3) de la Loi, ou

provided for the payment or discharge of its obligations and distributed its remaining property under subsection 211(7) of the Act. ☐ a constitué une provision suffisante pour honorer ses obligations et réparti le reliquat de l'actif selon le paragraphe 211(7) de la Loi.

Documents and records of the corporation shall be kept for six years from the date of dissolution by: Les documents et les livres de la société seront conservés pendant une période de six ans suivant la date de dissolution par :

Name – Nom	Occupation

Address – Adresse

Date	Signature	Title – Titre

FOR DEPARTMENTAL USE ONLY – À L'USAGE DU MINISTÈRE SEULEMENT	Filed – Déposée

CCA 1394 (02-89) 46

Form 17   ¶24-853

Canada Business Corporations Act

Articles of Dissolution
FORM 17
INSTRUCTIONS

Format
Documents required to be sent to the Director pursuant to the *Canada Business Corporations Act* must conform to sections 5 to 10 of the *Canada Business Corporations Regulations*

Item 1
Set out the full legal name of the corporation

Item 2
Set out the corporation number

Item 3
It is not possible to dissolve an insolvent or bankrupt corporation under the provisions of the Act

Item 4
Check the appropriate case.

Item 5
Set out the first given name, initials and family name, occupation and business address of the person who will be liable to produce the documents and records of the dissolved corporation under section 225 of the Act

Signature
A director or authorized officer of the corporation shall sign the articles

Caution
This form should not be filed at the same time as a Statement of Intent to Dissolve (Form 19)

Completed documents in duplicate are to be sent to:

The Director, Canada Business Corporations Act
Place du Portage
Hull, Quebec, Canada
K1A 0C9

Loi régissant les sociétés par actions de régime fédéral

Clauses de dissolution
FORMULE 17
INSTRUCTIONS

Présentation
Tous les documents dont l'envoi au directeur est exigé par la *Loi régissant les sociétés par actions de régime fédéral* doivent être conformes aux articles 5 à 10 du *Règlement sur les sociétés par actions de régime fédéral*

Rubrique 1
Indiquer la dénomination officielle complète de la société

Rubrique 2
Indiquer le numéro de la société.

Rubrique 3
Il n'est pas possible selon les dispositions de la Loi de dissoudre une société insolvable ou en faillite.

Rubrique 4
Cocher la case appropriée.

Rubrique 5
Indiquer le prénom, les initiales et le nom de famille, l'occupation et l'adresse d'affaires de la personne qui peut être tenue de produire, en vertu de l'article 225 de la loi, les documents et livres de la société dissoute

Signature
Un administrateur ou un dirigeant autorisé de la société doit signer les clauses

Remarque
Cette formule ne doit pas être déposée en même temps qu'une déclaration d'intention de dissolution (formule 19).

Les documents remplis en double doivent être envoyés au :

Directeur, Loi régissant les sociétés par actions de régime fédéral
Place du Portage
Hull (Québec) Canada
K1A 0C9

Form 18. Certificate of dissolution

FORM 18

FORMULE 18

**Certificate
of Dissolution**

**Certificat
de dissolution**

Canada Business
Corporations Act

Loi régissant les sociétés
par actions de régime fédéral

Name of corporation – Dénomination de la société   Corporation number – Numéro de la société

I hereby certify that the above-named
corporation was dissolved under the
Canada Business Corporations Act
pursuant to:

Je certifie que la société susmentionnée a
été dissoute sous le régime de la *Loi
régissant les sociétés par actions de régime
fédéral*, conformément :

(a) sections 210 or 211 of the Act as set out
in the attached articles of dissolution;

a) aux articles 210 ou 211 de la Loi, tel qu'il
est indiqué dans les clauses de
dissolution ci-jointes;

(b) section 212 of the Act; or

b) à l'article 212 de la Loi;

(c) the attached court order.

c) à l'ordonnance du tribunal ci-jointe.

Director – Directeur   Date of Dissolution – Date de dissolution

CCA-1405 (02-89) 46

Form 19. Statement of intent to dissolve or statement of revocation of intent to dissolve

		FORM 19 STATEMENT OF INTENT TO DISSOLVE OR REVOCATION OF INTENT TO DISSOLVE (SECTION 211)	FORMULE 19 DÉCLARATION D'INTENTION DE DISSOLUTION OU DE RENONCIATION À DISSOLUTION (ARTICLE 211)
Canada Business Corporations Act	Loi régissant les sociétés par actions de régime fédéral		

1 – Name of corporation – Dénomination de la société	2 – Corporation No. – Nº de la société

3 – The corporation intends to liquidate and dissolve ☐ La société a l'intention de procéder à sa liquidation et à sa dissolution

4 – The corporation revokes its certificate of intent to dissolve ☐ La société révoque son certificat d'intention de dissolution

Date	Signature	Title — Titre
CCA 1395 (02 89) 46		FOR DEPARTMENTAL USE ONLY - À L'USAGE DU MINISTÈRE SEULEMENT Filed – Déposée

Canada Business Corporations Act

Statement of Intent to Dissolve or Statement of Revocation of Intent to Dissolve
FORM 19
INSTRUCTIONS

Format
Documents required to be sent to the Director pursuant to the *Canada Business Corporations Act* must conform to sections 5 to 10 of the *Canada Business Corporations Regulations*.

Item 1
Set out the full legal name of the corporation.

Item 2
Set out the corporation number.

Item 3
Check item 3 if the corporation intends to liquidate and dissolve under subsection 211(3) of the Act.

Item 4
Check item 4 if the corporation intends to revoke under subsection 211(10) of the Act a certificate of intent to dissolve issued to it under subsection 211(5) of the Act.

Signature
A director or authorized officer of the corporation shall sign the statement

Caution
This form is not to be filed at the same time as articles of dissolution (Form 17)

Completed documents in duplicate and fees, if applicable, payable to the Receiver General are to be sent to:

The Director, Canada Business Corporations Act
Place du Portage
Hull, Quebec, Canada,
K1A 0C9

Loi régissant les sociétés par actions de régime fédéral

Déclaration d'intention de dissolution ou déclaration de renonciation à dissolution
FORMULE 19
INSTRUCTIONS

Présentation
Tous les documents dont l'envoi au directeur est exigé par la *Loi régissant les sociétés par actions de régime fédéral* doivent être conformes aux articles 5 à 10 du *Règlement sur les sociétés par actions de régime fédéral*

Rubrique 1
Indiquer la dénomination officielle complète de la société

Rubrique 2
Indiquer le numéro de la société.

Rubrique 3
Cocher la rubrique 3, si la société envisage de procéder à sa liquidation et à sa dissolution en vertu du paragraphe 211(3) de la Loi

Rubrique 4
Cocher la rubrique 4, si la société entend révoquer, en vertu du paragraphe 211(10) de la Loi, un certificat d'intention de dissolution délivré en vertu du paragraphe 211(5) de la Loi

Signature
Un administrateur ou un dirigeant autorisé de la société doit signer la déclaration

Remarque
Cette formule ne peut être déposée en même temps que des clauses de dissolution (formule 17)

Les documents remplis en double et les droits payables au receveur général, s'il y a lieu, doivent être envoyés au :

Directeur, Loi régissant les sociétés par actions de régime fédéral
Place du Portage
Hull (Québec) Canada
K1A 0C9

Form 20. Certificate of intent to dissolve

FORM 20

**Certificate
of Intent to Dissolve**

**Canada Business
Corporations Act**

FORMULE 20

**Certificat
d'intention de dissolution**

**Loi régissant les sociétés
par actions de régime fédéral**

Name of corporation - Dénomination de la société

Corporation number – Numéro de la société

I hereby certify that the above-named corporation intends to dissolve under the *Canada Business Corporations Act* pursuant to:

(a) section 211 of the Act as set out in the attached Statement of intent to dissolve;

☐

(b) section 212, 213 or 214 of the Act in accordance with the attached court order.

☐

Je certifie que la société susmentionnée a l'intention de procéder à sa dissolution sous le régime de la *Loi régissant les sociétés par actions de régime fédéral*, conformément :

a) à l'article 211 de la Loi, tel qu'il est indiqué dans la déclaration d'intention de dissolution ci-jointe;

b) à l'article 212, 213 ou 214 de la Loi, tel qu'il est indiqué dans l'ordonnance du tribunal ci-jointe.

Director - Directeur

Date Intent to Dissolve — Date d'intention de dissolution

CCA-1407 (06.88)

Form 21. Certificate of revocation of intent to dissolve

FORM 21

**Certificate of Revocation
of Intent to Dissolve**

Canada Business
Corporations Act

FORMULE 21

**Certificat de renonciation
à dissolution**

Loi régissant les sociétés
par actions de régime fédéral

Name of corporation – Dénomination de la société

Corporation number – Numéro de la société

I hereby certify that the above-named corporation revoked its intent to dissolve as set out in the attached statement of revocation of intent to dissolve, pursuant to section 211 of the *Canada Business Corporation Act.*

Je certifie que la société susmentionnée, conformément à l'article 211 de la *Loi régissant les sociétés par actions de régime fédéral,* a révoqué son intention de dissolution, tel qu'il est indiqué dans la déclaration de renonciation à dissolution ci-jointe.

Director – Directeur

Effective date – Date d'entrée en vigueur

CCA-1406 (02-89) 46

Form 22.   Annual return

FORM 22   FORMULE 22
ANNUAL RETURN   RAPPORT ANNUEL
(SECTION 263)   (ARTICLE 263)

FOR YEAR
POUR L'ANNÉE   19___

Canada Business Corporations Act
Loi régissant les sociétés par actions de régime fédéral

1. Corporation name and registered office address
Dénomination de la société et adresse du siège social

2. Corporation No. – N° de la société

3. Financial year end – Fin de l'exercice

4. Anniversary date of – Date anniversaire de
   ☐ Incorporation / Constitution
   ☐ Continuance / Prorogation
   ☐ Amalgamation / Fusion

5. Main types of business – Catégories principales d'activité commerciale

6. Has there been a change of directors?
   Y a-t-il eu changement d'administrateurs?
   ☐ Yes / Oui   ☐ No / Non
   If yes, has Form 6 been . . . – Si oui, la formule 6 a-t-elle été
   ☐ Filed / déposée   ☐ Attached / annexée

7. Has there been a change of registered office?
   Y a-t-il eu changement du siège social?
   ☐ Yes / Oui   ☐ No / Non
   If yes, has Form 3 been . . . – Si oui, la formule 3 a-t-elle été
   ☐ Filed / déposée   ☐ Attached / annexée

8. Date of last annual meeting – Date de la dernière assemblée annuelle

8. Does the corporation "distribute" its securities to the public?
   La société émet-elle ses valeurs mobilières par voie de souscription publique?
   ☐ Yes / Oui   ☐ No / Non

10. Has the corporation . . . . – La société a-t-elle . . . .
    A. Assets exceeding $5 million – un actif excédant 5 millions de dollars
    ☐ Yes / Oui   ☐ No / Non
    OR / OU
    B. Gross revenues this year exceeding $10 million – des revenus bruts excédant 10 millions de dollars
    ☐ Yes / Oui   ☐ No / Non

11. Does the corporation have 15 or more shareholders?
    La société a-t-elle 15 actionnaires ou plus?
    ☐ Yes / Oui   ☐ No / Non

Signature	Title – Titre	Date	Telephone No. / N° de téléphone

DEPARTMENT ONLY – MINISTÈRE SEULEMENT

Date received / Date de réception	Validation	Key code – Code clé	Cheque – Chèque	Amount – Montant

Note: A fee of $30 is required, payable to the Receiver General for Canada
Note: Un droit de 30 $ est requis, payable au receveur général du Canada
Please see instructions on reverse side
Voir les instructions au verso
RETURN THIS COPY
COPIE À RETOURNER

Canada Business Corporations Act

ANNUAL RETURN
FORM 22
INSTRUCTIONS

General

In accordance with section 263 of the *Canada Business Corporations Act* and subsection 4(3) of the *Canada Business Corporations Regulations*, a corporation must submit to the Director an annual return with the prescribed fee of $30 within 60 days after the anniversary date of its incorporation, continuance or amalgamation, as the case may be.

Item 3

State the date of the corporation's financial year end.

Item 4

This is the anniversary date of incorporation, continuance or amalgamation of the corporation under the *Act*.

Item 5

State the main actual business or businesses of the corporation, indicating, where possible, the corporation's standard industrial classification code (S.I.C.C.).

Item 6

Indicate whether there has been any change of directors since the last annual return and whether a notice of change of directors (Form 6) has been filed. Note that under subsection 113(1) of the act a notice of change of directors must be filed within fifteen (15) days of a change of directors.

Item 7

Indicate whether there has been any change of registered office since the last annual return and if a notice of change of registered office (Form 3) has been filed. Note that under subsection 19(4) of the Act a notice of change of registered office must be filed within fifteen (15) days after a change of registered office.

Item 8

Indicate the date of the last annual meeting.

Item 9

Indicate whether the corporation is a "distributing corporation", that is, a corporation that has made a distribution of its securities to the public within the meaning of subsection 2(7) of the Act.

Item 10

Indicate whether the corporation's total assets and gross revenues, including that of its affiliates, exceed $5 million and $10 million respectively pursuant to section 160 of the Act.

Item 11

Indicate whether the corporation has 15 or more shareholders. Part XIII of the Act requires any corporation that has 15 shareholders or more to solicit proxies.

Signature

A director or authorized officer of the corporation shall sign the return.

Completed form to be sent to:

The Director, Canada Business Corporations Act
Place du Portage
Hull, Quebec, Canada
K1A 0C9

Loi régissant les sociétés par actions de régime fédéral

RAPPORT ANNUEL
FORMULE 22
INSTRUCTIONS

Généralités

En vertu de l'article 263 de la *Loi régissant les sociétés par actions de régime fédéral* et du paragraphe 4(3) du *Règlement sur les sociétés par actions de régime fédéral*, toute société doit soumettre au directeur un rapport annuel accompagné du droit prescrit de 30 $ dans les 60 jours suivant la date anniversaire de constitution, prorogation ou fusion de la société, selon le cas.

Rubrique 3

Donner la date de la fin de l'exercice de la société.

Rubrique 4

Date anniversaire de constitution, prorogation ou fusion de la société sous le régime de la *Loi régissant les sociétés par actions de régime fédéral*.

Rubrique 5

Donner la ou les principales activités de la société en utilisant, si c'est possible, le code de classification des activités économiques.

Rubrique 6

Indiquer s'il y a eu un changement des administrateurs depuis le dernier rapport annuel et si un avis de changement des administrateurs (formule 6) a été déposé. En vertu du paragraphe 113(1) de la Loi un avis de changement des administrateurs doit être fourni dans les 15 jours suivant un changement.

Rubrique 7

Indiquer s'il y a eu un changement du siège social depuis le dernier rapport annuel et si un avis de changement du siège social (formule 3) a été déposé. En vertu du paragraphe 19(4) de la Loi, un avis de changement du siège social doit être fourni dans les 15 jours suivant un changement.

Rubrique 8

Indiquer la date de la dernière assemblée annuelle.

Rubrique 9

Indiquer si la société procède à l'émission de ses valeurs mobilières par voie de souscription publique au sens du paragraphe 2(7) de la Loi.

Rubrique 10

Indiquer si l'actif et les revenus bruts de la société, y compris ceux des personnes morales du même groupe, excèdent 5 millions et 10 millions de dollars respectivement, selon l'article 160 de la Loi.

Rubrique 11

Indiquer si la société a 15 actionnaires ou plus. La partie XIII de la Loi exige que toute société comptant 15 actionnaires ou plus sollicite des procurations.

Signature

Un administrateur ou un dirigeant autorisé de la société doit signer le rapport.

Formule complétée doit être envoyée au :

Directeur, Loi régissant les sociétés par actions de régime fédéral
Place du Portage
Hull (Québec) Canada   K1A 0C9 "

*Form 24. Insider report

* Forms 24 and 25 of Schedule I to the Canada Business Corporations Regulation (SOR/89-323) are revoked and replaced with a single Form 24. The amendment was brought into force September 20, 1990 by SOR/90-660.

INSTRUCTIONS

Where there is no ownership of or direction over securities of the reporting issuer, a report is not required in Quebec, Ontario, Manitoba, Saskatchewan or Alberta or under federal legislation (*Canada Business Corporations Act* and the *Bank Act*).

NOTE:

"Reporting Issuer", wherever it appears herein and in the form, has the same meaning as the words "distributing corporation" as defined in subsection 126(1) of the *Canada Business Corporations Act*.

1. Identification of the reporting issuer

Provide the full legal name of the reporting issuer. Use a separate form for each reporting issuer

2. Insider data

Indicate the relationship to the reporting issuer (see List of Codes). If more than one relationship, indicate all applicable codes.

Specify the date of the last report filed or if this is a first (initial) report, the date on which the holder became an insider.

3. Identification of the insider

Provide the following information about the insider: name, address, business telephone number, insider number and CUSIP number (corporate insider) if applicable

Insider Report forms in English or French are available from the federal, Ontario, Quebec and Manitoba jurisdictions.

4. Jurisdiction where the issuer is a reporting issuer or the equivalent

Indicate each jurisdiction where the issuer is a reporting issuer or the equivalent.

5. Insider holdings and changes

Show direct and indirect holdings separately.

Where a transaction is reported, both direct and indirect holdings of that class of securities must be shown.

For first (initial) report complete only:

Ⓐ designation of class of securities held,

Ⓓ present balance of class of securities held,

Ⓔ nature of ownership (see List of Codes).

Ⓕ identification of the registered holder where ownership is indirect.

If shares were acquired while an insider, complete all sections.

Ⓐ Indicate a designation of the securities traded that is sufficient to identify the class, including yield, series and maturity.

Ⓑ Indicate the number of securities or, in the case of debt securities, the aggregate face value of the class held, directly and indirectly, before the transaction that is being reported.

Ⓒ Indicate for each transaction

– the date of the transaction;
– the nature of the transaction (see List of Codes);
– the number of securities acquired or disposed of or, in case of the debt securities, the aggregate face value;
– the unit price paid or received on the day of the transaction, excluding the commission;
– if the report is in American dollars, check the space under "$ US"

Ⓓ Indicate the number of securities or, in the case of debt securities, the aggregate face value of the class held, directly or indirectly, after the transaction that is being reported;

Ⓔ Indicate the nature of ownership of the class of securities held (see List of Codes).

Ⓕ For securities that are indirectly held, identify the registered holder.

6. Remarks

Add any explanation necessary to the clear understanding of the report.

If space provided for any item is insufficient, additional sheets may be used. Additional sheets must refer to the item and must be properly identified and signed.

Only the insider is permitted to change a report.

7. Signature

The report must be signed and dated.

Two copies of the report must be filed with each jurisdiction within the time limits prescribed by the applicable laws of that jurisdiction. See addresses below.

One of the two copies must be signed by hand.

If the report is filed on behalf of a company, partnership, trust or other entity, the name must appear in printed form immediately following the signature. In the case of a company, there must be filed with each jurisdiction in which the report is filed a certified copy of the resolution or by-law authorizing the person or persons to sign. If the report is signed on behalf of an individual by an agent, there shall be filed with each jurisdiction in which the report is filed a duly completed power of attorney. The name of each individual signing a report shall be typed or printed legibly.

LIST OF CODES

Relationship to reporting issuer (Box no. 2)

Reporting issuer that has acquired securities issued by itself (or by any of its affiliates — *Canada Business Corporations Act*)	1
Subsidiary of the reporting user	2
Security holder who beneficially owns or who exercises control or direction over more than 10% of the securities of the reporting issuer (*Bank Act* and the *Quebec Securities Act* — 10% of a class of shares) to which are attached voting rights or an unlimited right to a share of the profits and to its assets in case of winding up.	3
Director of a reporting issuer	4
Senior officer of a reporting issuer	5
Director or senior officer of a security holder referred to in no. 3	6
Director or senior officer of an affiliate (*Bank Act*) or of a subsidiary under the *Quebec Securities Act* of the reporting issuer, other than in 4, 5 and 6	7
Deemed insider under the *Canada Business Corporations Act* or the *Bank Act*	8

Nature of the transaction (Box no. 5 Ⓒ)

Acquisition or disposition carried out in the market, excluding the exercise of an option	10
Acquisition or disposition carried out privately	20
Acquisition or disposition pursuant to a take-over bid	22
Change in the nature of ownership	25
Acquisition or disposition under a plan	30
Stock dividend	35
Acquisition or disposition of a call option	40
Acquisition or disposition of a put option	45
Expiration of an option	46
Acquisition or disposition by gift	50
Acquisition by inheritance or disposition by bequest	55
Short sale	60
Exercise of warrants	70
Exercise of rights	75
Exercise of options	76
Conversion or exchange	78
Capital reorganization	82
Stock split or consolidation	84
Redemption — cancellation	85
Issuer bid	87
Compensation for property	90
Compensation for services	95
Grant of options	96
Other (please explain in Remarks)	97
Correction of information (amended report)	99

Nature of ownership (Box no. 5 Ⓔ)

Direct ownership	0
Indirect ownership (identify the registered holder)	1

Alberta Securities Commission
21st Floor
10025 Jasper Avenue
Edmonton, Alberta
T5J 3Z5

British Columbia Securities Commission
1200, 865 Hornby Street
Vancouver, British Columbia
V6Z 2H4

Commission des valeurs mobilières
du Québec
C.P. 246, Tour de la Bourse
Montréal (Québec)
H4Z 1G3

The Director, Canada Business
Corporations Act
Place du Portage
50, rue Victoria
Hull (Québec)
K1A 0C9

Office of the Superintendent
of Financial Institutions Canada
13th floor, Kent Square
255 Albert Street
Ottawa, Ontario
K1A 0H2

Manitoba Securities Commission
1128 – 405 Broadway
Winnipeg, Manitoba
R3C 3L6

Ontario Securities Commission
Suite 1800, Box 55
20 Queen Street West
Toronto, Ontario
M5H 3S8

Saskatchewan Securities Commission
8th Floor
1914 Hamilton Street
Regina, Saskatchewan
S4P 3V7

Form 26. Statement of executive remuneration

Canada Business Corporations Act
Statement of Executive Remuneration
Form 26

Loi régissant les sociétés par actions de régime fédéral
Déclaration de rémunération de la haute direction
Formule 26

1. General

For the purposes of this form, "executive officer" of a corporation means the chairman and any vice-chairman of the board of directors of the corporation, where that chairman or vice-chairman performs the functions of the office on a full-time basis, the president of the corporation, any vice-president in charge of a principal business unit of the corporation, such as sales, finance or production, and any officer of the corporation or of a subsidiary who performs a policy-making function in respect of the corporation, whether or not the officer is also a director of the corporation or the subsidiary.

Remuneration of directors who are not also executive officers is taken into account only as provided in section 6.

2. Cash

(1) State the number of executive officers of the corporation.

(2) State the aggregate cash remuneration paid to the executive officers of the corporation by the corporation and its subsidiaries for services rendered during the most recently completed financial year.

(3) For the purposes of subsection (2),

(a) cash remuneration includes salaries, fees, commissions and bonuses and, in addition to amounts actually paid during and for the most recently completed financial year, the following:

    (i) bonuses to be paid for services rendered during the most recently completed financial year, unless these bonuses have not been allocated;

    (ii) bonuses paid during the most recently completed financial year for services rendered in a previous financial year, and

    (iii) any remuneration other than bonuses earned during the most recently completed financial year, the payment of which is deferred;

(b) remuneration paid to an individual for a period during which the individual was not an executive officer shall not be included in the determination of cash remuneration of executive officers; and

(c) remuneration paid during the most recently completed financial year that was disclosed in the filing of a document complying with the requirements of this form or a predecessor thereof in respect of a financial year other than the most recently completed financial year shall not be included.

(4) At the option of the corporation, the cash remuneration figure set out pursuant to subsection (2) may be broken down into categories, such as salaries, fees, commissions and bonuses.

3. Plans

(1) Describe briefly any plan pursuant to which cash or non-cash remuneration was paid or distributed to executive officers during the most recently completed financial year, or is proposed to be so paid or distributed in a subsequent year, and include in the description

(a) a summary of how the plan operates;
(b) the criteria used to determine amounts payable;
(c) the periods during which benefits will be measured;

(d) payment schedules;
(e) any recent material amendments to the plan;
(f) amounts paid or distributed during the most recently completed financial year; and
(g) amounts accrued for the group during the most recently completed financial year, inasmuch as the distribution or unconditional vesting of those amounts is not subject to future events.

(2) With respect to any plan involving options to purchase securities granted to executive officers during the most recently completed financial year, set out

(a) a summary of how the plan operates;
(b) the criteria used to determine the number of securities under option;
(c) the periods during which the benefits will be measured;

(d) payment schedules;
(e) all recent material amendments to the plan;
(f) the number of securities optioned during the most recently completed financial year;
(g) the designation and aggregate number of securities under option; and
(h) the average exercise price per security (when options with differing terms are granted, the information should be given for each class or type of option) and, when that price is less than the

1. Généralités

Dans la présente formule, « haute direction » d'une société désigne le président et les vice-présidents du conseil d'administration qui remplissent leurs fonctions à plein temps, le président de la société, les vice-présidents responsables d'un secteur de l'activité principale de la société, notamment les ventes, les finances ou la production, et tout dirigeant de la société ou d'une filiale qui exerce des pouvoirs de décision sur la politique de la société, qu'il soit ou non également administrateur de la société ou de la filiale.

La rémunération des administrateurs qui ne font pas partie de la haute direction n'est prise en compte qu'aux fins de l'article 6.

2. Rémunération en espèces

(1) Indiquer le nombre de personnes composant la haute direction de la société.

(2) Indiquer le montant global de la rémunération en espèces versé à la haute direction de la société par la société et ses filiales en contrepartie des services rendus au cours du dernier exercice.

(3) Aux fins du paragraphe (2):

(a) la rémunération en espèces comprend notamment le traitement, les jetons de présence, les commissions et les primes effectivement versés au cours et au titre du dernier exercice, ainsi que:

    (i) les primes à percevoir en contrepartie des services rendus au cours du dernier exercice, à moins qu'elles n'aient pas encore été attribuées,

    (ii) les primes payées au cours du dernier exercice pour des services rendus dans un exercice antérieur,

    (iii) toute rémunération, autre que les primes, gagnées au cours du dernier exercice, mais dont le versement est différé;

(b) la rémunération versée à un membre de la haute direction pour toute période pendant laquelle il n'était pas membre de la haute direction n'entre pas dans le calcul de la rémunération en espèces de la haute direction;

(c) la rémunération versée au cours du dernier exercice qui a déjà été déclarée dans un document déposé conformément aux exigences de la présente formule ou d'une formule antérieure relativement à un exercice autre que le dernier exercice n'entre pas dans le calcul de la rémunération en espèces de la haute direction.

(4) Au gré de la société, la rémunération en espèces visée au paragraphe (2) peut être ventilée selon des postes tels que salaires, jetons de présence, commissions et primes.

3. Rémunération sous forme de régimes

(1) Décrire succinctement tout régime en vertu duquel une rémunération, en espèces ou non, a été versée aux membres de la haute direction ou répartie entre eux au cours du dernier exercice ou est censée l'être au cours d'un exercice ultérieur et inclure les renseignements suivants:

(a) le sommaire du mode de fonctionnement du régime;
(b) les critères utilisés pour déterminer les sommes à verser;
(c) les périodes en fonction desquelles les prestations sont déterminées;

(d) le tableau des versements;
(e) toute modification importante récemment apportée au régime;
(f) les sommes versées ou réparties au cours du dernier exercice;

(g) les sommes portées au compte de la haute direction au cours du dernier exercice, dans la mesure où le versement ou l'acquisition définitive de ces sommes n'est pas subordonnée à un événement futur.

(2) À l'égard de tout régime en vertu duquel des options d'achat de valeurs mobilières ont été accordées aux membres de la haute direction au cours du dernier exercice, donner les renseignements suivants:

(a) le sommaire du mode de fonctionnement du régime;
(b) les critères utilisés pour déterminer le nombre de valeurs mobilières visées par les options;
(c) les périodes en fonction desquelles les prestations sont déterminées;

(d) le tableau des versements;
(e) toute modification importante récemment apportée au régime;
(f) le nombre de valeurs mobilières sur lesquelles des options ont été accordées au cours du dernier exercice;
(g) la désignation et le nombre total de valeurs mobilières visées par les options;
(h) le prix moyen de levée d'option par valeur mobilière (lorsque des options dont les conditions diffèrent sont accordées, ce renseignement doit être donné pour chaque catégorie ou genre

market price of the security underlying the option on the date the option is granted, provide the market price on that date.

(3) With respect to options exercised during the most recently completed financial year, provide, with respect to each class or type of option, in addition to the information prescribed by paragraphs (2)(a) to (f), the aggregate net value (market value less exercise price on the date of the exercise) of the securities under option.

(4) For the purposes of this section:

(a) remuneration pursuant to a plan need be taken into account only to the extent that the plan discriminates in scope, terms or operation in favour of executive officers **or** is not available to all full-time employees, other than those covered by a collective agreement;

(b) where an amount paid or distributed pursuant to a plan is disclosed under section 2, that amount shall not be included under paragraph (1)(f) if a statement is made under this section confirming that disclosure of the amount was made under section 2;

(c) amounts paid or distributed that are disclosed under paragraph (1)(f) shall not include amounts paid or distributed that have been disclosed in a previous filing of a document, other than a prospectus, complying with the requirements of this form under paragraph (1)(g) as accrued for the group in respect of a financial year other than the most recently completed financial year;

(d) ''options'' includes all options, share purchase warrants or rights, other than those issued to all security holders of the same class or to all security holders of the same class resident in Canada on a *pro rata basis*, and an extension of an option shall be deemed to be the granting of an option;

(e) ''plan'' includes any plan, contract, authorization or arrangement, whether or not set forth in any formal document, and may be applicable to only one person, but does not include the *Canada Pension Plan* or a similar government plan.

4. Other remuneration

(1) Describe all other remuneration not referred to in section 2 or 3 paid during the most recently completed financial year, including personal benefits and securities or property paid or distributed other than pursuant to a plan referred to in section 3, which remuneration is not offered on the same terms to all full-time employees, other than those covered by a collective agreement.

(2) For the purposes of describing other remuneration under subsection (1), the value to be given to such remuneration shall be the aggregate incremental cost to the corporation or subsidiary.

(3) For the purposes of subsection (2), ''incremental cost'' is the cost to the corporation or subsidiary of conferring a benefit on an individual, where that cost would not be otherwise incurred by the corporation if the benefit were not so conferred.

(4) Where the aggregate value of the remuneration disclosed under subsection (1) does not exceed the lesser of $10,000 times the number of persons in the group or 10 per cent of the remuneration stated under section 2, it is necessary to declare that fact only.

5. Termination of employment or change of control

Describe any plan or arrangement in respect of remuneration received or that may be received by executive officers in the corporation's most recently completed financial year for compensating such officers in the event of termination of employment (as a result of resignation, retirement, change of control, etc.) or a change in responsibilities following a change of control, where the value of such compensation exeeds $60,000 per executive officer.

6. Remuneration of directors

(1) Describe

(a) any standard arrangements, stating amounts, pursuant to which directors are remunerated by the corporation for their services in their capacity as directors, including any additional amounts payable for committee participation or special assignments; and

(b) any other arrangements, stating amounts, in addition or in lieu of any standard arrangement, pursuant to which directors were remunerated by the corporation in their capacity as director during the most recently completed financial year.

(2) Where remuneration is not in cash form, state the value of the benefit conferred or, if it is not possible to state the value, describe the benefit conferred.

d'option) et lorsque ce prix est inférieur au cours de la valeur mobilière visée par l'option à la date à laquelle celle-ci est accordée, le cours de la valeur mobilière à cette date.

(3) À l'égard des options levées au cours du dernier exercice de la société, indiquer, pour chaque catégorie ou genre d'option, outre les renseignements prévus aux alinéas (2) a) à f), la valeur nette totale des valeurs mobilières visées par les options (le cours moins le prix de levée d'option à la date de la levée d'option).

(4) Aux fins du présent article:

(a) la rémunération versée en vertu d'un régime n'est prise en compte que dans la mesure où le régime n'est pas offert à tous les employés à plein temps non régis par une convention collective **ou lorsqu'il** favorise les membres de la haute direction par son champ d'application, ses conditions ou son fonctionnement;

(b) lorsqu'une somme versée ou répartie aux termes d'un régime est déclarée en vertu de l'article 2, cette somme n'entre pas dans le calcul de la rémunération en espèces visée à l'alinéa (1) f) si une déclaration faite un vertu du présent article vient confirmer que la somme a été déclarée en vertu de l'article 2;

(c) les sommes versées ou réparties qui sont déclarées en vertu de l'alinéa (1) f) ne comprennent pas celles qui ont déjà été déclarées selon l'alinéa (1) g) dans un document, autre qu'un prospectus, déposé conformément aux exigences de la présente formule, comme sommes portées au compte du groupe relativement à un exercice autre que le dernier exercice;

(d) le terme «options» désigne les options, les droits ou les bons de souscription à des actions, autres que ceux qui sont attribués aux mêmes conditions et au prorata à tous les détenteurs de valeurs mobilières de la même catégorie ou à tous ceux d'entre eux qui résident au Canada; la prolongation d'une option est considérée comme l'octroi d'une option;

(e) le terme «régime» désigne tout régime, contrat, autorisation ou arrangement, qu'il soit ou non formulé dans un document officiel et qu'il s'applique à une ou à plusieurs personnes; est exclu d'un régime le *Régime de pensions du Canada* ou un régime public semblable.

4. Autre rémunération

(1) Décrire toute autre rémunération non mentionnée aux articles 2 ou 3 qui a été versée au cours du dernier exercice, y compris les avantages personnels et les valeurs mobilières ou biens accordés ou répartis autrement qu'en vertu d'un régime mentionné à l'article 3, et qui n'est pas offerte au même conditions à tous les employés à plein temps non régis par une convention collective.

(2) Pour la description des autres formes de rémunération visées au paragraphe (1), la valeur à indiquer est le coût marginal global supporté par la société ou la filiale.

(3) Aux fins du paragraphe (2), « coût marginal » désigne le coût supporté par la société ou la filiale pour accorder un avantage à un particulier, lequel coût ne serait pas par ailleurs engagé si l'avantage n'était pas accordé.

(4) Lorsque la valeur totale de la rémunération déclarée en vertu du paragraphe (1) ne dépasse pas le moins élevé des montants suivants: le produit de 10 000 $ fois le nombre de personnes dans le groupe ou 10% de la rémunération déclarée en vertu de l'article 2, il suffit de le mentionner.

5. Cessation d'emploi ou changement de contrôle

Décrire tout régime ou arrangement relatif à la rémunération touchée ou à toucher par les membres de la haute direction au cours du dernier exercice de la société, à titre d'indemnité en cas de cessation d'emploi (démission, retraite, changement de contrôle) ou en cas de changement de fonctions par suite d'un changement de contrôle, lorsque l'indemnité excède 60 000 $ par personne.

6. Rémunération des administrateurs

(1) Décrire:

(a) le mode normal de rémunération des administrateurs, en indiquant le montant de celle-ci, pour les services rendus en leur qualité d'administrateurs, y compris toute rémunération supplémentaire pour participation aux travaux d'un comité ou pour mission spéciale;

(b) tout autre mode de rémunération des administrateurs, en indiquant le montant de celle-ci, en plus ou à la place du mode normal, pour les services rendus en leur qualité d'administrateurs au cours du dernier exercice.

(2) Dans le cas d'une rémunération autre qu'en espèces, indiquer la valeur de l'avantage accordé ou, si cela est impossbile, le décrire.

Form 27. Application for exemption

Canada Business Corporations Act   Loi régissant les sociétés par actions de régime fédéral

"FORM 27
APPLICATION FOR EXEMPTION
(SUBSECTIONS 2(8), 10(2), 82(3), 127(8) and 151(1), SECTION 156 and SUBSECTIONS 160(3), 163(4), 171(2), and 187(11) of the Act and SECTION 75 of the Regulations)

FORMULE 27
DEMANDE DE DISPENSE
(PARAGRAPHES 2(8), 10(2), 82(3), 127(8 151(1), ARTICLE 156 et PARAGRAPHES 160(3), 163(4), 171(2) et 18 de la Loi: ARTICLE 75 du Règlement)

1 – Name of corporation – Dénomination de la société	2 – Corporation No. – N° de la sociét

3 – Type of application for exemption – Type de la demande de dispense

☐ Distribution to the public – s. 2(8)
Souscription publique – par. 2(8)

☐ Name of corporation – s. 10(2)
Dénomination de la société – par. 10(2)

☐ Trust indentures – s. 82(3)
Acte de fiducie – par. 82(3)

☐ Insider report – s. 127(8)
Rapport d'initié – par. 127(8)

☐ Proxy solicitation – s. 151(1)
Sollicitation de procurations – par. 151(1)

☐ Financial disclosure – s. 156
Divulgation financière – art. 156

☐ Affiliation exemption – s. 160(3)
Dispense de groupe – par. 160(3)

☐ Auditor exemption – s. 163(4)
Dispense d'un vérificateur – par. 163(4)

☐ Audit committee – s. 171(2)
Comité de vérification – par. 171(2)

☐ Continued reference to par value – s. 187(11)
Maintien de la désignation de valeur nominale ou au pair – par. 187(

4 – Name and address of applicant – Nom et adresse du demandeur

5 – Capacity of applicant – Qualité du demandeur

6 – List of documents – Liste des documents

Document Number – Numéro	Description of documents – Description des documents
1	Description and details of exemption sought Description et détails de la dispense demandée
2	Statement of facts Exposé des faits
3	Argument Exposé des motifs
4	
5	
6	
7	

The undersigned hereby certifies that the information given in this application and accompanying documents is true and complete in every respect.

Le(la) soussigné(e) certifie que les renseignements donnés dans la présent(demande et dans les documents l'accompagnant sont véridiques et complets à tous égards.

Signature of applicant – Signature du demandeur	Date

FOR DEPARTMENTAL USE ONLY – À L'USAGE DU MINISTÈRE SEULEMENT

Date received – Date de réception	Fee received – Droit reçu

CCA 1397 (02-89) 46

Canada Business Corporations Act

Application for Exemption
FORM 27
INSTRUCTIONS

Loi régissant les sociétés par actions de régime fédéral

Demande de dispense
FORMULE 27
INSTRUCTIONS

Format
Documents required to be sent to the Director pursuant to the *Canada Business Corporations Act* must conform to sections 5 to 10 of the *Canada Business Corporations Regulations*.

Item 1
Set out the full legal name of the corporation.

Item 2
Set out the corporation number.

Item 3
Check the appropriate box to indicate the provision of the Act to which the requested exemption relates.

Item 4
Set out the full name (first name, initial and family name if an individual) and address, including postal code.

Item 5
State the capacity in which the applicant acts; for example, a director, authorized officer or solicitor of a corporation, or a solicitor or agent of an applicant.

Item 6
Designate by a number each document accompanying the application and complete accordingly the table in Item 6. Each application must be supported by
(a) a description and details of the exemption sought;
(b) a statement of facts that states the issue and summarizes briefly the material facts; and
(c) an argument that states the legal, economic or other reasons why the application should be granted.

Signature
The applicant or the applicant's authorized agent shall sign the application. If the applicant is a corporation, a director or authorized agent of the corporation shall sign the Application.

Completed document and fees payable to the Receiver General are to be sent to:

The Director, Canada Business Corporations Act
Place du Portage
Hull, Quebec, Canada
K1A 0C9

Présentation
Tous les documents dont l'envoi au directeur est exigé par la *Loi régissant les sociétés par actions de régime fédéral* doivent être conformes aux articles 5 à 10 du *Règlement sur les sociétés par actions de régime fédéral*.

Rubrique 1
Indiquer la dénomination officielle complète de la société

Rubrique 2
Indiquer le numéro de la société.

Rubrique 3
Cocher la case appropriée pour indiquer la disposition de la Loi à laquelle la demande de dispense se rapporte

Rubrique 4
Indiquer le nom complet (prénom, initiales et nom de famille, s'il s'agit d'un particulier) et l'adresse, y compris le code postal

Rubrique 5
Indiquer à quel titre le demandeur agit, par exemple, administrateur, dirigeant autorisé d'une société, procureur ou mandataire du demandeur

Rubrique 6
Désigner par un numéro chaque document accompagnant la demande et remplir en conséquence le tableau de la rubrique 6 Chaque demande doit être accompagnée
a) d'une description et des détails concernant la dispense demandée.
b) d'un exposé des faits énonçant la question et décrivant brièvement les faits importants.
c) d'un exposé énonçant les motifs légaux, économiques ou autres qui justifieraient l'octroi de la dispense

Signature
Le demandeur ou son mandataire autorisé doit signer la demande. Si le demandeur est une société, un administrateur ou un dirigeant autorisé de la société doit signer la demande

Le document rempli et les droits payables au receveur général doivent être envoyés au :

Directeur, Loi régissant les sociétés par actions de régime fédéral
Place du Portage
Hull (Québec) Canada
K1A 0C9 "

Schedule II

Fees

[¶24-855]

1. (*a*) Revoked

   (*b*) Revoked

   (*c*) Each request for a name search or an analysis of a trade name database that cannot be effected by a standard computer search .... Cost plus 20%

   (*d*) Each request for a search or analysis of the Director's records .... Cost plus 20%
   (Am eff. Sept. 1, 1977. SOR/77-707)

2. Issuance by the Director of

   (*a*) a certificate of incorporation issued pursuant to section 8 .... $500

   (*b*) a certificate of amendment issued pursuant to subsection 27(5), section 178 or subsection 191(5) or 192(7) (except a certificate of amendment referred to in paragraph 82(2)(*a*) of these Regulations) 200

   (*c*) a restated certificate of incorporation issued pursuant to subsection 180(3) (unless issued with certificate of amendment) 50

   (*d*) a certificate of amalgamation issued pursuant to subsection 185(4) 200

   (*e*) a certificate of continuance issued pursuant to subsection 187(4) (unless subsection 268(8) applies) 200

   (*f*) a document evidencing satisfaction of the Director, as required under subsection 188(1) 200

   (*g*) a certificate of revival issued pursuant to subsection 209(3) 200

   (*h*) a certificate of revocation of intent to dissolve issued pursuant to subsection 211(11) 50

   (*i*) a certificate referred to in subsection 263(2) 10

   (*j*) a corrected certificate issued pursuant to subsection 265(1) .... same fee as would be payable for the certificate it replaces

(SOR/91-567, P.C. 1991-1904, s. 2.)

3.   Sending the annual return to the Director under
        subsection 263(1) $50

(SOR/92-729, P.C. 1992-2539.)

4.   Application to the Director for an exemption under
        subsections 2(8), 10(2), 82(3), 151(1), 160(3), 163(4), 171(2)
        or 187(11)   25

5.   Application to the Director for an exemption under
        subsection 156   100

6.   Uncertified copies of documents furnished by the
        Director under subsection 266(2), per page   1

7.   Certified copies of documents furnished by the
        Director under subsection 266(2), per certificate   35
        (Am eff. Apr. 6, 1979. SOR/79-316)

NOTE: All references to provisions are references to provisions of the Act, unless
        otherwise specified. (SOR/91-567, P.C. 1991-1904, s. 3.)

Table of Concordance
(Canada Business Corporations Act)

Based on R.S.C. 1970, c. 33 Section	Based on R.S.C. 1985, c. C-44 Section	Based on R.S.C. 1970, c. 33 Section	Based on R.S.C. 1985, c. C-44 Section
1–31	1–31	75	80
31.1	32	76	81
31.2	33	77	82
32	34	78	83
33	35	79	84
34	36	80	85
35	37	81	86
36	38	82	87
37	39	83	88
38	40	84	89
39	41	85	90
40	42	86	91
41	43	87	92
42	44	88	93
43	45	89	94
43.1	46	90	95
43.2	47	91	96
44	48	92	97
45	49	93	98
46	50	93	99
47	51	95	100
48	52	96	101
49	53	97	102
50	54	98	103
51	55	99	104
52	56	100	105
53	57	101	106
54	58	102	107
55	59	103	108
56	60	104	109
57	61	105	110
58	62	106	111
59	63	107	112
60	64	108	113
61	65	109	114
62	66	110	115
63	67	111	116
64	68	112	117
65	69	113	118
66	70	114	119
67	71	115	120
68	72	116	121
69	73	117	122
70	74	118	123
70.1	75	119	124
71	76	120	125
72	77	121	126
73	78	122	127
74	79	122.1	128

Based on R.S.C. 1970, c. 33 Section	Based on R.S.C. 1985, c. C-44 Section	Based on R.S.C. 1970, c. 33 Section	Based on R.S.C. 1985, c. C-44 Section
123	129	185.1	192
124	130	186	193
125	131	187	194
126	132	188	195
127	133	189	196
128	134	190	197
129	135	191	198
130	136	192	199
131	137	193	200
132	138	194	201
133	139	195	202
134	140	196	203
135	141	197	204
136	142	198	205
137	143	199	206
138	144	200	207
139	145	201	208
140	146	202	209
141	147	203	210
142	148	204	211
143	149	205	212
144	150	206	213
145	151	207	214
146	152	208	215
147	153	209	216
148	154	210	217
149	155	211	218
150	156	212	219
151	157	213	220
152	158	214	221
153	159	215	222
154	160	216	223
155	161	217	224
156	162	218	225
157	163	219	226
158	164	220	227
159	165	221	228
160	166	222	229
161	167	223	230
162	168	224	231
163	169	225	232
164	170	226	233
165	171	227	234
166	172	228	235
167	173	229	236
168	174	230	237
169	175	231	238
170	176	232	239
171	177	233	240
172	178	234	241
173	179	235	242
174	180	236	243
175	181	237	244
176	182	238	245
177	183	239	246
178	184	240	247
179	185	241	248
180	186	242	249
181	187	243	250
182	188	244	251
183	189	245	252
184	190	246	253
185	191	247	254

Based on R.S.C. 1970, c. 33 Section	Based on R.S.C. 1985, c. C-44 Section	Based on R.S.C. 1970, c. 33 Section	Based on R.S.C. 1985, c. C-44 Section
248	255	257	264
249	256	258	265
250	257	259	266
251	258	260	267
252	259	261	268
253	260	262–264	—
254	261	265	—
255	262	266	—
256	263		

Index

Paragraph

A

Absolute privilege
. inspector..24-282

Actions
. civil, effect of Act.................................24-350
. defined..24-319

Address
. registered office........................23-072–23-074

Adverse claim
. defined..23-192
. inquiry...23-329
. . fiduciary..23-331
. issuer's liability......................................23-333
. notice
. . broker's receipt after taking
     delivery...23-293
. . deemed given..23-254
. . duration...23-332
. . endorsement in bearer form.............23-283
. . fiduciary's duty....................................23-255
. . offeror to dissenting offeree.............24-052
. . staleness..23-256
. . title of purchaser...................23-251–23-252

Adverse claimant
. notice from issuer...................................23-330

Affidavit
. application for shareholders'
     lists...23-087–23-088

Affiliate
. defined..23-002–23-003
. financial statements...............................23-726
. . exemption..23-727

Agents — see also Brokers
. authority...23-066
. duties and rights.......................23-348–23-349
. liability...23-250
. warranty......................................23-249–23-250

Agreement
. unanimous shareholder
. . articles of incorporation.....................23-029
. . defined...23-002

Amalgamations
. agreement...23-830
. . termination..23-837
. articles — see Articles of amalgamation
. cancellation of shares............................23-831

Paragraph

Amalgamations — continued
. certificate...23-843
. . effect of..23-844
. notice..23-842
. shareholder approval................23-832; 23-836
. short-form
. . horizontal..23-839
. . vertical...23-838
. voting..23-834–23-835

Annual reports — see Financial statements

Annual returns
. submission..24-413

Appeals
. court order..24-343
. Director's decision...................................24-340

Application to court
. summary..24-342

Appropriate person
. defined..23-263
. determination...23-264
. endorsement of security.........................23-265

Arrangements and compromises
. approval application................................23-907
. articles of arrangement...........................23-910
. certificate...23-911
. . effects...23-912
. defined..23-905
. insolvent corporation's..........................23-906
. notice to Director....................................23-909
. powers of court..23-908

Articles
. amendments of...23-805
. defined..23-002
. director's refusal to file...........24-338–24-339
. . appeal...24-340
. filing...24-411
. termination...23-806
. . number name...23-806a

Articles of amalgamation
. approval and certificate...........23-840–23-843
. form...24-853
. sending to Director,
     procedure.................................23-840–23-843

Articles of amendment
. amalgamation, shareholders'
     approval....................................23-832–23-837

Paragraph

Articles of amendment — continued
. certificate.....................................23-822–23-824
. class vote..................................23-815–23-818
. constraints on share
   transfer..................................23-807–23-812
. delivery to Director...........................23-819
. effect on claims..............................23-824
. form...24-853
. notice of...23-814
. proposal of director or
   shareholder.......................................23-813
. reorganization....................................23-898
. rights preserved................................23-824
. share series...23-122
. special resolution..............................23-805
. termination..23-806

Articles of arrangement
. approval of arrangement.....................23-907
. corporation insolvent.........................23-906
. defined...23-905
. issuance..23-910
. notice to Director...............................23-909
. powers of court...................................23-908

Articles of continuance
. amendments.....................................23-845a
. notice deemed to be......................23-860a
. prescribed form.................................23-846

Articles of dissolution
. form...24-853
. submission to Director.........................24-167

Articles of incorporation
. by-laws..23-028
. continuance (import)...........................23-846
. delivery..23-030
. form...24-853
. provisions...........................23-027–23-028
. restated...............................23-825–23-828
. . form..24-853
. shareholders' agreement....................23-029

Articles of reorganization
. form...24-853
. powers of court...................................23-898
. prescribed form.................................23-900

Articles of revival
. form...24-853

Audit
. errors....................................23-786–23-789

Audit committee
. application for exemption.....................23-782
. directors...23-781
. errors detection, notice.............23-786–23-787
. functions...23-783
. meetings
. . auditor's attendance.........................23-784
. . calling...23-785
. members...23-781
. qualified privilege...............................23-790

Paragraph

Audit committee — continued
. review of financial statements.............23-783

Auditor
. appointment.........................23-736–23-737
. . acceptance.........................23-764–23-766
. . exemption...23-747a
. attendance at meeting..........................23-758
. ceasing to hold office..........................23-748
. court appointed....................23-756–23-757
. defined...23-002
. dispensing with...................23-745–23-747
. . exemption from appointing.............23-747a
. disqualification......................23-733–23-735
. examination...23-775
. incumbent...23-738
. independence.......................................23-732
. non-appointment...................23-745–23-747
. qualification..23-731
. qualified privilege.................................23-790
. removal...23-750
. remuneration..23-739
. report of other auditor.............23-776–23-778
. resignation...23-749
. right to information.................23-779–23-780
. statement..............................23-762–23-763
. unexpired term.....................................23-755
. vacancy, filling......................23-752–23-754

B

Bankruptcy and insolvency
. arrangement of corporation.................23-906

Bearer
. defined...23-192
. endorsement to.....................................23-267

Bearer form
. defined...23-195
. endorsement...23-283

Beneficial owner
. copies..23-689
. instructions...23-690
. limitation...23-693
. offence..23-694
. . officers..23-695
. proxyholder...23-691
. unknown..23-688
. validity...23-692
. voting of shares....................................23-687

Body corporate — see also **Corporations**
. bodies corporate..................................23-026
. defined...23-002
. holding, defined...................................23-005
. subsidiary, defined..............................23-006
. voting shares..........................23-620–23-623

Bona fide purchaser
. defined...23-192
. lost or stolen securities.........................23-345

Paragraph

Bona fide purchaser — continued
. recovery from..............................23-347
. title...23-252

Books and records
. access..23-081
. accounting, outside Canada..............23-079
. . offences.....................................23-080
. application to rectify................24-334–24-336
. auditing errors.........................23-786–23-789
. continued corporations.......................23-077
. copies..23-082
. directors'.........23-076; 23-078; 24-210–24-211;
                                            24-421–24-423
. . location......................................23-078
. dissolution, custody.................24-210–24-211
. form of..23-091
. keeping..23-075
. offences and penalties..........................23-093
. preservation...................................23-092
. rectification, application
    for.....................................24-334–24-336

Borrowing powers
. delegation.................................. 23-863a
. director.......................................23-863

Brokers — see also Agents
. defined......................................23-192
. delivery to..................................23-305
. warranties...................................23-261

Burden of proof
. contract for purchase of own
    shares......................................23-159
. validity of security.........................23-231

By-laws
. articles of incorporation....................23-028
. director's powers.............................23-428
. effective date.................... 23-430–23-431
. shareholder approval..........................23-429
. shareholder proposal.........................23-432

C

Call options — see also Put options
. defined......................................23-002
. insiders......................................23-565

Canadian resident — see Resident Canadian

Capital — see Stated capital

Certificates
. amalgamation.........................23-843–23-844
. amendment
. . articles.........................23-822–23-823
. . corporate name....................23-046–23-047
. . share series.......................23-123–23-124
. compliance, documents to
    Director....................................24-414
. compliance with conditions of trust
    indenture...................................23-391
. . statement by person giving
        evidence.................................23-392

Paragraph

Certificates — continued
. continuance (import)...........................23-845;
                                            23-847–23-849
. correction.............................24-416–24-418
. date...24-412
. discontinuance.......................23-860–23-861
. . date of...................................24-412b
. dissolution
. . effect............. 24-153; 24-169; 24-173; 24-178;
                                            24-207
. . issue.............. 24-152; 24-168; 24-172; 24-177;
                                            24-206
. incorporation........................23-031–23-032
. intent to dissolve...................24-158–24-159
. . revocation.........................24-164–24-165
. issue by Director.............................24-411
. options......................................23-127
. reorganization.......................23-901–23-902
. restated articles....................23-827–23-828
. revival...............................24-147–24-148
. rights.......................................23-127
. scrip, voting................................23-211
. security — see Security certificate
. share
. . contents...................................23-203
. . dissenting shareholder...........23-878–23-880
. . fractional.................................23-208
. . scrip......................................23-209
. signatures
. . corporation........................24-400–24-401
. . Director............................24-398–24-399
. take-over bid.................................24-816
. warrants.....................................23-127

Charter
. amendment....................................24-424a
. authorizing continuance.......................24-424c
. change of class of rights.....................24-424b
. defined......................................24-424

Claimants
. unknown, dissolution..............24-217–24-219

Commission
. sale of shares................................23-161

**Committees — see Audit committee;
            Directors committees**

Complainant
. actions, discontinuance........................24-331
. defined......................................24-319

Compliance
. certificate...................................24-414
. order...............................24-341; 24-348

Constrained share corporations
. defined......................................24-699
. directors' powers and
    duties............................24-705–24-715a
. disclosure of beneficial
    ownership.........................24-732–24-744
. disclosure requirements.......................24-702

Paragraph

Constrained share corporations — continued
. interpretation..24-699
. proceeds of sale................................23-175
. . costs of administration....................23-176
. . trust company..................................23-177
. . vesting in Crown.............................23-179
. references and definitions...................24-747
. sale of...23-171
. . effect of sale..................................23-173
. . obligations of directors...................23-172
. shares
. . sale of.......................24-730–24-730p
. voting rights, limitation..........24-717–24-729

Continuance
. article of, form...................................24-853
. authorization...................................24-424c
. certificate, form...............................24-853
. discretionary........................24-428–24-429
. dissent...24-425
. export — see Continuance (export)
. fees..24-430
. import — see Continuance (import)
. prohibited...24-433
. shareholders' dissent.........................24-425

Continuance (export)
. conditions...23-854
. discontinuance.................................23-860
. investment company.........................23-855
. notice deemed to be article...............23-860a
. prohibitions.....................................23-862
. rights...23-861
. shareholder approval........................23-858
. shareholders' meeting, notice...........23-856
. termination......................................23-859
. voting shares...................................23-857

Continuance (import)
. articles..23-846
. certificate...............23-845; 23-847–23-849
. issued shares...................................23-851
. . convertible....................................23-852
. . par value shares permissible..........23-853a
. limitation...23-853b
. rights preserved...............................23-850

Contracts
. director having interest,
    validity....................23-514–23-515
. pre-incorporation...................23-048–23-051
. prohibited loan by corporation...........23-167
. purchase of own shares by
    corporation.................23-158–23-161

Copies
. documents..24-403

Corporate names
. alternative.........................23-035–23-036
. certificate of amendment........23-046–23-047
. change directed............23-042; 23-044–23-045
. confusion of names..........................24-554

Paragraph

Corporate names — continued
. consideration of................................24-557
. continued...23-043
. designating number............23-040; 23-044
. exemption..23-034
. form..23-033
. interpretation...................................24-551
. misdescriptive, deceptively................24-584
. not prohibited............24-587–24-603
. not used..23-038
. prohibited................23-041; 24-563–24-581
. publication.......................................23-037
. reservation......................................23-039
. revocation.......................................23-045

Corporate seals
. omission...23-094

Corporations — see also Body corporate
. acquisition of own shares........23-134–23-138
. acts not applicable...........................23-017
. affiliate, defined..............................23-003
. annual return to director....................24-413
. applicant for list of holders of debt
    obligations.................23-385–23-386
. arrangement of insolvent....................23-906
. bankrupt.......................24-143–24-144
. businesses excluded..........................23-018
. capacity of person............................23-060
. . extra-territorial..............................23-061
. constrained share — see Constrained
    share corporations
. continued
. . lien on its shares held by
    debtor..................23-169–23-170
. . security certificate.............23-205
. defined...23-002
. holding own shares...............23-130; 23-154
. lien on its shares held by
    debtor..................23-169–23-170
. loans by
. . enforceability of contracts................23-167
. . permitted......................................23-166
. . prohibited.....................................23-165
. name — see Corporate names
. powers...............................23-062–23-063
. revival..........................24-145–24-148
. . return of property............................24-221
. rights...23-064
. signatures on certificate..........24-400–24-401
. statement of intent to
    dissolve................24-410–24-412b

Costs
. actions........................24-332–24-333
. investigation....................................24-274

D
Debt obligation
. defined..23-002

Paragraph

Debt obligation — continued
. holders
. . application for list of
holders......................................23-385–23-388
. . list...23-383–23-384
. issuers
. . certificate re compliance with trust
indenture...23-394
. . evidence, compliance with trust
indenture...............23-389–23-390; 23-394
. . list of holders...........................23-383–23-384
. reissue..23-157
. reorganization...................................... 23-899
. repayment..23-156

Debts
. directors' liability..................................23-505

Definitions
. Act...24-503
. action...24-319
. adverse claim..23-192
. affairs...23-002
. affiliate...23-002
. affiliated bodies corporate...................23-003
. appropriate person..................23-263–23-264
. articles..23-002
. associate...23-002
. auditor..23-002
. bearer...23-192
. beneficial interest..................................23-002
. beneficial ownership..............................23-002
. body corporate.......................................23-002
. bona fide purchaser...............................23-192
. broker..23-192
. business combination...............23-548; 23-571
. call...23-002
. Canadian...24-699
. complainant..24-319
. confusing...24-551
. constrained class...................................24-699
. constrained share corporation..............24-699
. constraint..24-699
. control..............................23-004; 24-699
. corporation...23-002
. court.................................. 23-002; 24-142
. court of appeal.......................................23-002
. debt obligation.......................................23-002
. delivery...23-192
. Director...23-002
. director...23-002
. dissenting offeree..................................24-049
. distinctive...24-551
. distributing corporation.........................23-545
. distribution to the public.........23-007–23-009
. document...24-503
. event of default......................................23-365
. evidence of appointment or
incumbency...23-317
. exempt offer............................. 24-023; 24-753

Paragraph

Definitions — continued
. fiduciary...23-192
. financial intermediary........................... 24-747
. form of proxy...23-664
. fungible.. 23-192
. genuine.. 23-192
. good faith...23-192
. guarantee of the signature...................23-315
. guarantor for issuer...............................23-196
. holder...23-192
. holding body corporate......................... 23-005
. incorporator..23-002
. individual... 23-002
. insider.............................23-545; 23-568–23-570
. interested person...................................24-048
. issuer..23-192
. liability..23-002
. maximum aggregate holdings.............24-699
. maximum individual holdings............ 24-699
. Minister.. 23-002
. negotiable instruments....................... 23-193
. offer...24-023
. offeree...24-023
. offeree corporation................................24-023
. offeror...24-023
. officer... 23-545
. ordinary resolution................................23-002
. overissue.. 23-192
. person...23-002
. prescribed...23-002
. proxy...23-664
. purchaser... 23-192
. put...23-002
. redeemable share................................. 23-002
. registered form.......................................23-194
. registrant..23-664
. reorganization....................................... 23-897
. resident Canadian..................................23-002
. secondary meaning................................24-551
. security...23-002; 23-192
. security interest......................................23-002
. send...23-002
. series...23-002
. share.........................23-545; 23-853; 24-023
. solicit...23-664
. solicitation by or on behalf of the
management of a corporation..........23-664
. special resolution...................................23-002
. statement..24-410
. subsidiary body corporate....................23-006
. take-over bid.............................24-023; 24-049
. trade mark...24-551
. trade name..24-551
. transfer..23-192
. trust indenture.....................23-192; 23-365
. trustee...23-365
. unanimous shareholder agreement.....23-002
. unauthorized...23-192

Paragraph

Definitions — continued
. use.. 24-551
. valid... 23-192
. voting share.................................... 24-699

Delivery
. constructive............................23-290; 23-303
. defined.. 23-192
. to broker... 23-305
. transferor's duty............................ 23-304
. warranties of intermediary.............23-259

Derivative action
. application to court......................... 24-320
. conditions precedent...................... 24-321
. powers of court.............................. 24-322

Director (Corporations Branch)
. alteration of documents..................24-415
. application for directions................ 24-337
. appointment.................................... 24-406
. certificate of..........................24-398–24-399
. . compliance................................... 24-414
. . correction............................24-416–24-418
. defined... 23-002
. exemption application.............. 24-834–24-843
. . notice of decision......................... 24-831
. records
. . copies.. 24-420
. . examination.................................. 24-419
. . form... 24-421
. . retention...................................... 24-423
. refusal to file document...........24-338–24-339
. signature on certificate............24-398–24-399

Director's circular
. take-over bid..........................24-033–24-037
. . approval...............................24-040–24-041
. . expert's consent..................24-038–24-039

Directors
. approval of financial statements.........23-717
. audit committee............................. 23-787
. authority... 23-066
. borrowing powers.......................... 23-863
. by-laws...................................23-428–23-429
. ceasing to hold office.................... 23-451
. change, notice to Director........23-470–23-471
. circular — see Director's circular
. committees — see Directors committees
. contract with corporation
. . continuing disclosure..................... 23-513
. . interest disclosure in.............. 23-509–23-511
. . time for disclosure.................. 23-509; 23-511
. . validity.................................23-514–23-515
. . voting, conditions........................ 23-512
. corporation branch — see Director
    (Corporations Branch)
. decisions, appeal from.................... 24-340
. defined... 23-002
. disclosure of interest.............. 23-508–23-509;
                                       23-511–23-515

Paragraph

Directors — continued
. dissent...............................23-524–23-526
. . take-over bid................................. 24-037
. duty of care.................................... 23-521
. duty to comply with Act.................. 23-522
. election... 23-445
. . voting... 23-450
. exculpation..................................... 23-523
. exemption from disclosure of
    financial statement......................24-693
. extraordinary sale, lease or
    exchange of property.................. 23-864
. indemnification..................... 23-528–23-530;
                                       23-532–23-534
. insurance.. 23-531
. liability.............................23-496; 23-500
. . actions... 23-501
. . conditions precedent.................... 23-503
. . issue of shares for other than
      money... 23-495
. . proxy solicitation.......................... 23-682
. . reliance on credible statements.........23-527
. . unsatisfied debt execution............... 23-505
. . wages...............................23-502–23-507
. managing.. 23-488
. meetings — see Directors meetings
. nomination
. . shareholder proposal..................... 23-601
. notice of incorporation, to
    Director.. 23-443
. notice re arrangement and
    compromises................................ 23-909
. number... 23-427
. . articles of incorporation.................. 23-027
. . increasing or decreasing................. 23-469
. offence... 23-133b
. powers
. . managing....................................... 23-426
. . unanimous shareholder
      agreement...........................23-644–23-646
. publication...................................... 23-563
. qualifications.................................. 23-435
. . residency............................23-437–23-438
. . shareholding................................. 23-436
. recovery of money or property
    from shareholder.................. 23-498–23-499
. removal... 23-457
. . class... 23-458
. . vacancy, filling.............................. 23-459
. remuneration, powers to fix.............23-535
. reorganization.......................23-899–23-902
. residency.. 23-437
. . committee..................................... 23-489
. . holding corporation....................... 23-438
. . meetings.............................23-474–23-475
. resignation..................................... 23-456
. resolution in lieu of
    meeting................................23-493–23-494

Paragraph

Directors — continued
. satisfaction of claim, contributions
   from other directors..............23-497; 23-507
. shareholder's resolution, statement
   opposing.................... 23-461–23-463
. shareholders meetings
. . calling..................23-634
. . right to attend..................23-460
. subrogation on liquidation....................23-506
. surrender of powers to receiver-
   manager......................23-407
. term of office
. . continuing, election failing................23-448
. . election.................. 23-445
. . incorporation..................23-444
. . staggered.................. 23-446
. unexpired..................23-468
. . unstated..................23-447
. vacancies
. . class..................23-466
. . directors vote to fill..................23-464
. . insufficient candidates.................. 23-449
. . removal..................23-459
. . shareholders' vote to fill.......23-464; 23-467
. validity of acts..................23-492
. voting, interest in contract....................23-512

Directors committees
. audit — see Audit committee
. authority..................23-490
. Canadian residency..................23-489

Directors meetings
. adjournment.................. 23-478
. attendance..................23-685
. Canadian residency.................. 23-474–23-475
. notice..................23-476–23-477
. one director..................23-479
. proxyholders' rights.............23-685a–23-685b
. quorum..................23-473
. resolution in lieu of..................23-493–23-494
. telephone.................. 23-480

Discontinuance (export)
. action for..................24-331
. certificate....................23-860–23-861
. prohibition..................23-862

Dissent
. amendment by court order..................24-327
. continuance.................. 24-425
. director, take-over bid..................24-037
. reorganization.................. 23-903
. shareholder — see Shareholders' dissent

Dissenting offeree
. defined..................24-049
. fair value for shares
. . application to court..............24-057–24-061
. . notice to offeror..................24-051
. . powers of court..................24-062–24-065

Paragraph

Dissenting offeree — continued
. transfer of shares......... 24-050–24-051; 24-054
. . payment..................24-054–24-056

Dissolution — see also Liquidation
. actions and applications to court........ 24-181
. . by shareholder..................... 24-179; 24-329
. application of Act..................24-143
. application to court..................24-182–24-188
. articles of.................. 24-167
. automatic.................. 24-432
. before commencing
   business....................24-149–24-153
. certificate
. . effect..................24-153; 24-169; 24-173;
          24-178; 24-207
. . form..................24-853
. . issue..................24-152; 24-168; 24-172;
          24-177; 24-206
. claimants, unknown..................24-217–24-219
. continuation of actions.................. 24-213
. . shareholder liability.............. 24-215–24-216
. court orders..................24-186–24-188
. court powers.................. 24-189
. court's final order..................24-204–24-205
. custody of records.................. 24-210–24-211
. Director instituted.................. 24-170–24-173
. form..................24-853
. grounds..................24-174; 24-179
. intent
. . certificate..................24-158–24-159
. . certificate, form.................. 24-853
. . certificate of revocation.........24-164–24-165
. . revocation.................. 24-163
. . revocation certificate, form..............24-853
. . statement..................24-157
. no property or liabilities..................... 24-150
. no shares issued.................. 24-149
. notice to Director.................. 24-175
. order..................24-176; 24-180
. property disposed of..................24-150a
. representative action..................24-216
. right.................. 24-166
. service of document on
   corporation, after..........24-214–24-214a
. shareholder proposal..............24-154–24-155
. shareholders' action..................24-179; 24-329
. show cause order.................. 24-185
. special resolution.................. 24-156
. statement of intent to dissolve
. . certificate.................. 24-412
. . certificate of discontinuance...........24-412b
. . defined.................. 24-410
. . execution and filing..................24-411
. . signature..................24-412a
. stay of proceedings under
   insolvency.................. 24-144
. unknown claimants..................24-217–24-220

Paragraph

Dividends
. declaration...23-162
. form of...23-163

Documents
. alteration by Director............................24-415
. copies............................. 24-403; 24-419–24-420
. Director's refusal to file............ 24-338–24-339
. filed by Director.....................................23-065
. format.......................................24-521–24-545
. inspection..24-419
. service on corporation after
    dissolution...........................24-214–24-214a
. verification...............................24-404–24-405

E

Election
. court review.. 23-641
. directors.. 23-450

Endorsement — see Security endorsement

Endorser
. immunity.. 23-270

Evidence of appointment or incumbency
. defined... 23-317
. notice to issuer........................... 23-319–23-320
. standards... 23-318

Exemptions
. Canadian ownership...............................23-133
. corporate name.......................................23-034
. disclosure of financial statement......... 24-693
. personal liability....................................23-051
. rules of procedure for
    applications............................ 24-819–24-843
. security distribution to public............. 23-009

F

Fees
. continuance... 24-430
. filing, copying and examining
    documents......................................24-846
. Schedule II...24-855
. security certificate................................. 23-198

Fiduciary
. adverse claims, inquiry by issuer........ 23-331
. defined.. 23-192
. duty, notice of adverse claim...............23-255
. endorsement..23-272

Financial statements
. affiliates....................................... 23-726–23-727
. approval by directors............................ 23-717
. consolidated............................. 23-713; 23-729
. . examination.............................23-714–23-716
. contents...23-710; 24-677
. copies to Director................................. 23-725
. copies to shareholders..........................23-719
. errors... 23-786–23-789
. exception.. 23-711

Paragraph

Financial statements — continued
. exemption from public
    disclosure...............................23-712; 24-684
. interim... 23-728
. offences and penalties..............23-720; 23-730
. prescribed circumstances for
    exemptions.............................. 24-690–24-695
. proxy circular.............................24-671–24-674
. publication.. 23-718
. review by audit committee.................. 23-783
. subsidiary... 23-729

Forms
. list of... 24-852
. prescribed under Regulations.............. 24-853

Fungible
. bulk, ownership of part.........................23-292
. defined.. 23-192
. securities.. 23-232

G

Guarantee of the signature
. effective assurance................... 23-314–23-316

Guarantor
. debt obligations, compliance with
    conditions of trust indenture.......... 23-390;
                                        23-394–23-395
. endorsement, warranties......... 23-286–23-289
. issuer's, defined.....................................23-196

H

Hearing
. investigations... 24-279
. . in camera.................................24-273; 24-279
. . publication of proceedings.................24-274

Holder — see Security holders

Holding corporation
. defined.. 23-005
. financial statements.................. 23-729–23-730
. residency of directors............................23-438

I

Incorporation
. certificate....................................23-031–23-032
. . form..24-853
. . of amendment.........................23-046–23-047
. . restated, form...................................... 24-853
. corporate bodies.................................... 23-026
. name of corporation................. 23-033–23-038
. . prohibited.................................23-041–23-045
. . reservation...............................23-039–23-040
. personal liabilities....................23-048–23-051

Incorporator
. defined.. 23-002
. eligibility... 23-025

Indemnification
. application to court................................ 23-532

Paragraph

Indemnification — continued
. corporation's derivative action............23-529
. director's..................................... 23-528–23-534
. insurance of directors and officers..... 23-531
. notices............................... 23-533–23-534
. rights.. 23-531

Information circulars
. soliciting proxies.................................... 23-599

Insider
. calls and puts...........................23-565
. civil liability...............................23-572–23-573
. defined.......................... 23-545; 23-545–23-547;
    23-568–23-570
. reports
. . body corporate....................... 23-553–23-555
. . constructive...23-551
. . distributing corporation.......23-549–23-550;
    23-552
. . exemption............................... 23-556
. . first.......................................24-605
. . offences and penalties........................23-558
. . publication...23-563
. short sales...23-564
. . exception..23-566
. trading — see Insider trading

Insider trading
. report
. . deemed......................................24-611
. . first...24-605
. . form...24-853
. . subsequent.................................. 24-608

Insolvency — see Bankruptcy and Insolvency

Inspection
. documents and reports..........................24-419

Inspector
. absolute privilege...................................24-282
. powers..24-277
. production of copy of court order...... 24-278
. report, copy to Director........................24-276

Insurance
. directors and officers............................23-531

Interest
. beneficial, defined............................. 23-002
. conflict of, trustee's................. 23-368–23-371
. directors' and officers' re
    contract with company.........23-508–23-514
. limited..23-253

Interim reports
. disclosure... 23-728

Investigations
. application to court............................... 24-269
. costs.. 24-272
. criminating statements........................... 24-281
. director's inquiries re compliance
    with Act.. 24-289
. exchange of information.....................24-277a

Investigations — continued
. grounds.. 24-270
. hearings
. . in camera................................24-273; 24-279
. . publication of proceedings.................24-274
. . right to counsel................................24-280
. inspectors'
. . court orders..24-278
. . exchange of information...................24-277a
. . report to director...............................24-276
. notice to Director...................................24-271
. ownership and control of
    securities.............................24-283–24-287
. powers of court..................................... 24-275
. right to counsel......................................24-280
. security for costs...................................24-272

Investment company
. continuance (export)..............................23-855

Issuer — see Security Issuers

L

Liability
. defined... 23-002
. issuer, unauthorized endorsement...... 23-285
. personal, pre-incorporation...... 23-048–23-051

Liens
. corporation on its shares held
    by debtor..23-169
. enforcement.. 23-170

Liquidation — see also Dissolution
. application of Act...................................24-143
. application to court.............. 24-182–24-184
. cessation of business and
    powers.................................24-191–24-192
. costs... 24-200
. court orders.................24-186–24-188; 24-190
. court powers... 24-189
. distribution in money..............24-208–24-209
. notice to Director.................................. 24-162
. procedure..24-160
. proposal by shareholders...................... 24-154
. . notice....................................... 24-155
. reimbursements by
    shareholders.......................24-215–24-216
. shareholder proposal................24-154–24-155
. show cause order................................. 24-185
. special resolution................................ 24-156
. stay of proceedings under
    insolvency.. 24-144
. supervision by court................ 24-161–24-162
. voluntary, supervision
    application............................24-182–24-188

Liquidator
. appointment...........................24-193–24-194
. duties..24-195
. examination of suspected
    persons...................................24-198–24-199

Paragraph

Liquidator — continued
. final accounts............................ 24-201–24-203
. powers.......................... 24-191–24-192; 24-196
. statements of experts............................ 24-197

Litigation
. recovery of transferred securities....... 23-308

Loans
. by corporation or affiliate
. . enforceability of contracts.................23-167
. . permitted.....................................23-166
. . prohibited....................................23-165

M

**Meetings — see Directors meetings;
Shareholders' meetings**

N

Negotiable Instruments
. defined.. 23-193

Notice
. adverse claim
. . broker's receipt after taking
      delivery.. 23-293
. . deemed given..................................... 23-254
. . duration... 23-332
. . endorsement in bearer form.............. 23-283
. . fiduciary's duty...................................23-255
. . offeror to dissenting offeree.............. 24-052
. . staleness... 23-256
. . title of purchaser.................... 23-251–23-252
. alteration by Director............................24-415
. amalgamation....................................... 23-842
. amendment of articles of
    incorporation......................................23-814
. application for investigation, to
    Director...24-273
. application to rectify records, to
    Director...24-335
. appointment or
    incumbency........................... 23-319–23-320
. audit committee meetings to
    auditor.. 23-784
. auditing errors.......................................23-786
. change of address of registered
    office... 23-074
. change of directors...... 23-470–23-471; 24-393
. corrected certificate.............................24-418
. deemed not served................................ 23-065
. . default, compliance with conditions of
      trust indenture................................. 23-395
. defect
. . security...23-233
. directors' circular......................24-034–24-036
. directors' meetings................................ 23-476
. . waiver...23-477
. discontinuance of action, to
    complainant....................................... 24-331
. dissolution.. 24-175

Paragraph

Notice — continued
. incorporators' list of
    directors.................................23-443; 24-393
. indemnification, application to
    court.....................................23-533–23-534
. issuer to adverse claimant.....................23-330
. issuer's agent, status............................ 23-349
. lost or stolen securities......................... 23-344
. of defect.................................. 23-233–23-236
. . staleness as...23-237
. offer for dissenting shares.................... 24-051
. record date...23-590
. refusal, shareholder proposal
. . application to court............................. 23-605
. . statement to shareholder.................... 23-604
. resolution, to dissenting
    shareholder... 23-876
. security defect........................... 23-233–23-236
. . staleness.. 23-237
. service upon corporation...................... 24-396
. service upon directors and
    shareholders............................ 24-392; 24-395
. shareholders meeting................23-591–23-597
. . amalgamation......................................23-833
. . auditor to receive............................... 23-758
. . directors to receive............................. 23-460
. . extraordinary sale, lease or
      exchange...23-865
. . list of shareholders................. 23-612–23-614
. . record date.............................. 23-587–23-589
. waiver..24-397

O

Offences and penalties
. accounting records in Canada..............23-080
. auditing errors.......................................23-789
. auditor, attendance at meeting........... 23-761
. financial statements..................23-720; 23-730
. general..24-347
. information re control of securities to
    Director.................................. 24-286–24-287
. list of holders of debt obligations........23-388
. proxy solicitation...................... 23-672–23-673;
                                                        23-681–23-682
. proxyholders' attendance at
    meetings..23-686
. record form and preservation...............23-093
. registrants, voting shares........ 23-694–23-695
. reports.......................................24-344–24-345
. shareholders list use..............................23-090
. statement of material facts....................24-345
. take-over bids............................ 24-045–24-046
. transfer of shares................................ 23-133b

Offeree
. defined.. 24-023
. dissenting
. . application re fair value of
      shares.....................................24-057–24-061
. . defined.. 24-049

Paragraph

Offeree
. dissenting — continued
. . offeror acquiring shares of.................24-051
. . payment for transfer of
   shares....................................24-054–24-056
. . powers of court re fair value of
   shares....................................24-062–24-065
. . transfer of shares................................ 24-049
. residency... 24-030

Offeree corporation
. defined... 24-023
. duties to dissenting shareholders........24-056

Offeror
. acquisition of shares of dissenting
   offeree..24-051
. defined... 24-023

Officer
. appointment... 23-520
. authority.. 23-066
. defined... 23-545
. disclosure of interest............................23-508;
                         23-510–23-511
. duty of care...23-521
. duty to comply with Act.......................23-522
. . exculpation.. 23-523
. insurance..23-531

Oppression
. application to court............................... 24-323
. grounds.. 24-324
. order to pay
. . dissolution... 24-329
. . limitation..24-328
. powers of court...................................... 24-325

Options
. certificates...23-127

Order
. restraining or compliance......................24-341

Organization meeting
. agenda.. 23-433
. calling... 23-434
. exemption.. 23-433a

Overissue
. defined... 23-192
. effect of payment.................................. 23-230
. validation..23-228
. . retroactive...23-229

Ownership
. beneficial, defined.................................23-002
. constructive...23-291
. part of fungible bulk.............................23-292

P

Penalties — see Offences and penalties

Person
. appropriate
. . defined................................. 23-263–23-264

Paragraph

Person
. appropriate — continued
. . determination..23-264
. defined... 23-002
. endorsement of security...................... 23-265
. interested, defined.................................24-048

Pledgee
. warranties...23-260

Prescribed
. defined... 23-002

Property
. disposed of, dissolution......................24-150a
. issued as dividend.................................23-163

Proposals
. shareholders.......................... 23-598–23-607
. . circulation... 23-603

Prospectus
. qualifications, document
   distribution..23-960

Proxy — see also Proxyholders
. circular
. . date and information.......................... 24-668
. . restraining order................... 23-696–23-697
. contents
. . dissident's proxy circular...... 24-653–24-665
. . management proxy circular.............. 24-644
. defined... 23-664
. deposit... 23-669
. dissident's circular................................. 24-650
. execution..23-666
. financial statement in
   circular..................................... 24-671–24-674
. form of..................................... 24-614–24-641
. . defined.. 23-664
. . restraining order................... 23-696–23-697
. management circular.............................23-599
. mandatory solicitation.............23-670–23-673
. revocation.. 23-668
. solicitation.. 24-614
. validity... 23-667

Proxyholders
. appointment... 23-665
. attendance at meeting...............23-685–23-686
. beneficial owner..................................... 23-691
. rights....................................... 23-685a–23-685b

Purchaser
. bona fide — see Bona fide purchaser
. constructive ownership........................ 23-291
. defined... 23-192
. notice of adverse claim........................23-293
. party to illegality...................................23-251
. right to requisites for registration.......23-309
. . rescission of transfer...........................23-310

Put options — see also also Call options
. defined... 23-002
. insiders..23-565

Paragraph

R

Receiver
. powers and duties.................... 23-405; 23-416
. . appointment under instrument........23-409
. . directions of court................ 23-408–23-409; 23-415

Receiver-manager
. powers and duties.................... 23-406; 23-416
. . appointment under instrument........23-409
. . directions of court.................. 23-408–23-409
. . director's..23-407

Record date
. fixing... 23-587–23-588
. . notice.. 23-590
. not fixed..23-589

Records — see Books and records

Registered holder — see Security holders

Registered office
. articles of incorporation.......... 23-027; 23-071
. change of address...................... 23-073–23-074
. notice to Director................................ 23-074

Registrant
. defined... 23-664
. instruction to.. 23-690
. voting of shares........................23-687–23-695

Registration
. effect... 23-215
. purchaser's right to
    requisites...............................23-309–23-310
. transferred securities................23-312–23-313
. wrong name.. 23-334

Regulations
. authority.. 24-407
. Canada Business Corporations
    Act.. 24-500
. publication................................24-408–24-409

Remuneration
. directors', officers, power to fix.......... 23-535

Reorganization
. articles, power of court............23-898; 23-900
. certificate... 23-901
. . effect.. 23-902
. debt obligations................................... 23-899
. defined... 23-897
. directors... 23-899
. dissent... 23-903
. form...24-853

Reports
. annual — see Financial statements
. errors, immunity................................24-346
. insiders
. . body corporate.....................................23-553
. . constructive.......................................23-551
. . distributing corporation.......23-549–23-550; 23-552
. . exemption.. 23-556

Paragraph

Reports
. insiders — continued
. . offences and penalties........................23-558
. inspection...24-419
. inspector, copy to Director...................24-276
. interim.. 23-728
. offences and penalties............. 24-344–24-345
. trading..24-605

Residency
. directors.. 23-437
. . committee... 23-489
. . holding corporation.............................23-438
. . meeting.............................. 23-474–23-475
. shareholder of offeree corporation..... 24-030

Resident Canadian
. class of persons prescribed.................. 24-548
. defined... 23-002

Resolution
. in lieu of meeting
. . directors........................... 23-493–23-494
. . shareholders......................23-630–23-631
. ordinary, defined............................23-002
. special — see Special resolution

Restraining order
. proxy circular, statement of
    material fact........................... 23-696–23-697
. under Act.. 24-341

Revival
. corporation................................24-145–24-148
. . return of property............................. 24-221

Rights
. certificates...23-127
. issue................................... 23-125–23-126
. transferability.................................. 23-128

S

Securities — see also Shares
. acquisition rights of corporation.........23-127
. adverse claims.................................... 23-254
. . fiduciary duty....................................23-255
. . inquiry.................................... 23-329; 23-331
. . notice.. 23-332
. . notice to broker............................... 23-293
. . notice to issuer..................................23-330
. . staleness as notice of........................23-256
. agents
. . liabilities..23-250
. . warranties...23-249
. alteration or completion...........23-247–23-248
. bearer form..23-195
. certificate — see Security certificate
. completion or alteration...........23-247–23-248
. conditional delivery............................. 23-236
. conversion...23-007
. defined.................................23-002; 23-192
. delivery, constructive........................... 23-290

                                    Paragraph   Paragraph
Securities — continued   **Securities**
. delivery on sale..........................23-303–23-305   . transfers — continued
. . to broker...23-305   . . registration..23-309
. . transferor's duty..................................... 23-304   . . rescission..23-310
. distribution to the public   . validation, retroactive...........................23-229
. . defined................................23-007–23-008   . validity
. . documents to Director.......................23-960   . . burden of proof.................................... 23-231
. . exemption...23-009   . . without notice of defect.....................23-234
. endorsement — see Security   . warranties
      endorsement   . . broker's..23-261
. exchange..23-007   . . intermediary's.....................................23-259
. fungibility..23-232   . . pledgee's...23-260
. holder — see Security holders   . . to issuer..23-257
. information re control to   . . to purchaser.......................................23-258
      Director................................... 24-283–24-287
. interest, defined.................................... 23-002   **Security certificate — see also Shares**
. invalidation..23-204c   . continued corporation...........................23-205
. issuer — see Security issuers   . destruction..23-218
. lack of genuineness...............................23-235   . fee..23-198
. lost or stolen   . joint holders..23-199
. . bona fide purchaser.............. 23-346–23-347   . proof of ownership.................................24-402
. . issue of new security............. 23-345–23-346   . restricted, liability of transferee..........23-204
. . notice to issuer.....................................23-344   . right of holder to obtain.......................23-197
. . recovery of new security.....................23-347   . share class or series..............................23-206
. negotiable instruments, defined..........23-193   . signatures.................................23-200–23-202
. non-delivery...23-236   . . unauthorized..23-246
. notice of defect..........................23-233–23-234
. . staleness.. 23-237   **Security endorsement**
. overissue   . appropriate person's................. 23-265–23-268
. . constructive...23-291   . assurance re effectiveness....................23-314
. . defined.. 23-192   . bearer form...23-283
. . effect of payment............................... 23-230   . blank..23-266–23-267
. . validation.................................23-228–23-229   . . conversion to special......................... 23-269
. purchasers   . certificate of dissenting
. . constructive ownership.......................23-291   shareholders.. 23-880
. . deemed notice of adverse claim.......23-254   . endorser's immunity...............................23-270
. . fungible bulk.......................................23-292   . evidence of appointment or incumbency
. . rights re endorsement.........................23-262   . . defined..23-317
. . title...23-251–23-253   . . notice to issuer........................ 23-319–23-320
. reclaiming possession................23-306–23-308   . . standards.. 23-318
. recovery on unauthorized   . fiduciary failing to comply..................23-272
      endorsement.......................................23-307   . guarantee of signature..........................23-315
. register — see Security register   . . standards.. 23-316
. registered form......................................23-194   . guarantor's warranties.............23-286–23-289
. registered holder — see Security   . . liability.................................23-287; 23-289
      holders   . issuer's liability.....................................23-333
. registration and recording.......23-212–23-218   . partial...23-271
. . in wrong name.....................................23-334   . purchaser's right to demand...............23-262
. . of transfer...23-309   . special..23-266; 23-268
. registration of transferred.......23-312–23-313   . to bearer...23-267
. retroactive validation of   . unauthorized..23-284
      over-issued...23-229   . . liability of issuers...............................23-285
. seizure..23-311   . . recovery of securities..........................23-307
. signatures, unauthorized.......................23-246   . warranties of guarantor, liability.......23-287;
. staleness as notice of defect.................23-237   23-289
. transfers.......................................23-225–23-226   . without delivery.....................................23-282
. . duty to register........................ 23-312–23-313
. . recovery for unauthorized   **Security holders**
      endorsement.....................................23-307   . appropriate person
                                                   . . defined.. 23-263
                                                   . . determination......................................23-264

Paragraph

Security holders
. appropriate person — continued
. . endorsement by.....................23-265–23-268
. certificate — see Security certificate
. constructive ownership........................23-291
. debt obligation
. . application for list of..............23-385–23-388
. . list...23-383–23-384
. holder, defined.................................. 23-192
. . joint... 23-199
. registered
. . constructive....................................23-220
. . dealings with.................................. 23-219
. . immunity of corporation....................23-222
. . infants...23-223
. . permissible.....................................23-221
. . surviving joint partner...................... 23-224
. . transmission....................23-225–23-226

Security issuers
. agents
. . duties and rights...............................23-348
. . notice to...23-349
. defences against purchaser for
    value......................................23-235–23-236
. duty to register transferred
    securities.................................23-312–23-313
. fiduciary..23-331
. inquiry into adverse claim....................23-329
. liability
. . registration of transfer....................... 23-333
. . unauthorized endorsement................23-285
. lost or stolen securities
. . duty...23-345
. . recovery of new security....................23-347
. notice to adverse claimant....................23-330
. registration in wrong name...................23-334

Security register
. branch.....................................23-213; 23-216
. central.....................................23-213; 23-217
. contents.. 23-212
. location.......................................23-214
. proof of ownership............................. 24-402

Shareholders
. approval
. . amalgamation.................................. 23-833
. . by-laws...........................23-429–23-431
. . continuance (export)........................23-858
. . effect in court action....................... 24-330
. . extraordinary sale, lease, or
    exchange............................. 23-864–23-870
. . property sale, lease or
    exchange............................. 23-864–23-869
. breach approved by, action.................. 24-330
. calling meeting — see Shareholders'
    meetings
. court action approval.................24-330–24-333
. defined, liquidation and
    dissolution.................................... 24-212

Paragraph

Shareholders — continued
. dissenting — see Shareholders' dissent
. joint voting................................. 23-623
. liability.......................................23-168
. . dissolution.....................24-215–24-216
. . proposal circulation.........................23-603
. lists — see Shareholders' lists
. meetings — see Shareholders' meetings
. notice to, service...................... 24-392–24-395
. proposal................................ 23-598–23-607
. . by-laws...................................... 23-432
. . exemptions...................................23-602
. . liability......................................23-603
. . nomination for director....................23-601
. . refusal to circulate................ 23-604–23-607
. . supporting statement................ 23-600
. unanimous agreement
. . articles of incorporation....................23-029
. . defined...................................... 23-002
. . restriction of directors'
        powers......................23-644–23-646
. vote to fill director's vacancy............... 23-467

Shareholders' dissent
. certificate
. . endorsement................................. 23-880
. . submission................................... 23-878
. class vote.................................... 23-872
. court fixing of fair value..........23-885–23-893
. notice of resolution........................23-876
. partial....................................... 23-874
. payment of fair value........................23-873
. . demand.......................................23-877
. . forfeiture.................................... 23-879
. . limitation................... 23-894–23-896
. . offer................................ 23-882–23-883
. . take-over bids................... 24-054–24-055
. . time.. 23-884
. rights.. 23-881
. written objection........................... 23-875

Shareholders' lists
. effects................................ 23-613–23-614
. examination..................................23-615
. furnishing to applicant............. 23-083–23-085
. . affidavit.................................... 23-087
. . holders of options or rights..............23-086
. notice of meetings.................... 23-612–23-614
. preparation..................................23-612
. use.. 23-089
. . offences and penalties........................23-090

Shareholders' meetings
. attendance........................... 23-685–23-686
. calling
. . court............................23-638–23-640
. . directors.................................. 23-634
. . procedure..................................23-636
. . shareholders...........................23-634–23-635
. notice........................... 23-588; 23-591–23-597
. . amalgamation................................23-833

Paragraph

Shareholders' meetings
. notice — continued
. . auditor to receive...............................23-758
. . continuance (export)...........................23-856
. . list of shareholders.................23-612–23-614
. place..23-584–23-585
. proxyholders' rights..............23-685a–23-685b
. quorum..................................... 23-616–23-619
. reimbursement of expenses...................23-637
. requisition............................... 23-632–23-633
. resolution in lieu of...................23-630–23-631
. time...23-586

Shares
. cancellation...23-152
. . amalgamation.................................... 23-831
. certificate
. . class or series...........................23-206–23-207
. . contents.. 23-203
. . dissenting holder.................... 23-878–23-880
. . restrictions.............................23-204–23-205
. . scrip.......................................23-208–23-209
. . transfer by dissenting offeree........... 24-053
. change in issued shares...........23-151–23-155
. classes.. 23-107
. . articles of incorporation....................23-027
. . certificate.. 23-206
. . change.........................23-151; 23-154–23-155
. . copies of conditions............................23-207
. commission for sale of.........................23-161
. continuance (import)............................23-851
. . convertible..23-852
. . defined... 23-853
. corporation's own
. . acquisition............................. 23-134–23-138
. . holding...................... 23-130–23-133; 23-153
. . purchase contract...................23-158–23-160
. defined.................................23-545; 24-023
. donation...23-141
. effect of unissued..............................23-155a
. form..23-105
. fractional
. . certificate.. 23-208
. . voting...23-210
. issue.. 23-109
. . constraint by special
    resolution..........................23-807–23-812
. . payment............................... 23-111–23-113
. issued as dividend...............................23-163
. . stated capital account........................23-164
. lien by corporation on
    debtor's...............................23-169–23-170
. nominal or par value...........................23-105
. . continued corporation......................23-106
. non-assessability.................................23-110
. payment to dissenting holders............23-884
. . take-over bid...........................24-054–24-055
. pre-emptive right..................................23-125
. . exception...23-126

Paragraph

Shares — continued
. prohibited transfers...........................23-133a
. purchasing contracts................23-158–23-160
. redeemable, defined.............................23-002
. redemption...23-139
. . limitation...23-140
. reserved...23-129
. restoration...23-152
. sale, commission................................23-161
. series
. . amendment of articles..........23-122–23-124
. . certificate.. 23-206
. . change.........................23-151; 23-154–23-155
. . copies of conditions............................23-207
. . issue...23-119
. . participation....................................23-120
. . restrictions......................................23-121
. stated capital account.............. 23-114–23-118
. transfer — see Transfer
. voting..23-108; 23-620
. . amalgamation........................ 23-834; 23-835
. . beneficial owners and
    registrants......................... 23-687–23-695
. . body corporate...................... 23-621–23-622
. . continuance (export)..........................23-857
. . extraordinary sale, lease or
    exchange...23-868
. . joint holders....................................23-623
. . pooling agreement........................... 23-643
. . procedure...........................23-628–23-629
. . proxyholder...............23-685–23-686; 23-691

Short sales
. insiders...23-564
. . exception...23-566

Signatures
. certificates
. . corporation..............................24-400–24-401
. . Director......................................24-398–24-399
. guarantee of...............................23-314–23-316
. . defined... 23-315
. security certificate....................23-200–23-202
. . unauthorized....................................23-246
. . warranties of guarantor........23-286–23-289
. unauthorized, defined..........................23-192

Solicitation
. by or on behalf of the management
    of a corporation, defined.................23-664
. defined.. 23-664
. exemption order..................................23-683
. . publication..23-684
. mandatory............................. 23-670–23-673
. procedure...........................23-679–23-682
. proxy...24-614

Solicitor-client privilege
. information to Director........................24-288

Special resolution
. amalgamation, classes and series
    of shares..................................23-836

Paragraph

Special resolution — continued
. amendment of articles.............. 23-805–23-806
. constraint on issue or transfer of
   shares.......................................23-807–23-812
. defined... 23-002
. dissolution... 24-150
. liquidation and dissolution...................24-156

Staleness
. notice
. . adverse claim.................................23-256
. . security defect.................................23-237

Stated capital
. reduction..........23-118; 23-142–23-143; 23-820
. . limitation...23-144
. . recovery................................. 23-145–23-147

Stated capital account
. change in issued shares........................23-151
. classes of shares..............................23-114
. continued corporation.............. 23-115–23-117
. reduction of capital..... 23-118; 23-148–23-150
. shares issued as dividend.....................23-164

Statement
. criminating, evidence before
   inspector...24-281
. defined.. 24-410
. filing...24-411
. financial — see Financial statements

Statement of material facts
. errors, immunity....................................24-346
. offences and penalties.............. 24-344–24-345
. proxy circular, restraining
   order.. 23-696–23-697

Statutory declaration
. amalgamation...................................... 23-841
. application for list of holders of debt
   obligations... 23-383
. compliance with conditions of trust
   indenture..23-391
. . statement by person giving
    evidence..23-392

Subsidiary
. amalgamation.............................23-838–23-839
. defined... 23-006
. financial statements.................. 23-729–23-730

T

Take-over bids
. amendment to...24-786
. application to court.............................. 24-047
. certificate with circular......................... 24-783
. circulars......................................24-756–24-759
. contents of directors' circular...............24-792
. date..24-029
. defined..............................24-023; 24-049
. directors' approval...............................24-040
. directors' circular.....................24-033–24-037
. . approval...............................24-040–24-041

Paragraph

Take-over bids — continued
. directors' circular — continued
. . expert's consent.......................24-038–24-039
. dissenter's status where no court
   application................................... 24-058a
. exempt offer circumstances
   prescribed..................................... 24-753
. exemption orders......................24-042–24-044
. experts statement................................24-780
. funds..24-031
. notice of directors' circular......24-795–24-801
. offences and penalties.............. 24-045–24-046
. report of chief financial officer............24-807
. sending..................................... 24-028
. shares of class
. . all.................................24-024; 24-026
. . less than all....................24-025–24-026
. shares of dissenting
   offerees......................24-050–24-051
. . fair value...................24-057–24-065
. . payment...................... 24-054–24-055
. share-for-share.............................. 24-032
. statement of directors' approval..........24-777
. where offeror has effective
   control...24-765
. where repurchase of own shares
   involved...24-771

Transfer
. constraint by special
   resolution.................................23-807–23-812
. defined... 23-192
. issuer's duty to register............23-312–23-313
. purchaser's right to registration
   requisites...................................23-309–23-310
. recovery...23-306
. . litigation...23-308
. . unauthorized endorsement................23-307
. rescission...23-310
. restriction...23-027

Trust indenture
. application of Act...................... 23-366–23-367
. compliance with conditions
. . certificate of compliance.....................23-394
. . declarations.......................................23-391
. . duty of issuer or guarantor.............. 23-390
. . evidence to trustee................. 23-389–23-394
. . notice of default.................................23-395
. . trustee's requirement.........................23-391
. debt obligations issued under
. . corporate applicant.............................23-385
. . duty of issuer.....................................23-384
. . list of holders............. 23-383; 23-387–23-388
. . statutory declaration.........................23-386
. . defined.........................23-192; 23-365
. Escheats Act application......................23-180
. offences..23-388
. reliance on statements..........................23-397
. trustee's conflict of interest,
   effects.................................. 23-368–23-371

Paragraph

Trust Indenture — continued
. trustee's duty re debt obligations....... 23-396
. . exculpation... 23-398
. validity, trustee's conflict of
   interest.. 23-370

Trustee
. conflict of interest...................... 23-368–23-369
. defined.. 23-365
. demand of evidence of compliance
. . certificate.. 23-394
. . notice of default.................................... 23-395
. . requirements... 23-391
. . with trust indenture.............. 23-390; 23-393
. duties.. 23-396
. exculpation.. 23-398
. liability...23-397
. qualification... 23-372
. removal for conflict of interest............. 23-371

V

Voting
. corporation holding its own
   shares...23-133f
. directors with interest in contract....... 23-512
. election of directors.............................. 23-450
. registrant..................................... 23-687–23-695
. scrip certificates.................................... 23-211
. share classes... 23-108
. . amendment of articles........... 23-815–23-818
. . dissent.. 23-872
. shares.. 23-620
. . amalgamation.......................... 23-834–23-835

Paragraph

Voting
. shares — continued
. . beneficial owners.................... 23-687–23-695
. . body corporate........................ 23-621–23-622
. . defined.. 24-699
. . extraordinary sale, lease or
    exchange...23-864
. . fractional...23-210
. . joint holders...23-623
. . pooling agreement.............................. 23-643
. . procedure..................................23-628–23-629
. . proxyholder............... 23-685–23-686; 23-691

W

Wages
. directors' liability................................... 23-502

Warranties
. agent...23-249
. broker...23-261
. delivered.. 23-259
. guarantor of endorsement....... 23-286–23-289
. pledgee.. 23-260
. to issuer..23-257
. to purchaser...23-258

Warrants
. certificates..23-127
. options and rights.................................. 23-127
. . reserved shares.....................................23-129
. . transferable rights............................. 23-128

War